The Last Place
on Earth

"One of the most enjoyable of all the studies of our misused wildlife."
—Cleveland Amory

"A book on ecology, no less expert and almost as romantic as Rachel Carson. Only a person as catholic as Harold Hayes could compose an essay as broad, instructive, necessary, and as utterly readable as *The Last Place on Earth*. I couldn't put it down."—Ned Rorem

"Excellent. . . . Could not be more timely. A fascinating, important book." —*The New York Times Book Review*

"An absorbing, important book."—*Saturday Review*

"This exceptionally well-written book will go far in making all readers more conscious of their place in the delicate balance of nature."—*Choice*

"A well-crafted piece of reporting that, like a Grant's gazelle, covers a lot of rocky ground with assurance and grace."—*Los Angeles Times*

SELECTED BY BOOK-OF-THE-MONTH AND MACMILLAN BOOK CLUBS IN HARDCOVER AND EXCERPTED IN THE NEW YORKER

Serengeti, in East Africa, a piece of land not much larger than the state of Connecticut, is as close to the Garden of Eden as any place in the world. It is still inhabited by some two million wild animals, the last great herds on earth. Except for a rather casual decision to accept an old friend's invitation, Harold Hayes says he might have lived out an otherwise self-absorbed life wholly oblivious of levels of existence so awesomely complex, so delicately calibrated, so impenetrably mysterious, and yet so tantalizingly rational in their order as to change completely his view of his and all men's place in the arrangement of things.

This book is, on the surface, the account of a latter day safari made by the author in the company of a second Noah, the great German zoologist Bernard Grzimek. Through their eyes we move from Kenya across General Amin's Uganda to the Serengeti Plain in Tanzania. The problem before them is that man needs more space, animals cannot live with less. Man and beast are both in danger. Between the needs of animals and the needs of man, who has the right of way?

Cleveland Amory has called *The Last Place on Earth* "one of the most enjoyable of all the studies of our misused wildlife." Tom Wolfe, not unexpectedly, said, "What I enjoy watching in *The Last Place on Earth* is the spectacle of all the human animals snorting and pawing the ground with egotism and ambition." William Conway, General Director of the New York Zoological Society, sums it up as "a grand book."

Harold Hayes is best known for his seventeen-year association with *Esquire* magazine. As editor, he has worked with many of the best writers in America, whose ranks he has joined with *The Last Place on Earth*.

The Last Place on Earth

HAROLD T. P. HAYES

5B

A SCARBOROUGH BOOK
STEIN AND DAY/*Publishers*/New York

For Pete Turner

FIRST SCARBOROUGH BOOKS EDITION 1983

The Last Place on Earth was originally published
by Stein and Day/*Publishers.*

Copyright © 1976, 1977 by Harold Hayes
All rights reserved, Stein and Day, Incorporated
Printed in the United States of America
Stein and Day/*Publishers*/Scarborough House,
Briarcliff Manor, N.Y. 10510

A portion of this book appeared originally
in *The New Yorker.*

Cover Design: George Lois/Dennis Mazella
Cover Photograph: Pete Turner
Typography and Type Design: Dennis Mazella
Maps: Rudy Hoglund

Library of Congress Cataloging in Publication Data

Hayes, Harold.
    The last place on earth.

    1. Natural history—Tanzania—Serengeti National
Park. 2. Serengeti National Park.   I.   Title.
QH195.T3H39   574.9678'27   76-15562
ISBN 0-8128-6087-X

After the flood God said to Noah, "And the fear of you and the dread of you shall be upon every beast of the earth, and upon every fowl of the air, upon all that moveth *upon* the earth, and upon all the fishes of the sea; into your hand are they delivered."

CONTENTS

FOREWORD

I am a southerner who has spent most of his adult life in New York City. Other than an affection for a succession of mongrel dogs I owned as a child, each of them giving way to the next through the limiting mechanism of the automobiles, I never paid much attention to the circumstances of animals of any kind; and I should imagine that, had I not gone to Africa in 1969, such would surely be the case today. However, I *did* go to Africa, and, as the reader will eventually discover, this book grew from that trip—as did my curiosity over the strange German, Bernhard Grzimek, and the Serengeti Plain, and its animals, and ultimately—inevitable progression!—the wonders and varieties of life still visible in that remote corner of the world.

Even in the first stages of writing this account, I had never quite anticipated the outcome. More remote than my interest in animals were the interrelated worlds of zoology, paleontology, ethology, ecology—the lot of it: I was a poor witness to the processes of natural history. Yet it is today inconceivable to me that—except for a rather casual decision in response to an invitation from an old friend—I might have lived out an otherwise self-absorbed life wholly oblivious of levels of existence so awesomely complex, so delicately calibrated, so impenetrably mysterious, and yet so tantalizingly rational in their order as to cause me now, half a century here, to view quite differently my own place in the arrangement of things.

I am acutely aware that my collateral reading was essential to my understanding of what I saw there, and to acknowledge the considerable contributions of others to this account, I have taken space elsewhere. Suffice to say here, David Ehrenfeld's *Biological Conservation*, suggested by the director of the Bronx Zoo as the best "overview" I would find, got me started, and John Bleibtreu's *The Parable of the Beast*, discovered through the offhand remark of a friend as I moved into the last stages of my manuscript, seem to me now to come as close as possible to being the first and last words on a subject that is, otherwise, endless. (Bleibtreu's last words are, "Being is transient, but life itself is immortal.")

So—this is the story of a man and a place, but more than that, if I have been lucky, it is an account of a state of being.

—H.T.P.H.
Stone Ridge, N.Y.
August, 1976

PART ONE

Into
Grzimek's
Hand

ONE

Siringet, the Masai core of the modern word *Serengeti,* meaning "an extended place," is as apt a phrase as any to reflect the rather vague impression held by most people of that section of East Africa known as the Serengeti Plain—several thousand square miles along the northern border of the United Republic of Tanzania. For those who have been there, however, it is a place extended in time as well as in space, an unexpected emotive experience of serenity drawn from deep in back of the unself-conscious mind, like loneliness, or extreme exultation. The scientist George Schaller, who studied lions there for three years, has written, "The plains, when verdant and covered with herds of wildebeest, zebra and gazelle from horizon to horizon, surely present one of the loveliest sights on earth." Fritz Jaeger, a German geographer who walked it off on foot in 1907, described it in his journal as ". . . grass, grass, grass, grass, and grass. One looks around and sees only grass and sky." Even without the presence of game it is an awesome sight: from Lake Ndutu, for example, slightly south of its center, the green plain extends outward without visual interruption for thirty miles, except toward the Nyarabo range, which is twenty miles away; toward Seronera to the northwest, it extends for sixty miles. To someone driving the dirt road from Seronera at about thirty-five miles an hour, which is a good going speed—not too hard on the vehicle and fast enough to sense the great distances—it does indeed seem like a sea of grass, sweeping out on all sides, rolling ever so slightly to the bottom of the sky. Serengeti is only a hundred and fifty miles below the equator, but it is situated on the Great Rift Valley's westward plateau five thousand feet high, and clouds come in low, as though in final approach, stacking up sometimes and causing the sun to cut through in shafts. The air is sharp and clear, the light so intense that professional photographers are unable to work with the assurance their film will reflect what they see, except during the hours between dawn and eight and from five until dusk. Traveling the plain on a summer day in January, one may scan the horizon across hundreds of delicate Thomson's gazelle, tails twitching, browsing the green but receding into the distance so that finally they are lost to view, brown specks to strain after but that can be confirmed only through binoculars, and then for the viewer to find that within the glass there is still a second degree of specks extending outward, on and on. Blue-gray overcast sky, green plain, golden light shafts, and the rust-brown animals—a celestial sight.

Serengeti is the last place on earth where large herds of wild animals gather in sufficient profusion to suggest the way one part of the world must have looked in Pleistocene times. There are more than four hundred and fifty species of birds there, one of the world's richest bird habitats, and seemingly an infinite variety of animals: lion, leopard, cheetah, buffalo, elephant, giraffe, wild dog, jackal, hyena, ratel, hippopotamus, crocodile, wart hog, hyrax, rhinoceros, mongoose, spring hare, porcupine, grass mouse, waterbuck, baboon, dik-dik, and colobus monkey, and three of the most poisonous snakes on earth, the puff adder, the spitting cobra, and the mamba. No one can be precise in such matters, but current estimates place Africa's large mammal population at ten million; two million of them are in and around the Serengeti Plain. Fifty-one hundred square miles of Serengeti is a national park, which means by the classical European definition of parks that the animals have priority within its borders and that humans are allowed in only as visitors or on official business. But the borders are man-made and arbitrary; the plain rolls on and so do the animals—the wildebeest, for example, using only fifty-one per cent of the park for its principal grazing grounds. The larger Serengeti ecosystem covers an area of fifteen thousand square miles, including all of the park; the Maswa-controlled area to the southwest; the Grumeti-controlled area to the west; the Salei plains to the east; Masai Mara north past the Kenya border; and, to the southeast, the Ngorongoro Conservation Unit, which, until 1959, was within the eastern boundary of the park. There are short grasslands, tall grasslands (in the wet season one species reaches five feet in height), and, in the north and west, bush and woodland plains. Some of Serengeti's streams run into alkaline basins and end there; others drain into Lake Victoria and may therefore be considered among the fabled sources of the Nile.

In the Ngorongoro area, to the east, where the plains rise slowly to the foothills of a chain of extinct volcanoes, the time sense is accelerated by land configurations only a few miles apart: Olduvai Gorge, where in 1959 Mary Leakey picked off the ground a

THE LAST PLACE ON EARTH

fragment from the skull of *Australopithecus boisei*, a form of near-human life dating back one million seven hundred and fifty thousand years; Ngorongoro Crater, an extinct volcano whose rim of near-perfect symmetry encloses, like the walls of an amphitheatre, a tiny peaceable kingdom two thousand feet below filled with one of the heaviest concentrations of large animals in Africa per square mile, all wandering about a lilliputian soda lake, acacia forest, and grassland plain—a Fabergé version of the Serengeti outside; and, on the far side of the crater, the near vertical drop of the western wall of the Gregory Rift, the massive prehistoric fracture that commenced in Russia about forty million years ago and split the earth's surface all the way to Rhodesia, its center sinking a mile at the slow-motion rate of six inches a thousand years and eventually forcing its walls thirty miles apart. All this is packed in together and traversed by the same one-track dirt road that leads from the plain, offering the visitor the eerie sense that he is being rushed from the Garden of Eden backward through the first six days of Creation. It all happens too quickly. From Seronera at the center of the plain to the Leakey camp in the gorge is a distance of only seventy miles; from the gorge to the top of the crater, twenty-five miles; from the crater to the floor of the rift, thirty-nine miles—in all, a hundred and thirty-four miles along a small road that rises and falls four thousand feet in altitude and twenty degrees in temperature, moves from tall grassland plains to short grassland plains, descends (at the gorge) to a lava riverbed, climbs through mountain woodlands to the crater rim, winds halfway around the crater and then drops through rain forest in a dizzying descent to the valley floor. In her battered old station wagon, hurrying on from Olduvai past all these wonders to Arusha, the first town beyond the rift wall where she will fill her monthly shopping list, Mary Leakey can make the trip in about four hours.

There is a sign at the Seronera airfield in the center of the park advising visitors to take care, for they are about to enter a world "young and fragile." By outside time, Serengeti is only eighty-three years old, having first been observed by a German explorer named Baumann in 1892 and soon thereafter found to be inhospitable to human settlement because of a variety of pestilences and wild animals. Today it is considered the greatest natural attraction on the African continent, the most celebrated national park in the world. Each of its three principal features—the plain, the crater, and the gorge—has its advocates among nature writers, who, reporting with care and restraint on data acquired through years of observation, ultimately give way to rhapsodic superlatives. While Schaller sees the plain itself as "one of the loveliest sights on earth," Henry Fosbrooke, a former conservator of the Ngorongoro Conservation Unit, maintains, "The Ngorongoro Crater in Tanzania is probably Africa's most beautiful reserve and one of the most spectacular wonders on earth." To the untrained eye, Olduvai doesn't seem to offer much competition: it is a sort of miniature Grand Canyon of scrub bush and raw earth formed over millions of years by evaporating lakes and rivers whose residual sediments have left, by the extraordinary coincidences of nature, fossils and stone tools scattered about on the surface of its gullies. Olduvai was discovered in 1911 by another German, a butterfly collector named Kattwinkel, who spotted on the floor of the gorge fossils of the three-toed horse, *Hipparion*. But it is the essence of time past on this tropical moonscape which is its wonder. On a recent occasion, strolling with a visitor and her five Dalmatians about her camp site, Mary Leakey looked to the ground, picked up a black object about the size of a walnut, and said, "Look at this! It's a molar from old Kattwinkel's *Hipparion!*"

Serengeti's herds are under constant but unobtrusive surveillance. From their laboratories at the center of the plain, scientists of the Serengeti Research Institute use computers, aerial cameras and other devices to monitor the animal population. They tend to class most of them in two broad categories: predators, or carnivores, such as the lion, leopard, cheetah, wild dog, jackal, and hyena; and prey, or herbivores, the majority of which are ungulates, or hoofed animals, such as the zebra, gazelle, and wildebeest. Vegetation sustains the prey and the prey sustain the predators. Although the classification is inclusive for the objectives of most of the Institute's studies, some herbivores manage to live out their existence without having to endure the wracking tensions that constantly beset the ungulates. For most predators, the elephant and rhinoceros are too big, the buffalo too mean, the giraffe too troublesome, and the ostrich too alert. But the zebra, gazelle, and wildebeest are prey of daily fare; constantly stalked, they are constantly on the verge of flight. Safety is sought in numbers and in a complexly interdependent warning system. It is the presence of these few highly visible species—at some times in small groups, at others in vast congregations—that, together with the extraordinary

18

recovery rate of the vegetation, characterizes the Serengeti as a unique habitat for African wildlife.

Ungulates wander the plain in fairly predictable patterns. Perhaps because there are simply more of them than any other, the wildebeest—an animal with the graceful body of the horse and the dull, listless face of the cow—take the lead. At last count, there were more than a million of them on the plain. With their constant attendants, the gazelle and the zebra, they graze selectively, each species taking the grasses at different heights, leaving something for all. The weather leads the wildebeest, and all other ungulates follow, the predators feeding on the lame, the aging, the newly born, and the unwary at the edges of the herd. After the long rains of late spring, they move from the east and center of the park to the bush country of the north and the west toward Lake Victoria, where there is permanent water; and they remain there until the short rains of November, when they form into columns and head back again. In some years (the precise date varying according to the weather), the grazing animals assemble into a single mighty horde and stand together, almost shoulder to shoulder, along the short-grass plains from Seronera to the foothills of Ngorongoro, spreading the plain twenty miles wide by thirty miles long. This phenomenon is known in East Africa—and elsewhere now as well, for there is no comparable sight left on earth—as the Great Migration. One is lucky indeed if he has timed his arrival in Serengeti to coincide with this spectacle, for it is then possible to drive out on the plain and actually cruise slowly among the herds. The animals part to make room for the intruder; and then, returning majestically to place on the flat grass endless reach, their number extending to silhouette mirages on the horizon, they create for one moment the illusion that wild animals have regained possession of the earth.

No one knows quite how much longer this fragile illusion will hold. The sea of grass is not endless, of course; at its widest point, the distance across Serengeti Park is only eighty miles. Cattle overgraze its harsh shores; to the southwest, small farms are edging closer; poachers take some forty thousand animals from the herds each year; and the people of the Wakuria, Waikoma, Wasukuma, and Masai tribes, who encircle it, add to their number in Malthusian leaps. Serengeti is scarcely more than a memory of our natural past surrounded now by the imperatives of modern civilization—the hunger of impoverished people sharpened by the scarcity of arable land—and, except for the added imposition of the animals, its dilemma is not unlike that suffered throughout much of the Middle East and Asia.

In East Africa, which includes Kenya, Uganda, and Tanzania, large families are considered a matter of necessity and a measure of prestige; half the population is under sixteen years of age. The population increases at the rate of 3.5 per cent a year; it is expected to double in twenty years and quadruple in forty. The subsistence income of the average East African is less than two hundred dollars a year. In Tanzania, four-fifths of the people live on one-fifth of the land, and Serengeti falls within that fifth. The pastoralists of Serengeti—particularly the Masai, who believe that God gave them all the cattle on earth—view the Serengeti's boundaries with mixed feelings. They have always lived peacefully among the great herds, but in times of drought, when their water holes dry up and their own grasslands wither, and as the privileged wildebeest graze serenely within sight of their dying herds across an invisible boundary line, there seems no other place to turn—a dilemma that has increased in agony with the almost predictable recurrence of such circumstances in Serengeti.

There is no other plain in the world comparable to Serengeti. Wild animals still graze in obscure corners of the African continent from Cape Town to Chad, but as civilization moves in, the animals are quickly crowded out; in Botswana, for example, the northwest corner was said up until 1973 to hold abundant game, but now the diamond industry is preparing to drill wells for its mines, the country is too poor to resist the opportunity, and the Okovanggo Basin, which has sustained the game, may be drained out. Every major civilization has eventually destroyed its wildlife, and civilization is fast overtaking Africa. Serengeti remains the great anachronism, its survival maintained through an odd, near mystical series of countervailing conditions that have thus far managed to tip a fragile balance slightly to the side of the animals: population increases vs. drought and famine; cattle proliferation vs. pestilence and disease; land pressure for cultivation vs. tourist income; scientific research vs. the vagaries of nature. Serengeti's agonies are local and for the most part unrealized by the rest of the world; its importance as a cultural resource for the world community, however, is unchallenged. Scientists see it as a sort of ecological paradise regained, however briefly, and not only for its importance as the last gathering place for the rich diversity of African wildlife

THE LAST PLACE ON EARTH

but as well for the light it may shed on the larger question of man's survival.

"Serengeti is basic to the concerns of conservation," says William Conway, Director of the Bronx Zoo. "The problem is not so much to save the animals there as to save the *habitat* of the animals. If animals can live there, so can man; if not, man cannot. It is a case of what we often hear referred to in our circles as the canary simile—the miners in Wales took canaries into the pits to serve as an early-warning system; when the foul air killed the canaries, the miners knew it was time to get out. There are some very practical aspects to all this. The production of the Salk vaccine required the destruction of six hundred thousand wild monkeys over a three-year period. Between this country and Japan, science is currently using them up at the rate of a hundred thousand a year." Peter Jackson, director of information of the World Wildlife Fund, says, "All our domestic crops and animals have been bred from wild stock, and especially among plants it is the genetic resources available in the wild which have helped to produce new wild yields." Conway asks, "Do we save animals for themselves or for ourselves? Another way to put it is: Will man set aside for tomorrow something he can use today? It hasn't happened yet. All of which, of course, leads to the key question: Does man truly *want* wildlife on earth, and is he willing to make the sacrifices necessary to keep it here?"

In the eighty-three years since Western man first discovered they were there, the animals of Serengeti have lived a touch-and-go existence, seldom regarded as much other than a cause of disease, a threat to life and property, a secondary food source, or, on rare occasions, a diversion for wealthy sportsmen. Large portions of East Africa are infested with tsetse, a mixed blessing. The tsetse is about twice the length of a housefly, with a painful bite, and as much surrounded by myth and danger as the python or gorilla, except that when it carries certain trypanosome strains, which cause sleeping sickness, the tsetse is considerably more lethal—to both man and his cattle—though harmless to plains game. The presence of tsetse in any area was enough to keep most people out; on the other hand, because tsetse was to be found in the company of wild animals, the prevailing opinion was that tsetse could be eliminated only by exterminating its hosts. In Uganda, at the turn of the century, some two hundred and fifty thousand people died from sleeping sickness, and subsequently, eighty per cent of the large mammals were destroyed; in Rhodesia, several hundred thousand head of game were destroyed. Tsetse has always been present in Tanzania, covering seventy-five per cent of the countryside—a principal reason for the majority of the population living in so small an area. Since tsetse was known to exist in the Serengeti (and still does in the woodlands to the west of Seronera), most people tended to stay clear of it.

They stayed out, too, because of the presence of rinderpest, another disease brought in by man, or, more precisely, by his cattle. Rinderpest is a viral infection that attacks ruminants of all kinds, both wild and domestic. It came to East Africa with Asian cattle in the late nineteenth century, and in a short time it swept across the continent. Serengeti's wildebeest herds were sharply reduced, but those surviving developed an immunity to the disease, and their continued survival suggested the conclusion that they transmitted not only sleeping sickness but rinderpest as well. Although Serengeti's animals were later proved innocent of both charges, the wildebeest *are* guilty of carrying a third infestation, known as malignant catarrh; this is a pestilence, spread on the grass by the afterbirth of the calf, to which cattle alone are susceptible—a warning as lethal as it is symbolic for cattle to keep out of Serengeti.

A further deterrent to settlement for which the animals could not in any way be held responsible, however, was the water of Serengeti. During the dry season much of the open water on the plain evaporates, that which remains becoming concentrated with salts and turning alkaline as it dries. At these times, apart from the presence of Grant's gazelle, oryx, dik-dik, and the ostrich, which obtain water from their food (and some enterprising Masai who in the past have dug a few fresh-water wells in the hard pan), the plain stands empty.

Wherever else such circumstances were not present, one reason or another has been found to eliminate most of the larger animals of East Africa. During the Second World War, the British drew upon them as a food source for their prisoners of war. By the late forties, as prophylaxis had reduced the death rate of both East Africans and their cattle, and as the population of both surged upward, the colonial government sought various ways to increase the productivity of the land held by the wild animals. One scheme called for the destruction of thousands of them to make way for peanut crops, an experiment eventually abandoned but only after the animals had

22

been slaughtered. Another called for the total extermination of wild ungulates throughout Tanganyika to eliminate rinderpest and create a beef-stock center for the Commonwealth.

Outside Africa, meanwhile, there was surprisingly little scientific interest in the wild herds. The study of animal behavior was still in its infancy, and not considered of much importance. As late as the end of the Second World War, what was known about African animals came mainly from the notebooks of hunters or from studies in zoos. The prevailing assumption outside of Africa was that the African continent still teemed with game—in the jungles of the Congo (where there had never been a lot) and along the great savannas to the east. In fact, what Africa teemed with mostly by now was cattle, and the destruction they were causing to the environment was—and still is—incalculable.

In East Africa, where the human population suffers a marked deficiency of protein, cattle are considered by many tribesmen to be too valuable to squander as food; they are an immediate index to wealth and social standing. Cattle have been present on the African continent since the earliest years of civilization, and have seldom been out of balance with their environment, primarily because there were too few of them to cause widespread damage. By the mid-fifties, however, with the systematic elimination of the principal cattle diseases, cattle had begun to increase in the same geometric intervals as man himself. (There is a larger biomass of cattle today on earth than man; in Asia they consume more protein than man.) In East Africa, as cattle began to spread over the savannas, encircling and diminishing the wild herds, those who watched closely saw an apparent paradox form: the same rich grasslands that had for hundreds of thousands of years supported hundreds of thousands of wild animals, from the small gazelle to the voracious hippopotamus, began now, under the grazing of cattle, to wither into scrub-bush desert. Small notice was taken at the time, even by those conservationists who had come to be directly concerned with the preservation of Serengeti's herds, for by the mid-fifties—it had seemed to have happened virtually overnight—the Serengeti had become an acute political problem.

The first conservationists in Serengeti were the first hunters—men like J. A. Hunter, Philip Percival, the American filmmaker Martin Johnson—and they were drawn there by the great profusion of lions. Only in Serengeti are lions apt to be encountered standing squarely in the midst of an open plain, as though at the center of a Rousseau landscape, supremely oblivious of their surroundings. Coming upon the creatures in such a setting—it is still a fairly common sight today—one may easily imagine the hunters' wonder at having arrived finally at the ultimate hunting experience. The sense of the lions' presence is heightened at night. Lying under thin canvas, one is awakened by their roars rolling across the plain— deep, throbbing warning for their migratory cousins to stay clear of the territory. It has never been difficult to kill a lion. On the few hunting safaris still permitted, the standard method is to string up the carcass of a zebra, wait at a safe distance until the lion comes to feed, and then shoot it. Earlier visitors tied the zebra carcass to the rear bumpers of their vehicles and shot the lions at their leisure from their car seats. In the twenties, a man named Saxton Pope wrote a book about his hunting experiences in the Serengeti, and toward the end he remarked, more or less as an afterthought: "We've now shot 52 male lions. I think possibly we're overdoing it a bit. Others will be coming after us." And indeed soon there would be, some driving down in Model T Fords, until the colonial government became so concerned from the complaints of professional hunters that it moved to establish protective restrictions. In 1929, nine hundred square miles at the center of Serengeti were set aside as a sanctuary for lions. In the thirties, additional land was gazetted, including the Ngorongoro Crater, and the list of protected species extended to include most of the carnivores, together with giraffe, buffalo, and rhinoceros. In 1940, the British declared Serengeti a national park, the first in East Africa.

Most of the game to come under the protective laws was believed by then to be centered about the central plain of Serengeti—it was widely accepted that this was the main grazing land for the migratory herds of wildebeest—extending outward to the shore of Lake Victoria to the west and onto the floor of the Ngorongoro Crater to the east, thus forming natural boundaries logical to the definition of the park. Vastly simplified, the park's first borders would look like the sketch on the facing page.

At that early time, the decision seemed an enlightened one for the colonial government to reach, except in one important respect: it did not take into account a handful of Masai who resided within the plain and had adapted themselves amiably to the hazards of bad water and disease. Although by European custom a national park delegates all rights within its borders to flora and fauna, excluding even the entry of man except as tourist or caretaker, the problem of

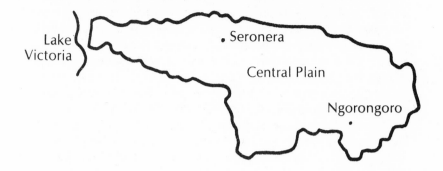

the Masai had not seemed pressing in 1940. Serengeti's herds obviously ranged far beyond the park's somewhat arbitrary boundaries; the tsetse was still a deterrent to permanent settlers; and the few Masai who lived there had occupied the area since long before the arrival of the British. In the Game Ordinance of 1940, the colonialists of Tanganyika had found it a matter of little consequence whether the Masai remained; in fact, there even seemed a certain logic to their presence. If the purpose of the park was to preserve nature, primitive man was a part of nature, and the Masai were primitive to the point of intransigence, rejecting Western ways; half-naked savages, some saw them, existing on a diet of cow's blood and milk. The Masai's presence in the park could be justified as simply another example of wildlife.

Soon enough, however, Tanganyika would become a protectorate of the United Nations and eventually, by 1961, would gain its independence. In 1964, Tanganyika joined with Zanzibar to form the independent Republic of Tanzania. While the transfer of power in this part of Africa would occur relatively amicably in contrast to other regions of the continent, political priorities would shift no less radically in favor of the needs of the Tanzanian people. Slowly, at first almost imperceptibly, and then with great swiftness, beginning as a local issue and ultimately turning international, the preservation of the Serengeti habitat forced the question that persists to this day: Between the needs of animals and the needs of man, which has right of way? By 1949, it was the pressure of the Masai—and by now there were believed to be some ten thousand of them in the park—seeking a place to pasture against the pressure of the animals seeking a place to graze that would bring this question to a head.

No people could have been less suited for the role of antagonist than the Masai. As nomadic pastoralists and comparatively recent settlers in vast sections of East Africa, they had themselves been increasingly pressed by the growth of modern agricultural interests, pushed downward from Nairobi and inward from the coast to the north-central region of Tanzania. They had been the most desirable of neighbors for the wild herds, living peacefully among them and roaming the plains without fear. Of the seven levels of development of the Masai male, only during the first two—when he would be expected to tend cattle alone on the plains through the age of twelve, and then into the rituals attending puberty—would he be obliged to prove his bravery; thereafter it was to be assumed. By 1949, the ten thousand Masai had been forced by land pressures onto the central plain and the floor of the Ngorongoro Crater, where they occasionally poached lion and rhinoceros (to demonstrate their bravery) and increasingly, with their cattle, blocked the wild herds from their water holes. Belatedly, the colonial government sought to impose restrictions against human settlement in the park, and the Masai were ordered out. The order was ignored. With Mau Mau disturbances now going on to the north, and because of an inherent sympathy for their plight, the colonial government decided not to push the point.

By this time, however, Serengeti had come to the attention of conservationists outside of Africa, and its reputation was established among them as a unique habitat—"the finest remaining assemblage of the plains game of Africa" was how the Encyclopaedia Britannica had described it at that time—and now it was the conservationists who began to press the issue. Why wouldn't the government honor its own regulations and move the Masai out? In 1956, harassed and confused, the colonial government announced with some uncertainty a new solution to the problem of the borders in favor of the Masai. If the Masai would not move, the borders would have to be changed to make room for them. The central plain—the acreage most vital to the migratory path of the herds—would be degazetted as parkland and opened legally to the Masai; the western corridor would become a small park in itself, and so would Ngorongoro and another, smaller crater, Embagai, at the eastern edge. In effect, the center of the park would be cut out. Now the Serengeti would look like the sketch on the facing page.

Instantly, the controversy spread beyond the continent. Some conservationists became so outraged they demanded the Serengeti

THE LAST PLACE ON EARTH

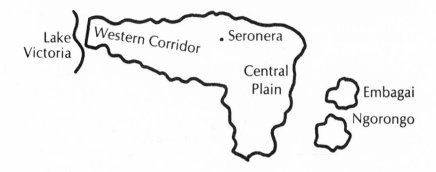

be removed from the administration of the British and placed directly under the supervision of the United Nations. Successive committees of inquiry were announced by the government, and a stream of expert witnesses filed into Arusha to testify, among them forestry and engineering officers from the British Colonial Office, L. S. B. Leakey, the paleontologist (living and working with his wife, Mary, at Olduvai, in the disputed area of the central plain), Masai elders, and officials of the New York and London Zoological Societies. In London, the Fauna Preservation Society commissioned a well-known botanist from London University, Dr. W. H. Pearsall, to visit the Serengeti, survey the ground in question and the movement of the game, and draw up his own recommendations along more scientific lines. In deference to Pearsall's credentials and with some relief at the possibility of being let off the hook, the government postponed its decision to await Pearsall's report. It was at about the time of the intersection of these events that a forty-eight-year-old German and his twenty-three-year-old son, Bernhard and Michael Grzimek, aghast at the government's equivocations, decided to take matters into their own hands. To begin with, they offered the governor of Tanganyika the money to *buy* the land and give it back to the animals.

TWO

The name is Polish, quite impossible to handle in English: "G," its elder bearer has patiently explained, "as in En*g*land,

> rz as in mea*s*ure
> i " " *I*ndia
> m " " *M*ombasa
> e " " *e*gg
> k " " *k*ingdom."

Most of his English-speaking acquaintances pronounce it "Jimek." It is a name which, since the late fifties, has come to be more closely associated with the rising and falling fortunes of the Serengeti today than any other. Dr. Bernhard Grzimek is a German veterinarian turned zookeeper who has devoted most of his life to the care and well-being of animals, the latter half of it particularly to the preservation of African wildlife, and especially to the wildlife and habitat of the Serengeti. Grzimek defines his purpose in life as "biophylaxis"—the protection of living species from extinction. His commitment has been constant since his earliest consciousness of hedgehogs and rabbits in the Upper Silesia of his childhood, and it has carried him through poverty, wars, and revolutions in Europe and Africa, personal loss, and public celebrity—all of which he has survived by making unequivocally clear to the world at large what his intentions are. ("First by soft line, then by hard line, next by bribery, and if necessary by outright blackmail," says John McDougall of the *Nairobi Daily Nation.*) Late in the spring of 1974, when he retired as Director of the Frankfurt Zoo, Grzimek described himself to the local press as "a showman of pity," an insight of precision which his career has supported since 1945, when, by his manipulation of the people and materials at hand, he restored the zoo from fifteen acres of bombed-out rubble and thirteen half-starved animals to its place as one of the leading zoological gardens in Europe.

Grzimek looks after animals—"Elephants can't vote," he is fond

28

of saying—and while he is not a religious man, he aligns himself with all those similarly concerned, secular or sacred, from Nietzsche to the authors of the Book of Genesis. "I sometimes ask myself," he once wrote, having just returned from an especially enervating trip to the Congo, "must one really and repeatedly make one's life so uncomfortable and wearisome? According to the Bible, one of our ancestors once built a big vessel and, as the waters rose, he saved from drowning lions and tigers, horses and cattle, giraffes and camels, and all the animals, two by two; by so doing, Noah bestowed upon future generations a gift richer than all the works of art, the discoveries and the knowledge, the religions and inventions of great men throughout the history of the human race. The swirling, ever rising tide of humanity is today drowning the wild animals just as surely as did the Flood in the Bible. But this flood kills more surely and lasts much longer. Creation is in dire need of a second Noah. Someone, then, must enter the lists on behalf of the animals; and not for the animals' sake alone, but for the sake of all mankind."

If elephants could vote, Grzimek would be a likely candidate. In their interest, he has been put upon by them—charged by rhinos, bitten by apes and wolves, infected with bilharzia—and has been held as a spy by the Sudanese and subjected to a bad scare during the Congolese revolt, when he barely escaped capture and probable execution. Because of his international identification with his constituency, he is now one of the few white men in the world welcomed by the heads of state of all black African countries. In 1972, while General Idi Amin Dada's bloody revolution traumatized Uganda, Grzimek flew into Kampala to lecture university students on animal behavior and to warn Amin himself on the damage of xenophobic policies to Uganda's tourist business, an important source of revenue for the economy from Amin's point of view, and for the wild animals from Grzimek's. The *idée fixe* of Bernhard Grzimek is animals. "People say I was a Nazi during the war," he says. "What they don't know is I wasn't *asked* to join the party. . . . What is important is that I would sit down to dinner with either Hitler or Stalin if it made any difference for my animals."

From a lifetime of standing off human adversaries, most of them politicians, Grzimek has himself become a political sophisticate, adapting his methods to the situation at hand to see his purpose through. He has outwitted, not necessarily successively, the German Army, the Allied occupation forces, the city fathers of Frankfurt, miscellaneous chicken and cattle breeders, the Canadian Parliament, Gina Lollobrigida, the leather industry in Offenbach, certain fellow-zookeepers in Europe, ministers of agriculture wherever they have crossed his path, and entrenched officials in the new, delicately sensitive governments of Africa. But especially ministers of agriculture, whose concern for the arable-land needs of people most often is directly opposed to the exclusive use of such land by animals.

Grzimek's method appears to be based on two unfailing perceptions applicable to most of the circumstances he has found himself in, from Labrador to New Guinea: (1) everybody likes animals unless immediately threatened by them; and (2) everyone has his pressure point, which Grzimek, if he is patient to seek it out, will be able to press. His success at what he has sought to do is measurable by many honors, among them gold medals from both the World Wildlife Fund and the New York Zoological Society, and by the esteem in which he is held by his peers. "He's a genius," says William Conway of the Bronx Zoo. "He has done more than anyone else to dramatize the plight of African wildlife." "He has undoubtedly been one of the greatest zoo directors and conservationists of our time," says C. G. C. Rawlins, Director of London Zoos. "I think that he did more to save the African fauna than any other person," says Dr. Heini Hediger, the Swiss zoologist. But beyond all this, if it is possible to compare such accomplishments, the grand obsession of Bernhard Grzimek, and unquestionably his most glowing achievement thus far, is the defensive war he has fought against time and man in protection of the Serengeti Plain.

By 1957, when the two Grzimeks began to concentrate their energies on the Serengeti, Bernhard Grzimek was better known throughout Europe than he was in Africa, although it was already known about him in Tanganyika that he followed a hard line on wildlife conservation and the offer to buy Serengeti was unlikely to be an idle gesture. The truth of the matter was that the money would come from Michael, who had it to spend, having earned it from filming African wildlife on an earlier trip with Bernhard. Both Grzimeks were strikingly attractive men, well over six feet tall, Bernhard with gray hair and Michael with blond, and both with wide turned-down grins. Michael had come to regard wild animals as part of the family, having been raised in the midst of visiting infants of various species—gorillas, kangaroos, wolves, and a group of chimpanzees whose occasional temper tantrums caused Bernhard to wear his old war helmet in their presence. Michael looked like his father and thought like him, and by the time he reached adolescence the two were inseparable. The Grzimeks had two other sons: Rochus, Michael's older brother, who had gone into business, and a boy named Thomas, whom the Grzimeks had adopted. But Grzimek seldom spoke of these two. It was Michael who was closer to him than anyone else. "Michael was not only my son," he would later write in an oddly revelatory moment, "but my only real friend."

In 1951, when Michael turned sixteen, Bernhard had carried him along on his first trip to Africa, and the two had traveled in an ancient truck through the rain forests of the Congo. Once, while in pursuit of forest elephants, the Grzimeks had become lost in the dense undergrowth and had wandered on foot for two days without food or weapons, existing on foliage they had observed chimpanzees eating. The trip was primarily a sightseeing expedition, but what is born in the bone is bred in the flesh, Grzimek later observed, and the two had returned to the west coast with two hundred animals—chimpanzees, monkeys, birds, snakes, and civet cats—all caged for shipment back to the Frankfurt Zoo. By sea, the trip to Hamburg would take longer than four weeks—more time than Bernhard could spare from his duties at the zoo. He arranged passage for his son and the animals on a small freighter, turned the expedition over to Michael, and flew on ahead. Later, in a school essay of the what-I-did-last-summer variety, Michael wrote an account of the experience that falls in the literature of boyhood adventures somewhere between *Captains Courageous* and *Swiss Family Robinson*:

> . . . For myself I had been given a small cabin directly over the stern. The door would not lock, and I got very angry at the way in which all the sailors kept on coming in and nosing around. Then I had a brain wave; I set free the large python which I kept in a box in my quarters, and let it roam about the cabin at will. After that, not a soul dared even open the door the tiniest crack! One day, incidentally, the python crawled through a hole in the steel wall and into the men's quarters, and there was a frightful hullabaloo. Everyone tried to get through the door at the same time, and two of the sailors were literally shivering with funk; actually I had to stand them a bottle of gin to make up for it, but I felt I had had my revenge for the way they were always laughing at me when I was seasick. . . .

Their second trip, two years later, was more ambitious and would provide the means for their later entry into Serengeti. Bernhard had wanted to bring back an okapi—the exquisite forest animal that seems a cross between a giraffe and a zebra, and whose existence was not discovered until 1900; he would write a book (he had, following the previous trip), and Michael, who had on his own arranged financial backing, would make a documentary film. Again the Grzimeks wandered the Congo, pursuing the okapi, living with Pygmies and gradually forming the perception that would come to obsess them both: there were too many people now, even in Darkest Africa, and no room left for the animals. Grzimek made it the theme of his book. "During the few minutes which it takes you to read to the end of this chapter," he began, "the number of people on earth will have increased by 4,000. By tomorrow at the same time the earth's population will have risen by almost 100,000. . . . To feed the new arrivals of a single month new arable land has to be found equal in size to the combined areas of Rhode Island and Delaware." He entitled the chapter, "Africa's Wild Animals Are Doomed," and the book, *Kein Platz für Wilde Tiere* (*No Room for Wild Animals*). The book was eventually translated into seventeen languages; Michael's film, with the same title and same theme, achieved a comparable success, winning in the Berlin Film Festival over Walt Disney's *The African Lion*. The film also gave the Grzimeks an opportunity to express their concern over impending events surrounding the Serengeti. Now, as Michael's profits began to mount, they made their offer to the British Colonial Office in Tanganyika.

To Frankfurt came a representative of the embarrassed British, Lieutenant Colonel Peter P. G. Molloy, bearing a counterproposal. "He suggested we should use the money for a much more important purpose," Grzimek later wrote. "The plains of Serengeti are said to harbor more than a million large animals, and these are constantly roaming in large herds. Sometimes there is one wildebeest beside the other as far as the eye can see; at others the same area is completely devoid of animals for months on end. There are many hypotheses about this migration, and the proposed new borders of the park are based on some of these theories. Up to now nobody has found how to follow the wandering animals. During the rainy season one often cannot drive even a station wagon over the few existing roads, let alone across swamped plains, mountains and ravines. The government has no funds to spare for such research—

but what government on earth ever had money to spare for lions, giraffes, zebras, and wildebeest?'' Because of the limited time the British scientist Pearsall would have on the plain, his survey would not be likely to provide the data needed. Molloy had suggested the Grzimeks devise some way to survey the Serengeti and the movements of the migration and then advise the government on the proper placing of the park's boundaries.

The Grzimeks were delighted, not only with Molloy's assurance of the government's good intentions but as well for the invitation to be part of the effort. They saw it as an unprecedented opportunity, as though having been invited to help save the great American bison herds of a hundred years ago, except that in this case the host government seemed genuinely committed to advanced principles of conservation. It would be the most ambitious scientific survey ever attempted in East Africa. The Grzimeks were uncertain as to how long their mission would take, but they were prepared to allow whatever time would be necessary to do it right. No matter what the scheme might cost them, they thought then, the result would be justified. The Grzimeks made their plans. They would have to improvise a laboratory of some sort in Serengeti, devise ways to capture and mark a variety of species, arrange some system of communication with scientists back home—endless details which had to be anticipated before departure. As before, Bernhard would write about the expedition and Michael would film it. But first, and most important, Michael insisted, they would have to learn to fly. To count such large numbers of game over so wide a territory would otherwise be impossible. And since they would be counting by eye, landing and taking off on rough terrain, they would need a plane suited to the mission. The Grzimeks ordered a Dornier-27 with a wingspan longer than the fuselage, capable of slowing the craft to thirty miles per hour at low altitudes. Only a few years earlier, and also at Michael's insistence, Bernhard had learned to drive. Now they both took lessons to learn how to fly their airplane, had it painted with black and white stripes, like a zebra, for easy identification, and on December 11, 1957, took off from Frankfurt, heading southeast for Serengeti, four thousand miles away, on the most extraordinary adventure of their lives.

"I remember my first encounter with them well," says Myles Turner, a Kenyan and former park warden of Serengeti who was living at the time with his wife and infant daughter at Banagi, in the heart of the wilderness plain. "Peter Molloy rang me up on the radio one day and said, 'Two Germans are coming over one of these days. Sort of look after them, will you? They're called Grzimek.' We'd never heard of them. I began making an airstrip nearby because Molloy said they had an airplane. One day a ranger and I were hauling away logs, trying to clear a place, and way in the distance I heard an airplane coming. This was a very rare thing in those days. We were *astonished!* We couldn't believe it. We only had four hundred yards cleared, the rest was trees lying around. It was nowhere near ready, and the ranger was pushing away underbrush with a bulldozer. Suddenly, over the trees came this Dornier plane striped like a zebra. We sort of stared back—we thought, They'll *never* land here. Michael just shoved on those great big flaps and down he came, and there the two of them were!"

Now, seventeen years later, Turner is still struck by the memory of them: "The thing that impressed me about them—they were a terrific pair, with *tremendous* vitality! They'd both got licenses in Europe. They were going to spend a lot of money on the game. They could have sat back on the profits of the film they had made, but no, they were going to do something for the game. From the moment they arrived, the *vitality* of those two—and the *work* they put into it—*tremendous!* . . .

"Another thing was the extraordinary relationship between Bernhard and Michael. They were more like brothers, really, than father and son. With Michael possibly a little ahead, making the decisions, and the old man agreeing, arguing a bit but usually giving in. It seemed to me Michael was running the show. A very strong personality, great charm. But they worked like a couple of close brothers, certainly not father and son. *Amazing!*"

"I think Bernhard would often let Michael run things. They were always playing like a couple of brothers," says Alan Root, a Kenyan filmmaker who began his career working with the Grzimeks in Serengeti. "They had this great thing of trying to catch the other guy unaware and slap him on the leg. You could be flying the plane and if Michael was asleep, Bernhard would notice this, and POW! he would whack him one. They wrestled a lot. Grzimek had Michael when he was very young, and he urged Michael to do the same, to marry straightaway so he could have grandsons to wrestle with. Michael had done this, and when they came to Serengeti he had one son and another on the way."

Myles Turner and another senior warden named Gordon Harvey

were responsible for supervision of the entire Serengeti area at the time—Turner for the Serengeti Plain, and Harvey for Ngorongoro. Even now, both having retired from Tanzania Parks, they give the impression of having been selected for their roles by a knowledgeable British film director. Turner is a small, wiry redhead with hooded eyes and a melancholy cast to his features; Harvey is older, with silver-gray hair and regular features. Both are politely distant until they become interested in the conversation, at which point Turner grows lyrical and Harvey turns brusque and deliberate, with heavy pauses and clipped, descending phrases. In predictable fashion for such men, both became conservators after some years of hunting the game. "I'd had enough," Turner says. "I loved hunting, I've shot ever since I was a kid, but you go on killing these animals and all this misery gets to you. You just get through it, and there comes the stage when you want to do something for the animals, and then you get mad on photography. And the final stage is to sit in your car, without your camera or anything, and just look at them." Both were sensitively aware of the delicate setting within their care. "My wife, Edith, used to set out watercress near the crater," Harvey says. "When we went down into the crater we'd plant shoots all about the place so we could treat visitors to watercress sandwiches when they came in on safari."

Turner and Harvey helped the Grzimeks put up a corrugated-tin shelter which would serve both as housing and as a laboratory during their stay in the Serengeti, and the Grzimeks set to work, flying grid patterns a thousand yards apart and counting the animals by eye from a height of one hundred and fifty to three hundred feet. There was room for four in the plane, and Turner and Harvey often flew with them, two counting from one side of the plane and two counting from the other. "You could only count in the months of February and March when ninety-five per cent of the ungulates—the wildebeest, zebra, and gazelle—were centered on the plains," Harvey says. "We would take off and fly quite low. We had a pad and a method. A dot meant ten, a cross fifty, and a circle a hundred. We got our count within ten per cent accuracy, and we kept practicing to get reliable estimates."

As the expedition progressed, Michael concentrated on his film, working with the young Alan Root and with a school friend who had come down to join them, Hermann Gimbel, a law student specializing in liability cases resulting from air crashes. The Grzimeks remained in the Serengeti throughout the year, experimenting with methods of animal observation that are now considered standard technique: they lassoed ungulates from their Land Rover, tranquilized them with the first crude dart guns, and marked them with dye for later aerial observation of their migratory movement. Grass samples were shipped back to a laboratory in Darmstadt to determine the grazing preferences of the animals.

"The Grzimeks went to great pains to be accurate," Harvey says. But it was for all of them a time of high excitement as well, and life on the plain was unpredictable. (On one occasion hyenas ate the rubber off the wheels of their airplane.) Michael was irrepressible and adventurous, both Turner and Harvey now recall, and they would not quibble the point: he was reckless. Once, while he was trying to lasso a zebra from the roof of the Land Rover, his rope pole slipped to the ground, jabbed backward into his throat, and knocked him off the vehicle. Grzimek flew him to Musoma for emergency treatment. Twice he seriously damaged the Dornier, and on one of these occasions he was obliged to leave his father alone on the floor of the Ngorongoro Crater at dusk in the company of an impressive variety of predators, all of which look on a man wandering alone at night (unless he is Masai) as an invitation to a banquet.

Gordon Harvey was with Michael on the occasion, and so was Myles Turner; both have had their share of narrow escapes with lions and other dangers of the bush, but the episode with Michael they look back upon as among their more sobering.

"We had been flying over wildebeest and we came in too low," Harvey recalls. "We felt a sudden violent blow to the plane—and I thought the tail had fallen off. Apparently we had hit an animal; there was a huge hole in the bottom of the plane, and the door had blown open. The plane was wobbling. Michael stayed very cool, got us a little higher, and straightened out the plane. One of the wheels was broken.

"We flew back over Grzimek, who was waiting for us on the floor of the crater. I wrote him a note on a piece of foolscap. I said we were going to Nairobi—this was Michael's idea, to get the plane fixed properly—and for him to get out of the crater as best he could. Turned out he didn't get the note. As a precaution, we flew over the lodge on the edge of the crater where our wives were and dropped them a note, too. They *got* this one and started down into the crater after Bernhard. But they told us later they had started too late. They took the long road into the crater and drove around with their lights on, but they couldn't find him.

"Meanwhile, we proceeded on toward Nairobi. Michael knew the operator in the control tower and the two of them jabbered back and forth over the radio in Polish and German. The operator told Michael to fly around until he'd exhausted his fuel. He instructed us to tie ourselves down and make sure there was nothing loose in the plane. He also told Michael to land on the dirt by the main strip because he didn't want his tarmac messed up.

"We flew around Nairobi and watched a soccer game below, and then we flew over a cemetery. We saw four freshly dug graves each right next to the other. Finally the motor started to sputter and Myles said to me, 'If you get out of this and I don't, watch after Kay. . . .'

"Then we came in. Michael landed on the one good wheel, carried the plane along on it until we had sufficiently slowed, and then let down on the left. We began to skid—sparks everywhere—turned a complete circle, and came to a stop on the tarmac. A spectacular bit of flying. Spectacular. Ambulances and fire engines pulled up with men in asbestos suits, and the first thing they did was give us hell for landing on the tarmac!

"As for old Grzimek, he wandered across the crater and just before dark ran into some Masai. He spoke no Swahili, but they figured he was in trouble. They took him to their *manyatta,* killed a sheep for him, and kept him through the night."

By the first week of January, 1959, with grim satisfaction, for their investigations had confirmed what they suspected about the inadequacy of Serengeti's proposed new borders, the Grzimeks had completed the major part of their study and were making plans for their return to Frankfurt. They had counted 366,980 large animals in the Serengeti area—194,654 Thomson's and Grant's gazelle, 99,481 wildebeest, 57,199 zebra, 5,172 topi, 2,452 eland, 1,717 impala, 1,813 black buffalo, 1,285 kongoni, 837 giraffe, 284 waterbuck, 178 stork, 115 oryx, 60 elephant, 57 roan antelope, 55 rhinoceros, and 1,621 ostrich—but not always were they to be found within the park's present boundaries, and, of course, when outside the boundaries they were free for the taking. The Grzimeks discovered that in the dry months of July and August, in fact, most of them weren't in the park at all but just above the western corridor in populated areas around the shores of Lake Victoria.

The Grzimeks had also established to their satisfaction the direction of the migration: they believed it moved south from the western corridor to the central plain near the foothills of Ngorongoro and back again. And they had determined the reasons for it. The wildebeest, zebra, and gazelle—the larger part of the migratory herd—grazed only certain grasses, and they took them when they were short. Hence, they would follow the rains moving eastward across the plains (at a rate of approximately twelve miles a day) as the first shoots were sprouting, and then double back after the grass had come up again. The Grzimeks' survey confirmed the worst fears of the hard-line conservationists, themselves included: the elimination of the central plain *would* destroy the migration— the single unexpendable element in the biological life of the plain. Moreover, they believed their evidence supported an argument not just for retaining the old boundaries, but for extending them.

The Grzimeks were later proved right in their conclusion but not precisely for the reasons they offered. At the time of the Grzimek count, scientists now believe, there were almost twice as many wildebeest on and about the Serengeti Plain. Not only were they bunched together in the northwest during the dry months but there were many more directly above the park as well, roaming north to the Kenya border and across to Masai Mara. The Grzimeks had flown over the north, but at times, apparently, when the animals were beyond their observation; and since the northern region was sparsely inhabited, there had been no documentary indications of their presence. But the Grzimeks' findings were to prove academic in any case. Sir Richard Turnbull, the Governor of Tanganyika, had decided not to wait for their report. Unbeknownst to the two of them, he had settled on a compromise solution that he hoped might please all parties. The contested central plain would become part of a greater Ngorongoro "Conservation Unit," a multiple-land-use plan permitting some agriculture, forestry, and grazing in the vicinity of the crater, but the central plain would be reserved for the game and any migratory movement within its boundaries. The western corridor would continue on as parkland, but added to it now—rather arbitrarily, almost as an afterthought for the concerned conservationists—was the large block of uninhabited land stretching upward from the central plain to the Kenya border. Thus was to occur another of Serengeti's curious, almost mystical ironies. Although seen as worthless at the time, the new northern extension would turn out to be the dry-season grazing grounds providing shelter to the huge herds the Grzimeks had somehow overlooked in

THE LAST PLACE ON EARTH

their 1958 expedition, absolutely crucial to the wildebeest migration. Not until a study completed several years later would this become apparent. But now, finally, a decision had been made and the borders fixed, including the providential northern extension, and they would, with minor but important modifications, remain the same to the present day:

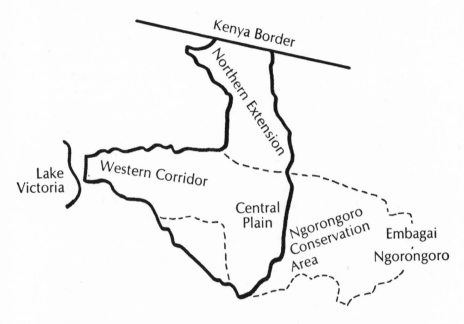

Word of these developments reaching Banagi brought shock and disappointment to the Grzimeks. They had invested considerable time and effort in their study, the better part of a year, with the understanding they would be serving some purpose. Now, apparently, whatever they might recommend, their findings would come too late.

On January 9th, the Grzimeks flew to Lake Natron to photograph flamingos for Michael's film. They had put down near the shore, and in the middle of the night a fierce rainstorm flooded the lake, threatening to swamp their plane. By the time they had moved the Dornier to higher ground, they were drenched and exhausted. Stripping out of their wet clothes, they wrapped themselves in their flying jackets and shivered through the night in the cockpit. Later

Grzimek would write about some of the things that went through his mind in the early morning of the tenth as Michael dozed fitfully beside him and the thunder crashed about their plane:

". . . If we had died that night nobody could have made sense out of our many notes on the life of the herds of animals in the Serengeti. Nobody else could have edited and cut the seventy thousand feet of colored film intended to produce *the* film of our dreams. The chances of survival of the Serengeti inhabitants would have been lessened.

"This probably seems unimportant to most people, to the people who would say: 'Those two didn't deserve any better. Why did they risk their necks for zebras and lions?' Men have other ideals for which they are willing to die: freedom, glory, politics, religion, the rulership of their classes, or the expansion of national borders. But in the long run Michael and I will be proved right. . . ."

Later that morning, the Grzimeks returned to their camp at Ngorongoro, dried out, and had a huge meal of fried steak and fresh pineapple. They would leave for Frankfurt on the next day, the eleventh, and now they began to make preparations for their departure. Around four in the afternoon, Michael flew off toward Banagi to pick up Alan Root and Hermann Gimbel, who had been photographing a sequence for the film. Flying quite low, in the vicinity of the Loliondo mountain range, the Dornier collided with a griffon vulture, the force of the vulture's body pinning the aileron cables along the leading edge of the right wing against the forward side of the main spar and sending the plane into a steep dive from an altitude of six hundred feet. A group of Masai were in the area digging water holes for their cattle, precisely the act of encroachment the Grzimeks were working so diligently to end. They saw the plane crash into the ground, and one of them ran to tell a nearby ranger.

Gordon Harvey was away in London on leave, and his replacement was the first to receive the news that Michael had died in the crash. "We made arrangements for the body to be collected, and a park's lorry was sent down to Ildonyogol," the warden recalls. "I followed on down to sort out the plane and get the place ready for the aviation people who would want to inspect it. We sent a message to Bernhard before I left to tell him what had happened and to break the news carefully to him. Possibly he would have arrived after the body had been brought up and this gave him the opportunity to pull himself together before viewing his son's remains." Michael's body was buried the next day on the eastern rim of the Ngorongoro Crater at a site overlooking the soda lake on the crater's floor below and beyond that—because the crater's shelf dips down along the facing western rim—the beginning of the central plain of the Serengeti.

THREE

Bernhard Grzimek returned to Frankfurt and completed the scientific report of their survey, which he published in a monograph entitled "Zeitschrift für Saugetierkunde." Next he wrote the book he had planned, ending it with Michael's death, and then he turned to the task of completing Michael's film. In late 1959, the book was published, and several months later the film was released. Both met with immediate success. The book was translated into twenty-three languages, and the film won an Oscar—the fifth in the history of the motion picture academy to go to a German film. Both carried as title a stern injunction: *Serengeti Shall Not Die.*

As a departing gesture, the British colonial government built, in Michael's memory, a laboratory in the Serengeti for the study of wildlife. By 1965, the Michael Grzimek Memorial Laboratory had become part of the major complex known today as the Serengeti Research Institute, the wildlife station housing from fifteen to twenty international scientists representing a variety of disciplines—geology, botany, zoology, behavior—all studying the interrelation of the Serengeti animals and their environment. The Serengeti Research Institute has since subjected the fifty-one hundred square miles of the Serengeti Plain to more careful scrutiny than has been received by any comparable wildlife acreage on earth. Moreover, since the Grzimeks first raised the alarm regarding its future, the Serengeti has drawn the concern and active attention of Niko Tinbergen, Konrad Lorenz, Peter Scott, the late Sir Julian Huxley, and the late Charles Lindbergh. It has received financial support from the Fritz Thyssen and Max Planck Foundations in Germany; from the Ford Foundation and the Canadian Agency for International Development; from the New York, London, and Frankfurt Zoological Societies; from the United Nations; from assorted conservation societies and universities; from numberless individuals, including African schoolchildren (whose donations helped construct the Michael Grzimek Memorial Laboratory); and from a group known as the Friends of Serengeti—wealthy American tourists for the most part, who, having seen it, want, like the Grzimeks, to try to save it.

Yet, while the care and support from outside agencies would prove important to the preservation of Serengeti Park, Grzimek realized in 1960 that the people who would ultimately decide its fate were not the people in charge of Tanganyika at that time—the colonial British, who were moving out—but the people who would soon reclaim it, the native citizens of the new nation eventually to be called Tanzania. Outside financing and scientific research were important, and Grzimek would play his role in seeing that both were made available to Serengeti. But in the longer view these matters were primarily tactical; Grzimek's concern was strategic, and by now he had gained an important edge. His experience in the Serengeti had been acquired at the expense of his son's life and the rejection of their research. Most men would have turned away in disgust and bitterness, but Grzimek simply decided to increase his efforts. Among emerging black African leaders he had earned the right to be regarded as one European different from all the rest: his sole concern was to help Africans conserve their own resources. In the political turbulence fast overtaking Tanganyika, Grzimek's sacrifices in the Serengeti and his success as an international spokesman for its problems would provide him a degree of influence that neither money could buy nor diplomatic power force. In nearly all the emerging African nations, as he had foreseen in *No Room for Wild Animals,* food and the arable land necessary to produce it had become instant priorities, especially in poor countries like Tanganyika. But even in independent countries with greater subsistence resources, such as Uganda, the reordering of national goals immediately increased the danger to wildlife, for not only would human poverty threaten the animals, but, paradoxically, so would economic progress as well. "Grzimek realized that as exports in these new countries increased—coffee, for example, or sisal—then industrialization would rise," says William Conway. "And when the gross national product of a country goes up, the value of land goes up, too. When this happens in countries like Tanzania, the value of animals on that land goes down."

By 1960, Bernhard Grzimek realized that if the Serengeti was to survive, he would have to provide the new Tanzanian leaders with hardheaded, practical reasons for conserving it. At first, tourism seemed the most likely way. By "civilizing" the experience—adding roads and lodges and modern conveniences—the government could draw an international audience to see the animals, providing revenue to equal that from coffee or sisal. But tourism, he soon perceived, could not always be counted on as a reliable source of support; there were too many variables. The only enduring course, Grzimek realized—certainly the one that appealed to him most—was the establishment of Serengeti as a cultural resource for the world, under the watchcare of the Republic of Tanzania. Coming late to modern society, the East African countries had little as yet to attract the interest of the industrial nations of the Northern Hemisphere. But their stock of wildlife was unique and irreplaceable. The great reserve of Serengeti, the last of its kind, could offer the rest of the world a glimpse into the past time of its own beginning, something worth treasuring in perpetuity against wars, plagues, drought—even famine. In Tanzania, his objective would be to instill a pride of possession for the world's sake. It would be a difficult argument to make; no other civilization had accepted it. Nevertheless, by 1960, Bernhard Grzimek had decided to see what he could do to put it over.

On my first trip to East Africa, in 1969, ten years after these seminal events, having come as a tourist to see the wildlife, I had never heard of the Grzimeks, nor had I much of an idea what to expect from the African countryside other than what I had read of Hemingway—not untypical of most Americans even though they are, by far, the predominant tourists to Nairobi. I took the "milk run," by now the well-traveled tourist circuit of two weeks' duration—from Nairobi southeast to Amboseli and Tsavo in Kenya, then back to the southwest and across the border to Ngorongoro and Serengeti in Tanzania, and then almost due north to Masai Mara in Kenya, swinging east again to return to Nairobi—a distance of about a thousand miles. It has come to be the most popular touring route in East Africa for several reasons: because it so efficiently yields the greatest riches of the savanna in the shortest time; because the roads in season (January through March, and September through November) are today reasonably navigable; and because the lodges, which are situated along that way about half a day's distance one from the next, are as sleek and extravagant as a rich man's retreat in the Caribbean. The year I was there, some eighty-five thousand visitors from around the world took the same route.

East Africa was not what I had expected it to be, neither jungle nor was there even at first glance much of a sense of wilderness. Tsavo, an early stop, reminded me oddly of the red-clay piedmont of

44   THE LAST PLACE ON EARTH

North Carolina. At the bookracks in the Kenya lodges, seeking to fix the place to an imagined impression, I kept looking for *The Green Hills of Africa*, but I couldn't find it, not even Robert Ruark's novels which I would have settled for. What was there and displayed most prominently was *Serengeti Shall Not Die*, by Bernhard Grzimek. I thought it curious that an English translation of a book by a German on conservation would be more in demand than anything by Hemingway on Africa, especially in a country so heavily visited by Americans. But I let it go at that; I was there after all to see, not to read, and I didn't feel unduly curious about Grzimek, even though at Seronera, halfway through the trip, I heard the strange guttural name again, this time affixed to one of the laboratories at the Serengeti Research Institute.

On another occasion—now in Serengeti for the third time and reporting on the trip for an American magazine—I was told of a scientist who regularly flew a glider from Ngorongoro over Serengeti to study the aerodynamics of the vulture's flight; and when I went to the Serengeti Research Institute to interview the man—a red-bearded Englishman named Pennycuick—he told me he couldn't pose for my photographer without Bernhard Grzimek's permission as Grzimek intended to make a film of his study and had first rights to any publicity deriving from his research. Pennycuick finally permitted the photographer to take his picture with the understanding that I would write Grzimek for his consent to publish it. I grew more intrigued by this man who apparently had established proprietary claim over life on the Serengeti Plain.

Back in upstate New York, my wife found at our local library a copy of one of Grzimek's several popular works translated into English, telling of his various experiences with animals in Africa. On a rainy afternoon I picked it up and began to browse. It was fluff reading but compelling, filled with bizarre facts about animals (the giraffe uses his neck as a lash and his head as a club, one blow can kill you), an occasional jeremiad (a hundred and twenty species of animals have become extinct since the days of Christ), and unpredictable, still-boyish adventures (how Grzimek confronted a live rhinoceros with a rubber dummy rhinoceros for purposes scientific, presumably, but unexplained). Having promised Pennycuick I would, I now wrote Grzimek in care of the Frankfurt Zoo and received, along with his consent, an unexpected request:

> . . . Please don't forget in your article the great contribution
> of African politicians to conservation of nature, which in my

opinion is a new branch of human culture becoming more and more important in the future. A country like Tanzania spends eight times more for conservation of nature than the United States of America, compared with their national income. Dr. Kaunda, President of Zambia, declared last year 15% of his country National Parks. Mobutu of the Congo in the last congress of his national party declared "We have certain advantages in being under-equipped. We have to be proud that we never made errors such as those which are regretted by some countries considered as completely developed. We are never disappointed, not to show our guests old cathedrals or monuments because the heritage of our ancestors is the natural beauty of our country, our rivers, large streams, forests, insects, animals, lakes, volcanoes, mountains and plains. In a world (sic), nature is the integral and real part of our originality and personality. We desire only that when scientists will have transformed the world into an artificial one that in Zaire an authentic nature will remain." If you write and speak about National Parks and Conservation of nature we should always praise not only the few Europeans like us working there, but also the responsible politicians. I would like that West German and American politicians in this new branch of human culture would soon reach the level of education of some Black African politicians like Dr. Nyerere, Dr. Kaunda, Mobutu, etc.

Mobutu has just created some more National Parks, among them the largest in the world, which for another fifty years will not be visited by tourists, but is just to protect nature and for scientific work. . . .

By now I had read *Serengeti Shall Not Die* and whatever else I could find by him in this country. I had learned that he was a professor of zoology at the University of Giessen; that he was the editor of a magazine about animals, *Das Tier*, with the largest circulation of any animal magazine in print (described by *The Times* of London as the best in the world, Heini Hediger and Konrad Lorenz are his coeditors); that his television program on wildlife, "A Place for Animals," was the most popular show in Germany; that the Frankfurt Zoo, which he had salvaged out of the war's rubble, was today considered one of Europe's best; and that he had organized two hundred scientists throughout the world to produce a massive, thirteen-volume encyclopedia of wildlife,

46   THE LAST PLACE ON EARTH

Grzimeks Tierleben: Enzyklopädie des Tierreiches, more comprehensive than any survey previously published, including the
nineteenth-century work, *Brehms Tierleben.* His expeditions to
Africa and elsewhere—New Guinea, Australia, South America—
have been the settings for most of his popular books about animals,
and a writer named Friedrich Gnosa had compared him to Albert
Schweitzer as that special breed of scientist who places practical
action above theory, a sentiment expressed in the English press by
Cyril Connolly. But of all the secondary material I was able to find, I
was most struck by the description Grzimek had given of himself to
a reporter, that he was "a showman of pity."

He seemed a man consumed by a single idea.

In my own case, my interests had been conditioned primarily by
my occupation as a magazine editor most of my adult life, a self-
fulfilling endeavor since it is a convention of such work to regard a
magazine's content as the extension of its editor's interests. The
magazine I worked for encouraged eclecticism ("Expect the Unexpected" was its oxymoronic bid to prospective subscribers), and I
had assumed that so long as I remained curious about the world I
shared with readers I would spend most of my time—if not always
deeply engaged—at least attentive and interested. My experience
had confirmed this: "work" had led from such unpredictably
interesting occasions as tea with Dorothy Parker to my brief
interview with Pennycuick in the Serengeti. For reasons unrelated
to this account, however, such work had recently come to an end
with the consequence that a choice of direction had to be made.
Having for so long skimmed the surface of so many interests, I
found it difficult to take any one of them as more steadfast than
another although Serengeti, the least likely and appealing more to
sensibility than to any other discernible prompting, had remained
one of the more persistent. Grzimek presented a new and bizarre
dimension to a pleasant past experience, a way back, perhaps, to a
place I longed to see again.

I wrote Dr. Grzimek that I would very much like to spend time
with him—some in Frankfurt but most of it, if possible, in East
Africa—in order to write about him and his continuing concern
with the Serengeti Plain. I would hope to go on safari with him. His
response was cordial but hardly encouraging: "I am a little bit
shocked that you want so much time. . . ." He would be leaving
soon for his annual visit to East Africa and he possibly could see me
for a brief interview in either Frankfurt or Nairobi, but extended

meetings were impossible; his schedule in Africa was indefinite but certain to be crowded. He included his private telephone number in Nairobi.

When I arrived in Frankfurt some weeks later, he had already left for Africa. None of his associates knew what he would be doing there, not even his secretary, nor where in East Africa he would be traveling—a characteristic departure, I was to learn. I spent my time talking with his associates and adding to my file, and then, toward the end of the week, I went to the Frankfurt Television Center to see an aging print of the documentary he had made with Michael, *Serengeti Shall Not Die.*

It was a cold, depressing day—the air over Frankfurt is as rancid as New York's—and I felt momentarily annoyed that I had provoked for myself so disturbing a disarrangement of time and place. The screening room was chrome and real leather, like the interior of a Mercedes, and when the lights went down I didn't know really what to expect. I had seen still photographs of both men, but they were of snapshot quality, unhelpful. By modern standards, the Grzimeks' documentary was crudely put together, and it seemed to move at a snail's pace. Still, it was in color, there was excellent footage of the animals, and early on, you could sense the great flat distances of the Serengeti. Michael's tall gangling presence was dominant: wrestling with zebras, flying his Dornier low over the wildebeest, laughing happily as a tiny bush baby crawled in and out of his shirt. The Grzimeks had re-created Michael's near-disastrous accident when he had fallen from the roof of the Land Rover, and there were other semidramatic episodes—Michael and Bernhard chasing poachers, and so on.

As in the snapshots, Michael seemed slightly unreal—old fashioned and almost too innocent, like a Tom Swift out of the twenties. His image on the screen was nevertheless visually consistent with the impressions I had formed of him, whereas Bernhard's associates had already corrected my first mental picture of the father. I had imagined him to be a single-minded man, given perhaps too easily to hyperbole and sentimentality, passionate but indulgent, essentially mild and rather easygoing—Icarus to Michael's Daedalus. The film supported the impression, but the man was different. In Frankfurt, Bernhard Grzimek is viewed with an odd mixture of respect and apprehension, as a single-minded and passionate man but not at all indulgent, shy, strung taut, tough, and very powerful. "In my view," said a local reporter, "he's a terrible

THE LAST PLACE ON EARTH

eccentric. I interviewed him once, and he kept some sort of wild cat in the room—the beast almost destroyed my tape recorder. Basically he is a missionary with a rather narrow perception, and usually he is stepping on one too many toes."

Bernhard Grzimek is a man of great energy: his typical day, as one associate describes it, is "to get up at five, do calisthenics, eat a light breakfast, be at the zoo by seven, spend the day there, come back to edit some of his film, read manuscripts for *Das Tier,* write thirty letters to scientists about his animal encyclopedia, then climb into bed and read himself to sleep."

Grzimek knows how to raise money for animals, and over the years he has learned how best to spend it; from his experience with television he also knows how to reach and influence the public. Through the assistance of the late George von Opel, the car manufacturer (who had his own private one-hundred-and-eighty-five-acre zoo) and a German official of the Common Market, he organized the financial community of Frankfurt into a revival of the Frankfurt Zoological Society—the Society of 1858—whose purpose was to relieve the zoo from total dependence upon the city budget. By the time of the zoo's centennial in 1958, his objectives having been met, Grzimek kept the money channel open to fund animal projects outside of Germany, mostly in East Africa.

Early in the fifties, he first appeared on television with a documentary entitled "Gorillas Need to Sleep, Too." Germans are entranced with animals: they lead the world in the rather recent science of ethology—animal behavior—and on a more quotidian level, I was surprised to see, they take their pets with them into the most exclusive restaurants. Grzimek and his animal shows were an immediate success. They have continued to be. Since 1959, his television specials appearing four to six times a year have consistently drawn between sixty and eighty per cent of the viewing audience. "When Grzimek is on the air," a local viewer observes, "the streets are empty." His shows are fashioned directly out of his views, anthropomorphic sometimes to the point of archness (his animal magazine is edited from the animals' point of view) but authoritative, and there is no nonsense about priorities—no music or other gratuitous embellishments, only Grzimek and the animals. Unlike animal shows in America, which are commercially sponsored, Grzimek's have only the animals to sell. Often he will talk on about a given subject while the film moves in another and unrelated direction. He puts the shows together himself, directs, cuts and talks over footage he himself has shot or (as in the case of Pennycuick) contracted for. He has film crews on assignment in various parts of the world, and sometimes he buys the films of others and adds his own comment.

Grzimek uses his television programs to raise more money. When he shows animals in jeopardy, he simply comes right out and asks for it. He directs the money received from viewers to another special fund called Friends of Threatened Animals. He then invites critics of his solicitations on state-owned television, if they care to challenge his intentions, to examine his books to see where the money goes. To date, he has raised six and a half million marks from his shows; he himself has given a quarter of a million marks from his own income to such causes. "You must understand that he is meticulously correct in his handling of these funds," says Dr. Richard Faust, his successor at the Frankfurt Zoo. "They are set up for the purpose of meeting wildlife crises anywhere in the world. We have no committees to contend with; there is no bureaucratic delay. When money is needed, we can send it out anywhere in the world, in seven days. We don't have fancy dinners to raise funds. That's too expensive in itself. We raise the money for animals, and 99.8 per cent of the money collected goes for the purpose intended." The fiscal construct of Grzimek's funding sources is as complex and orderly as a spider's web. At the center of it all is Bernhard Grzimek who, for the most part, decides how the money will be spent.

Thus, in the morgue of *The East African Standard,* I was later to find a steady stream of old news clippings attesting to his financial power in East Africa:

18 March, 1963—Sixty miles of a hundred-mile-long fire break through the Tsavo National Park have been completed. It was announced that the cost of this would be covered by a donation of 1400 pounds by Dr. Bernhard Grzimek. . . .

29 March, 1963—Dr. Bernhard Grzimek's influence with the Frankfurt Zoological Society has led to road development grants for two national parks in Northern Tanzania. . . .

6 January, 1967—Dr. Bernhard Grzimek has just given 5,000 pounds for the new Meru National Park. . . .

30 April, 1967—An amphibious vehicle has been given to the Murchison Falls Park by Dr. Bernhard Grzimek to aid in the apprehension of poachers. . . .

12 February, 1968—Dr. Bernhard Grzimek has made a gift of money to the relatives of a game scout who was killed by poachers on Rubondo Island in Lake Tanganyika. . . .

Donations on a larger scale seldom make the papers, because of the delicacy of the transaction. Grzimek and his various funds offered one East African nation a grant of fifty thousand pounds to establish land for a new park with the strict provision that no dawdling would be permitted: the money would have to be used by a deadline date, or forfeited.

Grzimek sometimes points out that the gifts come from one or another of his various organizations, as well as from himself, but insofar as most park wardens and conservators are concerned, it is Grzimek who is the source, and his annual arrival in East Africa is like a visit from a rich uncle. "I have to be careful what I ask him for," says one park warden who flies a plane partially funded by Grzimek, commands an antipoaching team salaried by Grzimek, and whose children are boarded in England through funds provided by Grzimek, "because I know he will give it to me."

But public opinion has become for Grzimek an even more important tool. "Very early on," says Dr. Dieter Backhaus, managing editor of *Das Tier,* "Grzimek decided there were several ways to accomplish what he was after—either you had to be a politician or be very rich, or you had to know how to use public opinion, and he chose the last way." Now, after nearly two decades as a television celebrity, and as one who can shape attitudes with intuitive brilliance, he still regards the will of the public with the respect and optimism of a cub reporter heading out on his first day at city hall. He knows that the expressed attitude of a mass audience can change things. What he seeks to do on television, therefore, is, according to his associates and to Grzimek himself, "make propaganda." Despite his distaste for politicians—"I would rather a prime minister go hungry than a lion," he once said—his use of the medium has gained him more political power than any single individual outside the German government, an advantage particularly galling to his enemies since, again, he has acquired it on the federal television system.

Grzimek's principal enemies are predictable: they are the enemies of animals—hunters, dealers in the hide and hair of threatened species, exploitative husbandrymen, and ministers of agriculture—especially ministers of agriculture—whose interests, both in Europe and Africa, always seem directly opposed to theirs. Often the fashion industry offends. Flashing on the screen behind him a photograph of Gina Lollobrigida in her new leopard-skin coat, Grzimek once sternly reminded his audience: "Leopard skins belong on the back of leopards, not cows."

He is not always successful, however, and in some important instances, less so at home than in Africa. West Germany is a poor example of effective conservation practices. Around Frankfurt there are seventeen per cent fewer plants than there were a hundred years ago; within the past fifty years, seventy-six varieties of animal have become extinct, and more than five hundred are currently considered threatened. Grzimek is said to be mortified by his failure to see established a single national park in Germany conforming to standards observed in Africa. There is one located in Bavaria and the government has sought to identify his name with it; but hunting and commercial forestry are allowed within its borders, and he has publicly renounced it. In 1969, Grzimek was appointed by Willy Brandt to prepare conservation legislation for the federal government in the newly created office of Commissioner for Nature Conservation. For four years he held the position, working with his own board of legal and scientific advisers to reconcile conflicting state conservation laws into a single federal law which would require ecological conformity for the planning of new construction in open places.

"Some people didn't like his independence," says Dr. Wolfgang Erz, his administrative assistant who works on in their old office in Bonn. "They started putting him off on his requests for legislation. There was another adviser there on conservation, and this man was completely loyal to the government, wouldn't talk against it. This didn't harmonize with the character of Professor Grzimek. He is too honest. A minister would come up to him and say how much he liked him and his show, and Professor Grzimek would say, 'The love of a minister is shown only in the budget.' He began to report to the public on the delays he was encountering—in the press and on his TV show—and no one expected he would do this. He asked viewers to write the prime ministers of Bavaria and Hessen. He showed their pictures, and he would say, 'These are the ones against conservation; you must write them. And not only you should write, but your uncle and aunt should write, too.' He was very outspoken."

In the end he was defeated—by the minister of agriculture. "When it became clear he was being blocked in the interest of

THE LAST PLACE ON EARTH

farmers and hunters," Erz continues, "he resigned. Grzimek leaves things as soon as he sees there is no more in it—when there is too much input for too little output. He is quite pragmatic. He says, 'If we can get fifty new laws, we take fifty; if we get a thousand, we take a thousand; if we get one, we take one.' Here, he could not get one." Another assistant, a Dr. Scherpner of the Frankfurt Zoo, says: "Grzimek knows exactly where to draw the line. When he sees there will be a disproportional return for the money or effort involved, he simply pulls out. He said to me once, 'We can't save everything. If we are not careful it will be next to use our time to save the turtle from turtle soup.' "

But on other occasions he has proved a formidable protagonist whose influence has been felt even beyond the reach of German television. In 1964, the slaughtering of Canadian seals had attained such proportions and caused so many protests that the CBC French network commissioned a film of the carnage. The producers sent it to Grzimek—German furriers were a major market for sealskins— and he put it on his program. "Don't write me," Grzimek warned his audience. "I can't do anything about it. Write the Canadian Prime Minister." Fifteen hundred letters arrived at the office of Lester Pearson from irate Europeans. Sealskin prices dropped from twenty dollars to three, and the Canadian minister of fisheries accused Grzimek of having trumped up the film by paying a skinner to make it secretly. Grzimek arranged for the cameraman to provide an affidavit of the film's legitimacy. Relations between Canada and West Germany became strained over the episode, and a German state secretary for foreign affairs announced to the Bundestag that Grzimek had faked the film. Grzimek called a press conference and issued a statement to the secretary: "I can't sue the minister of fisheries in Parliament if he tells lies because he is a deputy of Parliament. But if you repeat such damn lies you will learn your lesson of what will happen to you."

Eventually, the Foreign Secretary apologized but Grzimek kept up his campaign, now turning his angry audience on British fur dealers doing business in Germany, who in turn became so concerned over the possible damage to their trade that they brought an injunction against him. Ultimately, the matter was settled out of court to the advantage of Grzimek and future Canadian seals. A limit was put on the number of seals allowed to be taken, and restraints were imposed on the industry's methods of harvesting. In Germany, the fur industry agreed to sponsor the inspection of their methods by a veterinarian pathologist, to be appointed by Grzimek and paid for by the dealers. "I was careful how I went about this," Grzimek would later tell a reporter. "I knew what could be the reaction of people outside Germany. 'After killing six million Jews, you Germans will advise us of how Canadians should deal with little seals?' I appointed a scientist from Oxford."

Serengeti Shall Not Die had come to an end and now I was about to see the latest of Grzimek's television specials. It would be my first look at the man as he has become today, and again I was unprepared. Without music or accompanying titles he suddenly appeared on the screen, fourteen years older than the doting father I had viewed minutes earlier; now he was a well-tailored Lutheran minister of stern countenance, cold eyes behind gold-rimmed glasses, a faint smile—either ironic, bemused, or slightly patronizing, I wasn't quite sure which—with gray hair and long mod sideburns. He was seated behind a desk. He spoke softly but firmly, as though to misbehaving children, into a camera frozen rigidly at attention. There were no "two-shots" or close-ups. Just Grzimek filling the screen head-on. As he talked on, a cheetah suddenly appeared at stage left, leaped on the desk, walked between Grzimek and the camera, and stopped. Grzimek continued talking. After several moments, the cheetah moved off to the right and the screen filled again with Grzimek's face. The hard look was still there.

The picture on the screen now shifted to scenes of chicken hatcheries and cattle stalls. His producer, a short, earnest young man with horn-rimmed glasses, who had arranged the showing, tried to keep up a running translation for me:

"He's telling about the cruelty imposed upon domestic animals to get maximum production yields. . . . He is talking about the force-feeding of cattle and livestock, synthetic diets, and deliberately overcrowded conditions. . . . He says it persecutes the animals and reduces the food value for the consumer. . . . Now he is showing a chicken egg with a rubbery shell. He says this comes from the use of synthetic foods. . . . He is showing how cows are force-fed with tubes down their throats. They are kept in their stalls. They get no exercise. . . . That is a ball of hair he is holding up. It was taken from the stomach of a cow. Licking is instinctive to cows, he says. It is how they take in necessary minerals. But in such close quarters they have nothing to lick but themselves. . . ." Grzimek is still on camera, holding the grotesque object in his hand.

54   THE LAST PLACE ON EARTH

It is about the size of a volleyball. "Grzimek is denouncing the members of the government responsible for permitting these conditions, mostly the minister of agriculture. . . . He asks the audience to tell their families and friends to write the minister and protest these things. . . ."

Abruptly the picture shifted to an idyllic scene of the East African plain, gazelle and waterbuck nibbling grass side by side. The producer whispered, "He doesn't like the people to think it is that way for all animals."

Afterward, at the commissary of the television studio, a smooth looking fellow with close-cropped hair came over to our table. The producer introduced us and said the man was a free-lance camera-man who occasionally worked for Grzimek. He seemed comfortable to the room—ageless in common with the effect sought by all film people although his sweater and corduroys placed him a generation beyond the blue-jean and sheepskin minglers. His English was excellent.

"Grzimek has a lot of film people on contract," the cameraman said, "he can't go everywhere, you know. He has a team right now in Rwanda studying the gorilla. He has contracts with all these people in various places, and he takes every chance he can to extend himself." I recalled the trouble I'd had taking a picture of Pennycuick. "I don't like to call it business because he does it for the animals. He gives his money, too," the cameraman said. He smiled as he talked but the tone of his voice was more apologetic than admiring. "It's of no use if some great doctor works as a specialist in one area and never goes out to the public with what he finds, just sits on in his museum. Grzimek believes you have to bring it to the public.

"He's very hard on people who do not care about animals. He will tell the audience what to do about such people—he is the only one on television who would dare to do so. He asks for help, too. I know a lot of people who don't have much money but spend it on animals because of Grzimek. Very often he will say, 'I received five marks from an old lady in Hessen. Thank you very much. We will spend it on an airplane for the wardens of Serengeti.' "

He did not seem to think I was convinced; I tried not to anticipate him. "Grzimek is fighting for the *space* of animals, their room to live," he said. "He doesn't care much *which* animals. . . ."

The young producer remained silent. The cameraman said: "He had a lot to do with bringing tourists to Africa. The zoologists say we have to save the animals from the human beings, we should keep the human beings out. But Grzimek says no, you have to use the tourists. Then Grzimek will say to the Africans, 'We are bringing you the tourists. There were sixty thousand Germans in your country last year, and in this way I helped bring many thousands of marks into your country,' and on this point they can talk on—that if they go on allowing the animals to be shot or overcrowded, no tourists will come. This is the way Grzimek deals with *them*."

"Do you know any personal friends of his I should talk with?"

A long pause, and: "No."

It was the same blunt response to a question I had asked of others. Was it that the people about him were so protective, or was it really possible that he had no friends? I began to realize the hazards I faced in seeking background across cultures. Still, this was the first German I had met without permanent ties to Grzimek, the first to acknowledge, however obliquely, there was something forbidding about my subject. At least he would appreciate the difficulty of my logistical problems. I told him of my brief unsatisfactory exchange with Grzimek, and that all I had to go on was the vague promise of a single interview. What could he suggest?

"He will see you, I think, but you will find that he is a hard person to talk with. It takes a long time to get through to him." And then, hesitating again, staring hard at me as though to be sure he was getting across, he said something which fixed the curious, ambivalent impression I had begun to form about a man I hadn't met:

"First come the animals, and then for a long time comes nothing. And then come the human beings.

"But," he hurried now to reassure, "I don't think you will have trouble. He doesn't like the German writers who are always trying to probe into his private life. I would recommend that you get on with his ideas and what he has done and what he wants to do now, and the private part I would leave until the end when you have everything else you want. And I think it is best to let him talk. Yes. He talks a lot and he likes to talk. I think it is a very good idea to meet him in Africa. He must be a different man there, unlike the man he is in Germany."

FOUR

The visible time levels of Serengeti are unexpected. In one corner of the Ngorongoro Crater there are mysterious graves of a long-faced, long-headed people dating back three thousand years; to the northwest of the plain there is a Beau Geste–style fortress built by the Germans during their occupancy of Tanganyika at the turn of the century; at the center, near Seronera, pottery remnants from thirty thousand years ago have been traced to ancestors of the Wanderobo, a tribe still living in Serengeti; the giraffe, leopard, and hyena have lived there for two and a half million years without significant evolutionary change, the crocodile for a hundred and forty million years. Some of the rocks near Banagi are the oldest on earth—three thousand million years old. It is the sense of space, however, that is most immediately striking: sky traces the flat, green horizon for three hundred and sixty degrees, at once frightening and oddly liberating, as though one could wander for days in any direction without coming to the end of it.

Even the dirt underfoot is exotic; a kind of clay called black cotton soil, it is nonporous and does not immediately absorb the crashing rains that may fall with only a moment's notice. At the end of the dry season when the plain is grazed out or leveled by brushfires, rain summons the green shoots to reassemble: the red oat grasses grow an inch in the first two days of rainfall. Winds descending from the active Lengai volcano swirl loose lava sediments into huge black hills some twenty feet in height; the hills inch their way across the grass. Otherwise the plain is impeccable, policed by a chain of scavengers from lion through maggot flies, each taking its turn, so that a buffalo dying will be reduced in a matter of days to horn and skull glistening white against the dark-blue sky. One feels an instinctive sense of identification, of having *felt* the place even though never before having seen it. Once, when we wandered off the road and slowly over the plain, with hundreds of thousands of animals all about us parting leisurely to make an avenue for our vehicle to pass, the sky suddenly turned black and the rain pounded down in opaque flats turning the plain almost instantly into a shallow sea bottomed by the stubborn cotton soil. We made it back to the road but that, too, was quickly flooded out, and to go forward, one of us had to walk shin deep through the new sea to guide the road's edge. At such times is the wrenching strength of the place frighteningly visible; where the streams run, bridges are washed down, and water snaps white at elbows of the raging streams.

Another time, tenting out near Seronera west of the center of the plain, I was by myself fixing breakfast when I heard a low rumble, like thunder, off across the plain to the east. There were yellow-fever trees between me and the source of the noise, and as I squinted into the sun, I saw the first of an enormous herd of wildebeest emerging from behind the trees on a course directly across the right front of my camp site. On and on they came, thousands of them, and they were running at full stride, all out, shoulder to shoulder. When at last they had gone, the sense of quiet and space returned, and Serengeti's sense of timelessness.

Serengeti's wildebeest are the last substantial gathering of the animal on earth, the last vast herd of any land mammal, and there are so many of them, they directly condition all forms of life on the plain. They are everywhere, feeding the lion at one end of the food chain, and at the other, tiny larvae inside the decaying wildebeest skull which, emerging as caterpillars, feed on the inner stuffs of the horns before they turn into moths and fly away. In the west, where the wildebeest churn the lakeshores to mud, fish come near the surface seeking clearer water; awaiting them are a variety of birds that have trailed the wildebeest in anticipation of the feast.

"The wildebeest *is* the Serengeti," says Myles Turner, the former warden of Serengeti. "From November till May, they're on those central plains. They sort of ebb and flow over two thousand square miles of grasslands, those great armies, going wherever the rain falls. It's the calving time; after birth, a wildebeest calf can stand in five minutes; in fifteen, it can run as fast as its mother. But the predators are out—hyenas killing the calves; wild dog, cheetah, and lion get in there among the migration. It seems just endless.

"Then, suddenly, about the beginning of June—but you can never be precisely sure—suddenly the northeast wind gets up, you can feel it coming across those plains, and straightaway there's a

THE LAST PLACE ON EARTH

change in the whole herd. They know the dry weather is coming, and that the water is drying up. The calves are suckling and the mothers need the water; and then the dry weather *really* sets in with this terrific northeast wind beginning to blow night and day, and you see the *whole lot* turn to the west and move out in long lines. And then they form up usually in the Moru country around Seronera for a couple of days, into *gigantic* armies, and you never know quite which route they're going to take—the southern route around the Duma from Seronera, or through the Mbalageti Valley, or past Kamunya and down behind Kubukubu Hill onto the Masabi Plain. And always Kay and I would be flying out every day and watching. It was a great thing to see. Once we knew their route, we'd go out on a hill and then you'd see them coming, at times so closely packed in the valleys you could walk across their backs. The migration takes place the whole year but the actual movement from the plains into the central ranges is the great spectacle. It's all over *in three days!* Eight hundred thousand wildebeest have gone, and you've lost them in that bush country.

"They stay in the west through August and then they start heading north up in the Mara country around Kenya—they take a different route now there is so much farm settlement there. They stay there until November, when the thunderclouds start to build up over the plains again, and when it starts to rain a hundred miles to the south, they start back again. I've often wondered how they *know* to move from that far away. I think it must have something to do with the lightning in the distance at night. They see it, and the thunder they hear in the distance, and they just aim for it, just as elephants do in the northern frontier in a dry spell.

"Sometimes they stampede—that's what you saw—and when they get going they don't stop for anything, not even rivers. Up on the Mara River, eight or nine thousand will form up on the bank. The leading wildebeest suddenly plunges in, and everybody behind comes after. The condition of the river makes no difference. If it's in flood, and it usually is then because of the sudden rains, they are just washed away in the hundreds. I found over five hundred dead in one pool on the river one day. Once the rush starts, even when the leading ones are washed away, the others behind won't stop. They'll keep coming until everybody has crossed or been washed downstream. You can see them plunge in turning upside down with their legs in the air and floating away downstream, with the odd one getting to the other side, and the more pouring in until it's absolutely black in the river—probably thirty, forty yards wide of solid wildebeest. . . . And then they wander back in long lines to Seronera and start the whole cycle all over again.

"*Goddamn it,* the migration is the *wonder* of the Serengeti! *Forget* everything else. Must have been like your bison in eighteen seventy before your hunters shot it out. Nothing like it anywhere else on this earth. To see that number of animals—it's absolutely incredible. I saw it year after year and it never failed to thrill me, flying over it or moving through it. Absolutely unique. You can see lions other places, elephants, buffalo—but you can't see a million wildebeest anywhere else on this planet. If you could only see it as we've seen it, following it through all the stages of its yearly cycle, it's just one of the wonders of the world. It's incredible! *That* is the thing that makes Serengeti unique."

In one fashion or another, whether through the prospect of the wildebeest migration or the serenity of the endless grasslands, it was apparently the virginal sense of place—this obscure plain holding evidence of the natural past—that had compelled the attention of men with such disparate backgrounds as Myles Turner, the Kenyan hunter turned park warden, and Bernhard Grzimek, the German veterinarian turned zookeeper. From my own coincidental perspective, the wonder of it was that any visitor, whatever his point of origin (and I considered myself typical), was susceptible—arrested, even disoriented by this unexpected glimpse into the past. For those who hadn't been there, hadn't seen or felt it, however, it was unreasonable to assume Serengeti to be more than an abstraction. Transformation would have to await the visitor's presence. I had been there three times before. Now, on the sleepless overnight flight across the Sahara, tracing the course of the Grzimeks' tiny zebra-striped craft of fifteen years earlier, I was going there again, jetting backward beyond memory to a private experience that each successive trip had somehow come to intensify (rather than diminish—the expected disappointment of revisiting a treasured place).

An indulgence to see it this way, perhaps, under the circumstances. For the first time I would have to deal with Serengeti in hard contemporary terms, as local acreage under threat—as no more than an abstraction; Grzimek's Serengeti. By choosing to track the

THE LAST PLACE ON EARTH

passions of Bernhard Grzimek I had made the choice. On the other hand, even this prospect beguiled: such devotion to be inspired by a place! That men like Turner and Grzimek, having found it almost half a lifetime ago, would remain so faithful to the effort to preserve it.

But—from what? One could only vaguely sense the magnitude and variety of its problems now. In 1958, when the Grzimeks had flown into Serengeti to begin their survey, there were nine and three-quarter million people in the U.N. protectorate of Tanganyika. Now there were said to be fifteen million. There were new governments in East Africa and untried institutions with unpredictable policies and desperate needs. What future could there be for wild animals in such circumstances? It would be naive to assume East Africa less pragmatic than nations of the West. Usefulness would be measured there, as elsewhere, in terms of economic productivity—Conway had warned of this. The animals could prove their right to exist only by paying their own way. In this respect, then, the Serengeti of Tanzania, although the most important national park in the world, could not be seen as appreciably different in its claim for a future than had been Grzimek's bombed-out zoo grounds in 1945—only less conspicuous to the Western nations.

My own context further argued the futility of their task. America was still the wealthiest of nations but what claim could be made back home for the wildebeest of Serengeti? The wave of attention Grzimek had drawn with his book and Michael's film to the boundary disputes of fifteen years ago was by now forgotten, or unknown. Serengeti in my country was at best a parochial affair, one of a thousand interlocking problems of world ecology, subsumed under Wildlife Conservation (*deadly* abstraction!), of concern to people who worked in museums, zoos, and a few foundations, who were themselves separated by the labyrinth of bureaucracy and its more immediate priorities.

Serengeti Shall Not Die, Grzimek's title had bravely insisted, but I guessed from my conversations with his associates in Frankfurt that the translator may have taken liberties. The German is "Serengeti Darf Nicht Sterben," but when Faust or Backhaus referred to the book, they said, "Serengeti *Must* Not Die," less an injunction than a fearful warning. As a sober counterpoint to Myles Turner's witness to the wildebeest of Serengeti, it would be important to keep in mind that most of the people one knew back in the West didn't know of Serengeti, where it was, or what a wildebeest looked like.

From January through March, Bernhard Grzimek lives at his second home in the upper-middle-class suburb of Westlands, roughly five miles from the center of Nairobi. It is the best time of the year in East Africa, the spell between the short rains of the fall and the long rains of the spring; and to the mild discomfort of residents, the city is filled with visitors from all over the world, flooding the hotels, taking over the restaurants, and jamming the roundabouts from all directions.

Over the years since the Grzimeks' Serengeti expedition, Nairobi has drastically changed. In those days, as the main axis of supply for the British colonies, it was still a frontier town. Farmers timed their shopping trips to allow for drinking and gossip at Saturday noon in the Long Bar of the New Stanley or the Lord Delamere Room at the Norfolk, and because of the Mau Mau scare they often came in wearing six guns or carrying shotguns over their shoulders. The few visitors were mostly rich hunters who could afford the accommodations provided, at a steep price, by professional outfitters: two trucks, a Chevrolet pickup modified into a shooting car, ten in service, and generators to allow light in the tents and ice in the drinks. Most of the hunting is over now because of increasing restrictions with the result that the big outfitters, like Ker and Downey, must either lease hunting privileges on the few remaining privately owned farms or ship their clients out to Chad or Ethiopia, where there are fewer restrictions (but also less game).

Nairobi today is a city of over half a million inhabitants; a major distribution center for international manufacturers; the capital of Kenya, the last East African economy based, however tenuously, on free enterprise; and a lively resort town filled with hotels and swimming pools, a gambling casino with a topless floor show, an international convention center, drive-in movies, supermarkets, and, spread about in key density areas, three Kentucky Fried Chicken houses. For the native Kenyan moving in from the bush, whom the tourist seldom sees, it is becoming dangerously over-crowded—in some sections as many as a thousand people to an acre. Tourism provides Kenya with its largest source of foreign exchange.

Tourists come to Nairobi to see the wild animals, which are to be found in the immediate vicinity (the Nairobi National Park

THE LAST PLACE ON EARTH

borders the airport) and in national parks scattered about the three East African nations at a radius of up to a thousand miles. To some of the major parks, the distance at first seems unmanageable—from Tsavo in Kenya, the last great reserve of black rhino, to Ruwenzori in Uganda, the last great reserve of hippopotamus, for example, it is a distance of nine hundred miles. But there is a macadam highway most of the way, and a touring car can make the trip in about twenty-two hours. Following the conventional travel circuits, it is possible to spend less than half a day driving from one park lodge to the next, leaving after breakfast, lunching at another lodge along the way, and arriving before dinner at the next well in time for a hot shower and a change before meeting for cocktails in the lounge. Coffee is served on the terrace after dinner as the animals gather about an illuminated water hole within safe viewing distance.

Most of East Africa's wildlife lodges were constructed in the sixties, and each of them is striking and unique; built of rough stones or local hardwoods, with vaulting ceilings and split deck planes and walls opening to rock terraces and parapets outside. At Lobo, in the northern Serengeti, wood shafts and glass walls emerge from random crevasses of a rock kopje, with acacia trees rising through the floor of the dining room and continuing on through the ceiling to flower above the roof. One may tour East Africa's parks in almost any fashion and at any price, by light aircraft or chauffeured Peugeot, or by minibus with groups of eight or ten. Until the mid seventies, most of the traffic flowed in the parabolic route from Nairobi to southeastern Kenya, through northern Tanzania, and back to Nairobi—the "milk run" I took on my first trip. It is less popular now because of border problems between Tanzania and Kenya. Since both countries seek tourists, and the tourists' dollars support the national parks, this poses ambiguities that would take me the better part of my stay to understand.

At the height of the season—the months when Grzimek is there—tourists collect from all over the world, the circuit sees its heaviest traffic and the lodges, having been booked six months in advance, are full. Darting through the parks in search of some new sight, the minibuses attract their own, particularly in the flat scrub bush of Amboseli lying directly in the shadow of Kilimanjaro—commuting distance from Nairobi. It is a common occurrence, and not very appealing, to see them crowding the animals. On one occasion I saw a minibus spot a lion stalking three wildebeest lagging behind their herd. Within minutes there was a fleet of small buses crossing in and out as the lioness edged forward for a better view. Some were equipped with roof hatches and their occupants crowded up from below, chattering happily over this primeval spectacle. Increasingly now, and particularly in the overcrowded areas like Amboseli, tourists outnumber some of the predators—more than a nuisance for the latter, which sometimes go hungry because of the traffic. Recently, the Hilton Hotel chain bought twenty-eight thousand acres in southeastern Kenya to assure the presence of game in reasonable distribution to the number of guests. The builders called themselves African Ponderosa. By the winter of my arrival, Holiday Inn was said to be planning twenty-five hotels throughout Kenya to take advantage of the tourist boom. For local conservators who had lobbied long and arduously for increased facilities to attract the tourist who, in turn, would bring the income justifying commercially the presence of the game—and by no means excluding Bernhard Grzimek—Nairobi's tourist industry had begun to seem an illusory advantage.

Nairobi encourages other illusions. The service class is black and still obeisant toward whites, almost a caricature of blacks in the Deep South a generation ago. There are some seventy thousand whites still residing in Kenya, and they accept the deference. Nevertheless, this, too, is an illusion only resort-deep and evident soon enough by the reverse order of racial designations here. "Black" is as disagreeable a term to the majority in Kenya as "Negro" has become to the American black. "Kenyan" is preferred—Kenyans own their country, American blacks do not. Whites are called "Europeans" even though many of them are Kenyan citizens and nearly all of British extraction—still observing British colonial customs, still employing Kenyan servants.

But the service class is an arm of the tourist industry. Kenyans are definitely in charge of their country now, and one need spend little time with Europeans to realize their shared sense of impermanence. They await Africanization, a delicately ambiguous euphemism meaning throughout East Africa the transfer of authority from the colonial to the independent governments—shorthand now, fifteen years after the fact, for the replacement of whites, in whatever capacity, by blacks. The process has been delayed in Kenya longer than anywhere else for the practical reason that whites continue to serve a useful purpose. How much longer this will be so is the occasion for their concern.

In their rootlessness, tied by customs largely anathema to their host governments and by whatever compulsion to stay on in face of an unpromising future, they are uneasy residents. While it is not always accurate within Nairobi's lexicon of euphemisms to describe them as expatriates, it is somehow more fitting to regard them as such. It is certainly a description literally accurate of Bernhard Grzimek, however, a citizen of Frankfurt who seldom spends more than three months here out of the year; and within a very few days it would come to be for me the only appropriate way to look on the small dwindling community of British post-colonials about Grzimek now struggling desperately, with him or against him, to save the animals of Serengeti.

FIVE

On the Sunday evening following my talk in the commissary with the free-lance cameraman, I called Grzimek's private number from my room at the Norfolk Hotel in Nairobi.

"*Bitte?*" came a metallic voice out of the receiver.

I told him who I was and that I was anxious to meet him. He was decidedly unenthusiastic. He would not be free for the next few days, he said; he was going tomorrow to Dar es Salaam to see Tanzanian officials. His English was heavily accented but distinct. He said he would call me toward the end of the week but he seemed anxious to get off the phone. I wondered whether he had associated my name with our correspondence, and if he had, whether it made any difference. I hung up and fished from my notes that earlier, unpromising letter: "Of the time when I worked in Ngorongoro and the Serengeti together with my late son," he had written, "nearly nobody is more in East Africa, because all the administration is Africanized in the meantime. The only one left will be Myles Turner and his wife . . . maybe also Gordon Harvey. . . ."

At lunch in the hotel dining room the next day, Gordon Harvey said, "Well, he's right. John Owen is gone—Africanized out. Hugh Lamprey—Africanized out. Myles Turner was transferred out of Serengeti six months ago. He has a small post in northern Tanzania now but in six months he'll be gone, too."

John Owen, Hugh Lamprey, and Myles Turner are clearly principals to any modern account of the Serengeti Plain, Harvey says, having formed the nucleus of expatriates working under the independent government to develop the Serengeti and the Tanzanian Parks Department in the wake of the departing colonials. John Owen and Hugh Lamprey were Oxonians, scientists by training. John Owen replaced Peter Molloy, the man who had first invited down the Grzimeks, as director of Parks. Lamprey had moved over from the colonial game department, as a biologist, to Parks under the new government to become in 1966 the first director of the Serengeti Research Institute. Lamprey touched up Grzimek's En-

66

glish in his monograph on the Serengeti expedition. As operations warden of Serengeti for eighteen years, Myles Turner had come to know more about the acreage of Serengeti than anyone else.

It was John Owen who had developed the Serengeti Research Institute (out of the Michael Grzimek Memorial Laboratory) into a center for international scientists, and Lamprey who had administered their research. Out here, Hugh Lamprey is generally considered the scientist most knowledgeable about the wildlife of East Africa. They all had been quite close to Grzimek, who was busy funding and promoting their efforts in Europe.

"John Owen was a brilliant man," Harvey said. "We all liked him. He was a very fair man . . . a very fair man." A part of Owen's organizational ability lay with his talent for raising money outside of East Africa to assist Tanzania in meeting the cost for projects he himself had often proposed.

"He could bite anyone's ear for money. Foundations. Rich Americans. He must have got tens and tens of thousands of pounds for the parks—one reason he lasted so long, I think." When Owen came in 1961, there was one national park in Tanzania—Serengeti—and when he left in 1971, there were seven. All together the animal reserves in Tanzania now equal the land size of Belgium. So far as Gordon Harvey was concerned, this was mostly John Owen's doing.

Harvey made no effort to conceal his indignation over the Africanization of these men. They should have been viewed as different from the colonials, for they were working for the animals, under hire to the new government, and they still knew more about them (and about Serengeti) than anyone else. He had no idea where they were now. He believed John Owen and Hugh Lamprey were connected in some way with an international conservation agency, but he couldn't be sure of that. They had been out of it for several years.

As for Myles Turner, he was stationed on top of Mount Meru, some two hundred miles to the south near Arusha, Tanzania. "You ought to go down and talk with him, he keeps copious diaries, has a record of everything that's happened."

Harvey made you wonder how typical he himself was of the missing expatriates. He is an impressive-looking man of about sixty, of Scottish extraction, silver-haired and quite handsome, with a bad back disciplined to a military bearing. He came out here many years ago, worked as an accountant in order to fish and hunt, and then one day in the mid-forties he was invited to join the colonial game department, an experience which shaped his outlook ever after. He had got into Parks in much the same fashion as Myles Turner, and the two of them had provided ground expertise for the Grzimeks through their Serengeti expedition of 1958. Harvey has been out of it, too, even longer than the others. In the mid-sixties, he resigned his post and returned to Kenya to become a tour leader. But he had kept in touch with Grzimek, even though he was no longer in a position to offer him much assistance.

In outlook Harvey is both amiable and dour, a strange mixture. His recollections are attenuated, too spare, and punctuated by a meditative silence, the end of which is sometimes signaled by repetition of his last phrase. ("Grzimek could be a stubborn man. Hard to change his mind once he made it up." Silence. "Once he made it up.") He skims the years of the sixties too quickly for my needs, his Serengeti a cryptic history dominated by expatriates; African names are conspicuously missing.

Sifting reflections, Harvey chewed his food now and meditated. There were a few others that might be of interest: Michael Wood, the head of Flying Doctors—he was about to be Africanized off his farm at Kilimanjaro . . . the Leakeys, perhaps . . . strange chap named Ian Parker, an ivory trader and game cropper . . . George Dove, he ran a camp in Serengeti, but he was about to leave, too. Derek Bryceson, he supposed. But they were all spread out to hell and gone, names without faces, and fading. A meager list.

"Alan Root," he said, brightening. "He lives near here, in Naivasha."

Alan Root's name appears in the translated works of Bernhard Grzimek on his African adventures more often than any other expatriate's. In *Among Animals of Africa,* Grzimek includes a letter from Root relating a frightening and bizarre accident that in the telling serves as introduction to a side of Africa still beyond the domestication of the tourist industry:

> I am now out of hospital at last but am still very weak and my arm and hand are still swollen and painful. It happened at Joy Adamson's camp in the Meru Park. I found the [puff adder] snake, about 4 feet long, near her camp and caught it to show her and an American that we had with us. I opened

its mouth and milked it a bit to show them the amount of venom these snakes have, and then I put it down whilst she was changing film in her camera. I then went to catch it again but the snake was by now very angry and as I grabbed for its neck it turned and bit me. Because I was bitten years ago and had injections of antivenin I knew that I would be sensitive to further antivenin, and therefore I delayed the injections for a while in order to see how severe the bite was going to be. Because I had already partly milked the snake I did not think that I had got a very big dose of poison. However, the arm swelled rapidly, I became dizzy and nauseated, so Joan gave me the 3 injections (3 ccs.) intramuscular whilst flying back to Nairobi.

As we expected, I reacted violently to the antivenin, vomiting and my heart beat and respiration going up rapidly. When we got to the hospital in Nairobi the doctor thought that these conditions were due to the snake bite and gave me another 10 ccs. of antivenin intravenously. I immediately went into anaphylactic shock and they had quite a battle with antihistamines, cortisone, adrenalin, and oxygen to keep me alive.

Over the next 3 days my condition deteriorated. The hand was three times normal size and covered with enormous black, blood filled blisters. My arm swelled to the size of my leg and was also full of blood, and I had great bloody swellings stretching from my arm pit down to my waist, across my shoulder blades and in front as far as my throat. On the fourth day my haemoglobin count had gone down to 36. 40 is considered to be the lowest permissible level. I was given a transfusion of 4 pints of blood which made me feel a lot better and from that day on I started to improve.

Joan got Prof. David Chapman, an expert on snake bite treatment, to fly up from South Africa to see me and his advice was of great value. During these first 4 days the doctors had been seriously considering amputating for they had not been able to feel a pulse at all in the arm, and the hand and fingers were so swollen and damaged that they considered it would never be of any use to me again. However, now, 4 weeks after being bitten, the arm is almost back to its normal size and my hand has made a miraculous recovery. It is still very swollen and painful, but my thumb and 3 outer fingers are all in reasonably good shape. I can move them and I have most of the sensation back now.

My index finger, which one fang obviously went deeply into, is not so good. The whole top surface was destroyed by the venom right down to the tendons. Within the next couple of weeks I will be having new skin grafted on to this finger and it will then be a matter of time before we know whether it is going to be of any use to me. You told me about your finger that the chimp bit and I have noticed that you are able to use that hand very well despite it being stiff. It will obviously be anything up to 2 months before I will be able to do anything with my hand again, and though I am impatient already I really should be grateful that I have got away so lightly.

If Gordon Harvey is typical of the expatriates around Grzimek, Alan Root is archetypical. He flies his own airplane, sails his own hydrofoil, drives his own Range Rover (a luxury version of the Land Rover), scuba dives, shoots rapids, and operates the only hot-air balloon in East Africa. I knew of him from my first trip to Serengeti when as proprietor of our outfitters (Root & Leakey Photographic Safaris) he flew into our camp with his blond, elegant wife, Joan, a pet lynx cradled in her arms.

The Roots took our party to a small conference room of the Serengeti Research Institute and showed us two of their films—the escalation of life, from insects to elephants, living off a baobab tree, and the aquatic underworld, from crocodiles to hippos, of a volcanic spring named Mzima, near Tsavo. The cover of an issue of *National Geographic,* in a still from the sequence, shows the diminutive Joan snorkeling alongside a rock python three times her length. Everything about them is extravagant. They live on the shore of Lake Naivasha in a house tracing back to a turn-of-the-century colonial named Ewalt Grogan who, to prove his worth to his girl friend's father, walked alone from Cape Town to Cairo. He brought his bride back to Naivasha because it was the most beautiful place along the length of his trip, and he built there the house the Roots live in today. Sixteen acres about it enclose Root's private menagerie: lemurs, honey badgers, gazelle, a spotted hyena into whose mouth Root sometimes playfully sticks his nose to the horror of his visitors (the torque of a hyena's jaws is greater than a lion's), and an aardvark named Milly, or Million ("Aardvark a million miles," Root explains without being asked, "for one of your smiles"). Such humors are consistent with his nature. He did eventually lose his index finger from the puff adder's bite, and on a trip to London he bought a plastic finger in a novelty shop. Upon his return, shaking hands all around, he would sometimes leave it behind within a startled greeter's grasp. Following a forced landing of his balloon atop telephone wires near Naivasha and upon learning subsequently that President Kenyatta was having trouble with his phone service to Naivasha, he remarked: "Tell the President Mr. Root was on the line."

Root is considerably more flamboyant in deed than manner, however. He looks like an untenured history instructor in old clothes working around his barbecue. Joan sweeps her blond hair up into a baseball cap and dresses similarly. Wherever he goes, whatever he does, she does, too. They are both informal and affable but extremely shy. Alan Root is the finest nature photographer on the continent. Since 1972, he has been filming the wildebeest migration on foot, by Land Rover, light aircraft, and from his balloon. It is said to be his best work to date.

Root is about the same age as Michael Grzimek would be now. He was brought to the Grzimeks in Serengeti by Myles Turner, who explained that Root wanted to learn how to make films. Michael and Alan had become close friends and they had talked often of their plans to make nature films for television, an ambition that Root, whose films are shown now throughout the world, has masterfully attained. It was Alan Root whom Michael was flying out to meet when he collided with the vulture. Root is closer to Grzimek than anyone else in East Africa, has trapped animals for his zoo, made films for his television program and accompanied him on his most dangerous expeditions.

In the sixties, at the time of the Lumumba uprising, Root drove Grzimek into the Congo to check on the welfare of the animals in King Albert Park. By a coincidence of timing, they narrowly escaped capture. Three days before their arrival, the rebels had moved through the park ahead of them. "I was told they had with them the prime minister of Kivu Province, the man who had invited us," Grzimek has since recalled. "He was in a wooden cage, his teeth broken, and his moustache torn from his face. They said to hold any Europeans in the area until their return." Root and Grzimek escaped through the park to safety over the Uganda border.

Not very long thereafter, having wandered off course in a flight by light aircraft over Lake Rudolf, they made a forced landing in the desert and were taken prisoner by Sudanese soldiers suspecting them to be part of a local insurrection. They were held incommunicado for weeks, part of the time in Torit in an office once occupied by John Owen, who had been the last district commissioner under the colonial government in Sudan. Root managed to persuade a South African mercenary pilot, there to train the Sudanese, to radio their whereabouts to the outside; Julius Nyerere, the President of Tanzania, appealed to the Sudanese government to release them; and Grzimek and Root helped by tracking down a copy of *Serengeti Shall Not Die* in a local bookshop, persuading their captors they were harmless naturalists.

"Michael was the kind of guy I am now, I suppose," Root has remarked, placing his own position within the expatriate community. "He was crazy about animals, determined to do his own thing. A bit mad. Crazy pilot. Just someone determined to live life to the full." More than anyone else Alan Root was believed to have become for Bernhard Grzimek in East Africa a sort of surrogate for Michael—if it should be even remotely possible that anyone could take Michael Grzimek's place.

By coffee time, Gordon Harvey had moved briskly to the politicization of modern Serengeti. "Impossible to maintain discipline in the park—even under the British the administrators were on the side of the Masai. Catch a poacher flat-handed and it was impossible to convict him. . . . Impossible.

"And after independence it was worse—insubordination, trade unions, government policies. Intolerable. You couldn't sack a fellow from your staff without giving him warning in writing five times. But before you could give him a letter of warning, you had to go before the local tribunal—four or five elders who sat in a circle and heard his case. The way it is now, for an African anywhere, he is *never* wrong. They have a word, *lakini,* which means 'but.' Always an excuse. I had been out in the country far too long to take kindly to all that, so I resigned. . . ." Harvey stared across the dining room and thought about it. "Yes, I resigned.

"Then, when John Owen left, this chap named Bryceson took over—a fighter pilot for the R.A.F. in World War Two, member of Tanzanian Parliament now—very difficult fellow. Always likes to be on the right side of the fence. No help at all. Anyway," he sighed, "it's all Africanized now."

THE LAST PLACE ON EARTH

East Africa's *fin de siècle*. Harvey's world had vanished.

"But what about Grzimek's role now?" I asked.

"Grzimek is very important, of course. His whole heart is in Serengeti." He began to meditate again. Trying to move him along I said: "I hoped to see him today but he's in Tanzania for most of the week."

Harvey looked up. "No, he isn't," he said. "Grzimek is in Nairobi. I talked with him this morning. He's coming here for tea this afternoon. Right here. In your hotel."

Now we both meditated. At length Harvey turned to the scientific problems of caring for Serengeti's animals but he might as well have been talking to himself. Although offered casually enough, his late news on Grzimek caused me such concern that I could keep contact only with the rhythms of his stop-and-go conversation. Grzimek knew about the problems of reporters—he was an editor himself. Surely he was aware I had come halfway around the world just to see him?

". . . No, I *don't* think you could always say the scientists were a help in Serengeti. No. Not at all . . ."

My attention stayed frozen to Harvey's news. Why the duplicity—to what end? Why hadn't he simply said it was more convenient to see me at the end of the week? And if he did intend keeping the interview, why hadn't he set a date? Gordon Harvey, I observed with impatience at my lack of concentration to what he was saying now, had a tattoo on his arm.

". . . We called these chaps 'boffins.' Some of them were nice enough, but they were completely ruthless, did exactly what they wanted. I found myself in the invidious position of being against them. One of them asked me if he could dart a topi. I said if he did, I'd shoot it. I wouldn't have it within five miles of my office. I didn't want topis around with red flags coming out their ears. That's not what people come to Serengeti to see. To find out what an animal ate, it wasn't necessary to shoot it on your *doorstep.*"

The scientist as spoiler?—momentarily the indignant Harvey came back into focus.

"The fellow I really didn't approve of was George Schaller. He spent three years in Serengeti studying the social life of the lion. One day I saw three lion cubs about as high as this table. They couldn't get down to the water to drink, too weak from lack of food. They were just dragging their hind legs. Schaller would sit in his Land Rover and let them die. I used to say to John Owen, 'Why doesn't he feed them?' And he would say, 'He shouldn't interfere—let nature take its course.' A damn shortsighted view, in my opinion." Harvey said he had to grant the other side: if the lion cubs were left to their fate, the lion population of Serengeti would seek its own level in relation to the environment. But he couldn't accept it. "A national park is not really a natural place, and what's more, the total number of lion is declining sharply. . . . It is declining sharply!" Much later I was to realize that Gordon Harvey had been leading me to a conflict of intent in Serengeti more critical than the partitioning of the park in 1957, which had first drawn the Grzimeks there. But I was a restive audience. I thanked him for his help, for the list of names, and hurried back to my room to begin tracking them by phone if possible; something more productive to do, I thought, until teatime.

I peeked in the lounge around five—there he was, giving me the slip—and had my first look at him. He was dressed casually in a sports shirt and slacks and was seated with three elderly women who were doing all the talking. I hardly recognized him from his television show. The gray hair was combed stylishly over his head to cover a bald spot, accenting his mod sideburns, and the stern visage was not so much ironic or even bemused as sad and distracted. The corners of his mouth drooped. He was staring at his teacup. I wondered again, this time with better reason, if he intended to see me at all. But there was not very much I could do about it in any case. As far as I was concerned to Bernhard Grzimek, Grzimek was in Tanzania and he would be there until the end of the week.

SIX

Harvey's list was right: the impress of these few on Serengeti was considerable. Grzimek's own involvements could not be measured in any meaningful way without taking them into account. The next morning, having arranged to see a native Kenyan Parks deputy to discuss wildlife policies from an African government's vantage, I was received with such open suspicion I quickly abandoned the possibility of seeking other governmental views. At least for now. Grzimek's concerns were mainly with Tanzania anyway, I told myself, and even if they were not that exclusive and my subject had been as cooperative as Harvey, I lacked the grounding in his own political references to make much sense out of what he might tell me. But I turned back to Harvey's all-white list (hurried back—at least we shared cultures) with misgivings, aware that I risked moving away from the centers of decision rather than closer to them, that xenophobia in East Africa was more my problem than the East Africans'.

Still, Harvey's list was right. Concern over the welfare of Africa's animals has created an establishment of interests out here— magazines, publishing houses, conservation societies, and funding offices—and every European in town is aware of the pecking order; they confirm his list. At one point, most of Harvey's list lived inside the Serengeti; the fact that most of them are no longer there in no way qualifies their expertise. They are scientists, ex-hunters, a businessman, a filmmaker, a doctor, and a politician—a microcosm of outside interests, but apparently as indigenous and as unexpected, for the outsider at least, as the improbable Grzimek himself.

By standards of the larger European community they are not at first glance so unexceptional. All are of British extraction, having come out during colonial times or having been born of such parents—a second generation. Restless, adventurous people, they had been drawn by the presence of game, or by paleontological digs, or simply by the chance to pioneer a last frontier. All are self-reliant in the ways of people who have learned to make themselves comfortable amidst wild, often hostile settings; and all are quite versatile—nearly all of them expert pilots, for example, against the need to shorten the great distances of the savanna. But again, such is the case for many Europeans out here (one farmer inspects his vast pasturelands by light plane and when he arrives home after dark his wife puts out two lanterns, one marking the beginning of the landing strip, the other the end).

It is as against this background that the Serengeti people—Harvey's list—are seen here as something rather more special: more ingenious, more self-reliant, more deeply involved—drawing the gossip in this gossip-hungry town with the vibrance reserved in the West for film stars and remote literary figures. In short order, escalating toward myth, the Nairobi version of them takes form.

The Serengeti expatriates are like the members of a large, talented, difficult family; all too self-absorbed, quarreling often (sometimes bitterly), and driven nearly to distraction over how to save the property. Each has become defined by his own experience, each in his own way an expert. Some have acquired international celebrity, drawing a steady stream of representatives of Western media. (Not all of them welcome the intrusion, one of them having hid out in the bush of Olduvai to escape a writer from *Playboy.*) Articulate and facile, each has his own version of their common experience, and nearly all of them are said to be writing books: scientific studies, conservation theories, adventure stories—in one case, a work of philosophy. Very probably no one of these books will conform to the views of any one of the others.

All are said to agree, however, on Serengeti as paradigm for the future of wild animals in East Africa. "The conservation of Serengeti is a complex question out here," one of them, a scientist, would remark, adding a warning both ominous and vague: "Wildlife in East Africa is now big business. It is extremely difficult to thread your way through the morass of interests here. The situation has become polarized. . . ."

Whatever the complexity of these interests, it is common knowledge in Nairobi that time is running out not only for the wildebeest herds but for the Serengeti expatriates as well. However they may have commended themselves by their past good works—and there are many stories recounted along these lines—or by their eagerness to serve the new government now, their physical presence is too visible a reminder of the recent supremacy of the white man in East Africa. In Nairobi, the Serengeti expatriates are looked on as

76

endangered, disappearing now or already gone. A lost patrol. Even Grzimek, at the very center of the expatriate myth, has become a rather remote figure here.

Nevertheless, they are still considered the most reliable index to the modern problems of Serengeti; the most astute local observers of Bernhard Grzimek; and in these important respects each seemed to deserve more amplification than that provided by the austere Harvey. Waiting through the long few days until I might see Grzimek, I assembled about each of them as much as I could put together of his own story:

John Owen

About the time of the transfer of authority from the colonials to the independent government of Tanganyika, on his way to take his new job as director of Parks, John Owen had stopped off in Frankfurt for Bernhard Grzimek's advice. "He screened *Serengeti Shall Not Die* for me—Michael's presence in the room was palpable—and then he told me not to be deterred by his son's accident, but to learn to fly," Owen has since recalled. "It would be the only way to survey those distances. I did, and had my wardens learn, too. It revolutionized the administration of African parks." A large, pipe-puffing, avuncular man, John Owen dominates the next stage in the Serengeti, bringing in the money, equipment, and manpower to open the plain to modern travelers. Owen's father, a missionary, had been a friend of Jomo Kenyatta, and had become so ardent in his defense of locals' rights against the government, he was known to settlers as "the arch demon." Mild and congenial in manner, Owen apparently had been well cast for the role of fund-raiser, looking the very opposite of the slick, big-city entrepreneur. In Nairobi one morning, as he recounted the severe problems of Serengeti, a financier was so moved he gave Owen twenty-five thousand pounds over the breakfast table. He is described variously as emotional, paternalistic, ambitious, a man of great drive—yet none of these is felt to do him justice. In some frustration, Myles Turner would later take from his files a quote of W. H. Murray once given him by Owen that, Turner thought, summed Owen himself up best:

> Until one is committed there is hesitancy, the chance to draw back; always ineffectiveness. Concerning all acts of initiative (and creation) there is one elementary truth, the ignorance of which kills countless ideas and splendid plans; that the

moment one definitely commits oneself, then Providence moves, too. All sorts of things occur to help one that would never otherwise have occurred. A whole stream of events issue from the decision, raising in one's favor all manner of unforeseen incidents and meetings and material assistance, which no man could have dreamt would have come his way.

I have learnt a deep respect for one of Goethe's couplets:

"Whatever you can do or dream you can, begin it.
Boldness has genius, power, and magic in it."

Of all Owen's fertile enterprises, his most significant contribution—picking up, in effect, where the Grzimeks had left off—was his conversion of the tiny Michael Grzimek laboratory into the Serengeti Research Institute, a priceless asset of the Serengeti Plain. There is nothing comparable to it in the West. While important studies of the various species have come out of its inquiries, like the work of Schaller, Kruuk, Watson, and others, a greater value may eventually lie in what it will reveal about the dynamics of comparable arid and semi-arid regions in the Northern Hemisphere. As the great wildebeest herd is unique, so is the setting that sustains it, with implications significant within the larger context of world ecology. Exactly *how* significant, scientists themselves are still not certain, although some among them view this incomparable setting as a sort of object lesson to man of the bounties available from nature only so long as man himself stays out. In any case, the existence of S.R.I. offers at least the opportunity for scientists to measure the rate of spoliation that accompanies man's presence.

HUGH LAMPREY

"In 1962, John Owen began to see that the biology of the Serengeti was very little understood," Hugh Lamprey has said since. "Owen began a tentative inquiry into the nature of the setting. He recruited three biologists, and they studied the most obvious elements—the grasslands, the large mammals and their food supply. It was not long before they realized you couldn't study grassland production without a botanist. Grassland production depended on two important factors: climate and soil. So they had to have climate studies and soil studies. Grzimek pointed out you couldn't study animal diseases without a veterinarian, so they added a vet, and so on. It soon became apparent to all of us that this incredible ecosystem was held together through mechanisms of self-

THE LAST PLACE ON EARTH

regulation. We didn't know how or why this was so, and the explanation for this became our first task."

Owen had placed Hugh Lamprey in charge of the Institute to coordinate such studies, a logical move since Lamprey had been the first resident biologist in the old colonial game department. (His responsibility was "pest control," which at that time meant the control of crop-raiding elephants, and the way you controlled them was to shoot them.) Lamprey, too, is said to be an extremely modest man, square-jawed and earnest, and exquisitely polite ("Bit of a boy scout, if you ask me," one of the locals says).

Within a very short time, some seventeen scientists had gathered from all over the world to study, under Lamprey's supervision, the population dynamics of zebra, gazelle, impala, and elephant; the social behavior of impala; the grazing preferences of the wildebeest; the vulture as scavenger (Pennycuick's specialty); disease and parasites in the larger animals; and the effect of predators on residents of the woodland communities. Botanists were measuring the impact of fire and elephant on the vegetation; the vegetation itself was being mapped through aerial observation; and computers had been brought in to assist in the long-range monitoring of the entire ecosystem.

What was thought then to be the point of all this research would soon become a matter of dispute among some of the other Serengeti expatriates, however, one of whom—Ian Parker—held there was no point to it at all, that it had resulted only in the irresponsible squandering of invaluable years and hundreds of thousands of pounds. ("Forget about Parker," one European said, "until you know more about the rest of them.")

MYLES TURNER

Another expatriate who was not always sympathetic with Lamprey's scientists was Myles Turner, the operations warden of Serengeti. He shared some of Gordon Harvey's misgivings. Turner had observed more natural history of the park in his long years there than most of the young "boffins" put together. " 'Smash and grab' is the phrase we used for them," Turner has said. "It was just a mad rush of youngsters coming in, grabbing a subject and disappearing with it. If you were lucky, you might see their Ph.D. thesis, but you rarely did because there were seldom copies of their work. And you know, roaring around in their Land Rovers, their long hair flying in the wind—it was just all wonderful." But Turner had come to live with the situation, working like Lamprey under the benevolent Owen, and having had, finally, time for little else than his central concern, which was the protection of Serengeti's animals from poachers.

Turner's fear was that Serengeti would eventually be poached out if not constantly protected by paramilitary defenses against the encroachments of surrounding tribesmen whose numbers and needs were increasing in alarming proportions. Once, in the southwest of the plain, when he had found over a thousand snares in a single day, he happened across a lone kongoni. "I raised my hat to him," Turner told George Schaller, the scientist. "I really did. Any animal that managed to survive there was something special." Even despite his best efforts, and with relatively sophisticated equipment provided by Owen's funding efforts in the West, Turner estimated the loss to Serengeti to be in the tens of thousands of head of game each year.

Now Owen and Lamprey were gone and Turner would soon follow.

"The Africanization process took all of them," a European hunter out here says. "You know—this business of returning their natural heritage to the Africans. John Owen was very, *very* upset—lost that twinkle in his eye, that two-fisted drive. When he left he was a broken man. Hugh Lamprey wanted to make the Serengeti Research Institute into the leading wildlife research center in the world, which he did. The same spirit isn't there anymore. One of Myles Turner's characteristics was to fight for whatever he believed in, and this is not the way to deal with things now. All those people, they looked on those parks as their children. It's too bad. The Tanzanian parks system lost a magnificent, irreplaceable group of men."

THE LEAKEYS

Mary Leakey and George Dove live on the Serengeti Plain like old neighbors in a small town, Mrs. Leakey at Olduvai Gorge in the central plain thirty-five miles from George Dove's tented camp at Lake Ndutu to the southwest. They first met forty years ago when Mary Leakey was driving alone in the Serengeti and the clutch to her vehicle burned out. Dove happened along and fixed it. An experienced construction worker, he has done small chores for her since; presently he is building her an enclosed laboratory to replace her thatch-roofed lean-to. Mrs. Leakey lives alone, walking out early to her digs, where rhinos sometimes graze, in the company of her five Dalmatians. She has lived in this way, overseeing Tanzanian assistants, since the death of her husband, L. S. B. Leakey, two years ago. Her frequent reports on newfound fossils of early hominids, or "near-man," are followed with avidity and some bewilderment by scientists outside of Africa—all the more so for the fact that a great many of the major paleoanthropological discoveries of the past fifteen years have come from within the family of Louis and Mary Leakey. In 1959, Mary found the fragments of the left temple of an australopithecine, dating the possible origin of near-man to 1.75 million years; other discoveries have followed. Almost as much has been made of Olduvai in central Serengeti as of Mary Leakey's finds, for the freakish configuration of the earth in that area throws up to the surface remnants of stone tools and hominid fossils of enigmatic variety. More than a small irony, some say, that so much of the evidence of early man is to be found in one of the last natural settings.

The Leakeys had raised their children in Serengeti: naked and armed only with animal bones, Louis and his son, Richard, once scavenged a zebra carcass from encircling hyena to demonstrate early man's capability to compete with predators. Home-trained, Richard first tried the tourist business (as partner with Alan Root in the Root & Leakey Company), then turned to paleoanthropology, soon to become as well known for his discoveries as his parents. In 1972, Richard discovered a hominid skull of earlier origin than Mary's find (2.8 million years) and more directly related to modern man. Conservation of wild animals was not the primary interest of the Leakey family as it had been for the park people—Owen, Lamprey, and Turner—but they were nevertheless prominent within the East Africa community for their identification with such efforts. Louis Leakey had testified at the hearings of 1957 against the plan to partition the central plain, and subsequently it was his advice to Jane Goodall that set her into her studies of the chimpanzee at Gombe Stream in southern Tanzania, a seminal project which has since narrowed the ethological space between that species and near-man, the Leakeys' family franchise. Richard has become even more closely identified with the conservation community. He succeeded his father as director of the National Museum of Kenya and just recently, people say, dared to organize a street march of five hundred schoolchildren against the sensitive Kenyatta government, protesting the brutal poaching of elephant going on to the southeast, around Tsavo.

GEORGE DOVE

George Dove keeps an eye out for Mary Leakey now that she is alone, although it won't be too long before he himself will be gone from Africa for good. The word in Nairobi is that George Dove is fed up, "about to pack it in." Dove is a rather fierce-looking fellow—orange-red all over, like the lions he used to hunt, with hulking chest and arms, and a red, waxed, cat-whiskered moustache, cantilevered almost twice the width of his face. He cultivates a fierce scowl and dyspeptic manner, although this is regarded as a rather lame effort to disguise a too-amiable and generous nature. Expatriates come and go at Dove's tent camp—Jane Goodall wrote *In the Shadow of Man* there; presently there is a young Dutch girl staying there to study the biology of the civet cat; and a young American works for him as a guide when tourists stop by (infrequently these days). For many years Dove led hunting safaris—he had apprenticed with the first and the most famous hunters, J. A. Hunter and Philip Percival—until in the early sixties he turned back to his earlier trade to help in the construction of the new lodges going up for tourists in Tanzania.

Dove's present tent camp at Lake Ndutu is a model for the sort of tourist dwelling the expatriates now tend most to favor in the interest of the animals: the tents are permanently pitched, require little maintenance, and blend into the setting, a modest contrast to the big resort lodges at Seronera and Lobo to the west and north, requiring whole communities to maintain. Dove thinks he knows as much about Serengeti's animals as anyone else, and he shares Gordon Harvey's distress about the diminution of the lion population. Whereas he once hunted them to shoot, he now feeds them from his camp kitchen, and when he sees they are diseased, as is often the case, he treats the meat he will throw them with antibiotics. From time to time he has done what he could to preserve the setting—on one occasion organizing a letter-writing campaign among former clients to protest human incursions into the park.

"You know, I've been here a long time," he says, in explaining to a visitor the circumstances of his impending departure. "I can remember Seronera when there wasn't a single thing there of any sort. When the first park warden came in, I went over and helped him build the first little hut. We had no equipment, no *nothing*. We wanted to make a road down the corridor, and we used to tie a big log of wood onto the back of a Land Rover and pull it, so that it helped make a path.

"One day not long ago, Derek Bryceson was by here. I mentioned that poaching was very bad now. Bryceson went back and had the army skirt the whole area. One of the first places they came was to *my* camp. I had an elephant skull with two tusks in it out front— had it since 1958, and the game department had okayed my having it. They carted me off to the crater and kept me in custody for four days, charged me with stealing property from the Tanzanian government. 'No *way*,' I said, 'will I plead guilty to that.' They finally threw out the case, but in the meantime the paper published the story that I was a bloody poacher!

"And then Derek Bryceson came here after that and said, 'Well, when I started this thing I didn't know *you'd* be the first one to be caught.'

"I said, 'Well, have no fear. It's had its desired effect. You've had your little fun and now it's over. I'm leaving.' He came down here half a dozen times to plead with me to stay. No *way*. I will miss the animals. I will miss them the most."

Dr. Michael Wood

In a somewhat roundabout fashion, George Dove has Derek Bryceson in common with Dr. Michael Wood, another of Dove's neighbors, who lives about two hundred miles to the northeast. Dr. Wood is a plastic surgeon who came down from London after the war and bought a farm on the northern slope of Mount Kilimanjaro from Bryceson. Bryceson had received it as a compensatory gesture from the British government to R.A.F. pilots wounded during the Second World War, of whom Bryceson was one. Beyond the gesture, the British had hoped to stop incursions of the nomadic Masai in the vicinity by settling the area with colonials.

Bryceson was unable to make a go of the farm, however, sold it to Wood, and moved to the capital of Tanganyika where he entered Julius Nyerere's T.A.N.U. party, soon to form the new independent government of Tanzania. Over the years, Dr. Wood devised ingenious methods of arresting erosion along the slopes of the mountain, succeeding where Bryceson had failed and converting the hills into richly arable fields of wheat, corn, and seed beans. Now, within a very few months, the Bryceson/Wood farm would be appropriated by the Tanzanian government, of which Bryceson was now a prominent member, and split up among native Tanzanians, including—yet another irony—the Masai the British had sought to discourage some twenty years ago by giving the land to Bryceson.

Dr. Wood flies his Cessna back and forth to his office in Nairobi. Across the African continent, his skills as a physician are far more widely known than his talents as a farmer. He is one of the founders of Flying Doctors, a pioneering system of medical delivery devised and operated by a small group of physicians who provide medical care, free for those unable to pay, across the several East African nations.

Operating out of Nairobi with a shortwave radio hookup, a fleet of small planes, and a network of bush-cleared landing strips, Flying Doctors manage to cover thousands of miles of wilderness where there are neither roads nor medical facilities. Dr. Wood himself is said to oversee some forty-five thousand cases a year in this fashion, including one Masai he tells of who, wounded by a rhino, walked sixty miles to the landing strip carrying part of his intestine in his blanket toga. In his one day of the week at the Arusha hospital near his farm, Wood may perform as many as forty operations.

Dr. Wood's concerns, relating to those of Bernhard Grzimek, are less direct than the others', though hardly less urgent, having to do with the health of the African people as a problem greater in magnitude than that of their animals. "Not only are there too many people in East Africa for the resources available to them," he has said, "but most all of them are sick. They have all the diseases we have in the Western world, plus all the tropical diseases—leprosy, tuberculosis, cholera, the plague. If you did a random search of human blood from Kasa to Kampala, you'd find that the hemoglobin count is about fifty per cent [seven grams of hemoglobin per one hundred mililiters of blood], so that you are dealing with people who are half-alive or half-dead, whichever way you want to think of it. We always reckon that any African coming to us with a specific problem has at least six other diseases as well."

Under the circumstances of having devoted twenty years to establishing his farm at Kilimanjaro, Dr. Wood is said to be unperturbed about having now to give it up, viewing the nationalization of his property as an inevitable consequence within the logic of recent and impending events—an attitude expressed by others among the expatriates, Owen, Lamprey, and Turner particularly. (When the word finally comes to move, however, someone in Nairobi says, Dr. Wood and his family will be given twenty-four hours to get out.)

DEREK BRYCESON

Derek N. M. Bryceson considers himself African. He is the only white man left holding office in an East African nation. Some in Nairobi feel he is also capricious and self-serving, but in fairness it should be kept in mind that part of their resentment may grow out of Bryceson's security in a setting which so many others are now being forced to give up. Whatever the case, it is clear that nobody much likes Bryceson though none will say as much for the record. It is too risky, especially for those who have worked for the Tanzanian government or are still dependent on its favor. "Since he was an unsuccessful farmer," one of the locals bitterly observes about his entrance into Nyerere's government, "naturally he would be appointed Minister of Agriculture."

Bryceson is tall, prematurely gray, crippled from his war wound, and bluntly aggressive toward the other expatriates. But at the time of independence, had he been a blood relative of all of them, he would still have drawn their wrath for the office he held—that of Minister of Agriculture—is the role of antagonist to those concerned with the preservation of wild animals, and especially, it was emphasized, to Bernhard Grzimek, who has been feuding with ministers of agriculture over the world most of his adult life. In Germany, they defeated his plan for that country's first national park; in Rhodesia, Uganda, and Tanganyika, they destroyed hundreds of thousands of animals, perhaps millions, to eliminate tsetse or rinderpest, or just to grow peanuts; in East Africa, they are responsible more than any other agency for encouraging the cattle explosion which is turning the savanna into desert. The enemies of wild animals—farmers and cattlemen—are the constituents of ministers of agriculture. "Elephants can't vote, but Masai can," Grzimek says out here, over and over, and their votes shape the policies of ministers of agriculture. In consequence of all this, Grzimek's reaction against ministers of agriculture through the critical period of the sixties is said to have become reflexive: they were the enemy. Inevitably, in East Africa, on one occasion after the next, he would run head-on into Derek Bryceson.

The fact that both men are Europeans seeking the favor of the

African President, Julius Nyerere, that each thinks his way best not only for the people but for the country as well (and Grzimek for the continent)—these things have done little to ease the strain between them. And since it had been awkward, even suicidal, for the other expatriates to expose Bryceson openly, Grzimek the outsider too often has had to take it upon himself to do so. His method has been essentially the same as perfected in Europe (pressing the right button at the right time) but directed not so much at public opinion for its effect as toward the single source of Julius Nyerere, who, apparently, alone makes the difference.

According to one widely told story, in 1962, the first year after independence, when there had been a wave of rhino poaching in Ngorongoro, Grzimek and Alan Root had persuaded all the tourists in the area to write Dr. Nyerere protesting the slaughter, had written letters themselves over fictitious names, and then, after a suitable delay, Grzimek had written Nyerere over his own name saying he had heard about the displeasure of the tourists. He suggested respectfully that if the poaching continued, the new tourist industry in Tanzania could be irreparably damaged. Nyerere had taken the appropriate action in time. Thus it had become a matter of course that Grzimek would use variations of the same technique subsequently against Derek Bryceson, the Minister of Agriculture.

Bryceson never quite seemed to catch on. He would authorize some modification to Serengeti's border restrictions, and each time, even though Grzimek might be in Frankfurt, he would strike. "I have five thousand people who will write when I ask them," he has said, and the letters would pour into the beleaguered Nyerere protesting Bryceson's latest transgression. Then would follow Grzimek's own letter, a statesmanlike communication from the respectful conservationist whose only concern was that Tanzania treat her animals wisely, always of course in her own best interest. And always the stratagem worked. There was some reason to believe Nyerere himself was amused by Grzimek's methods.

On at least one occasion, however, it had all got out of hand, escalating within hours into an incident of international concern comparable to the row of the late fifties. Indeed, on precisely the same acreage that had brought the Grzimeks flying to the rescue twelve years earlier—the central plain of Serengeti and the foothills of Ngorongoro—Derek Bryceson in 1969 announced his intention to

86

permit cattle grazing. The fact that there had been none previously, even though the central plain had been excluded from the park by the British, was due to the establishment of the Ngorongoro Conservation Unit. This was the land-usage plan which permitted controlled farming, grazing, and forestry to be carried on in small selective portions of the unit while the better part of it—the central plain, Olduvai, and the Ngorongoro Crater—remained reserved for the animals. It was a new and bold experiment which had worked well enough and had even been welcomed by most, for it had allowed the dust to settle after the furious controversies of the fifties. Following independence, the Tanzanians had seen no reason to change it.

But now Derek Bryceson was declaring the government's intention to reverse the priorities of land usage, giving over 3,040 square miles of the unit to the Masai for their cattle, and leaving only 160 square miles reserved for the wild animals. It was exactly the threat to the Serengeti that Bernhard Grzimek had feared might someday come should the park's borders be interfered with in any way. With a simple administrative order, Derek Bryceson, the Minister of Agriculture, would destroy the Serengeti Plain and the migration.

Grzimek was in Frankfurt at that time, and the progress of his movements, as read in and between the lines of *The East African Standard,* traces his quick counterattack.

On September 1st, datelined London, a report appeared, beginning,

> A flood of angry reaction has greeted the Tanzanian government's plan to promote farming for the Masai in the Ngorongoro Conservation Unit. . . .

And it went on to list some of the more prominent expressing alarm:

> . . . among others, Peter Scott the naturalist; the Secretary of the Fauna Preservation Society; and Sir Hugh Elliott, the UK Representative of the International Union for the Conservation of Nature.

Bryceson, according to this account, dismissed their fears as "absolute nonsense." Then, on September 4th and 5th, the following:

PROFESSOR GRZIMEK JOINS
PROTEST ON NGORONGORO

London—Sept. 4. Professor Bernhard Grzimek, who launched the phrase, "The Serengeti Shall Not Die," yesterday joined the protest on the latest Tanzanian plans for Ngorongoro, calling them "disastrous and tragic."

The German zoologist whose book made the name Serengeti famous throughout the world appealed to President Nyerere to reverse the government's decision to excise the bulk of the Ngorongoro Conservation Area and hand it over to range development authorities.

He said it was impossible to see how turning marginal land over to the Masai for their herds could advance their welfare. It was a disservice to wildlife without any advantage to human life, including tourism.

"I trust it is not too late for the President to correct this disastrous, tragic decision," Professor Grzimek said.

He was obviously personally distressed by news of the plan because he has dedicated several years of his life and seen his son, Michael, die in the cause of conserving the wildlife of the Serengeti.

His television programs on wildlife have top television ratings throughout Europe and he constantly persuades his audience to donate money for conservation projects in East Africa, particularly Tanzania. He himself makes over half his fees for his programs to these projects.

Many millions of marks have been raised in this way, but it was his deep personal interest in the area rather than the money, which caused Professor Grzimek's distress.

It is understood that the Director of Tanzania's National Parks, Mr. John Owen, was now in London and is due to brief the officials of the World Wildlife Fund on Friday. Until then the organization is reluctant to comment.

Tanzania's Minister of Agriculture, Mr. Bryceson, is due in London next week and is bound to be closely questioned by leading conservationists who are still reserving their opinion although their first reaction was one of horror.

And on the next day:

Sept. 5. Tanzania's new plan for the Ngorongoro area would not only harm rather than help the Masai, it would impair the country's image overseas where it has enjoyed an excellent reputation, Professor Bernhard Grzimek said in a letter to *The East African Standard.*

Professor Grzimek, who has a long association with conservation measures in the Serengeti/Ngorongoro area, has already written personally to President Nyerere to make his views known. He had earlier described the news as "disastrous" and "tragic" to a *Standard* reporter who called him at his Frankfurt home.

In his letter, he said he had always championed the record of Independent African states, particularly Tanzania, in game conservation. This work "may be one of the main contributions of Black nations to the civilization of mankind," he said.

But the latest developments had led to many criticisms of his judgment and of the pro-African propaganda he had used in his books and television programs (which have an estimated audience of 40 million in Europe).

It was, however, Tanzania's last European governor, Sir Richard Turnbull, who started the rot by allowing his administration to cut Ngorongoro out of Serengeti National Park. Now it was the only European minister, Mr. Bryceson, who had finished the job. . . .

Once again, Julius Nyerere's government pulled back. Grzimek had won, Bryceson lost, and the plan been abandoned. But Grzimek and Bryceson had fought on so long and so loudly that, as some in Nairobi observed now, both men had come to lose influence with Dr. Nyerere, himself a quiet and intense socialist who seemed always left in the middle of their controversies, somewhere between the needs of his people and the survival of his nation's wildlife. This opinion was strengthened considerably a few years later when Derek Bryceson was relieved of the post of Minister of Agriculture and assigned a new office. It was a move of little consequence to the outside world but of deep concern to the Serengeti expatriates, who saw it now as a cruel joke played by Nyerere, or an impatient attempt to neutralize the problems both men had caused him, or, as a newspaperman here remarked, Nyerere's way of making each side see more clearly the problems of the other.

Derek Bryceson now became the new director of Tanzania's national parks, the office once held by the exalted and revered John Owen. It was the single office most critical to the welfare of the Serengeti after Julius Nyerere's. To the shocked and appalled expatriates forced by political events to relinquish their stewardship and preparing now to leave Serengeti for good, it seemed as though Dr. Nyerere had deliberately set a fox in the coop to guard the chickens.

But it is perhaps misleading to suggest that the Serengeti expatriates draw quite so obsessively the attention of everyone in the Nairobi community. One's understanding is qualified by the subject matter flowing from one bystander to the next, each obligingly worrying old issues which have not been resolved and may never be; then each moves on to other matters.

At the moment, it is the latest adventure of the intrepid Alan Root that is the center of attention. The Roots have just set a world record by sailing their balloon over Mount Kilimanjaro, the highest mountain in Africa. For most of the community it is largely an entertainment; for the newly arrived visitor, an insistent metaphor of the exhilaration of place, obscuring for the moment East Africa's ruder problems.

The Roots had had trouble finding the right weather conditions. Then one morning about dawn, a light plane had flown up first to check from above—the top of the mountain is almost always obscured by clouds—and when word was radioed down that conditions seemed favorable, the Roots had launched. Flying in a balloon is like no other mode of travel, for excepting the occasional roar of the burner there is no sound of machinery—no groaning joints as in a wind-borne glider—only the natural sounds; in the Roots' balloon, the sounds of East Africa. At first light in the early morning chill, with calls of the night animals about them and the dark ground, falling away, forming to silhouettes, the Roots began their ascent.

They climbed the eastern wall of Kilimanjaro to a height of twenty-four thousand feet, and by then the clouds had burned off; they sailed down the long axis of the mountain, across Uhuru Peak, toward the west—perfect visibility. From their tiny wicker basket

90   THE LAST PLACE ON EARTH

they could see all of it—the savanna, the volcanoes, the sharp slice of the Great Rift Valley; a few miles to the south the smaller Mount Meru, near whose peak is the house of the Myles Turners; at the foot of the mountain the small town of Arusha where John Owen (and now Derek Bryceson) kept his office; and due west, some two hundred miles, toward the Serengeti Plain where Mary Leakey worked her digs and George Dove grumbled over his morning coffee.

Not too high above the mountain snows but at peak altitude now they are using oxygen masks but Joan's reaction time is too slow and, growing logy, she discovers that in the excitement she has failed to connect the air line of her mask to the tank in the corner of the basket. It is a wonderful experience, by forgotten coincidence an echo of the declared intention of young Michael Grzimek to fly his Dornier to the top of Kilimanjaro someday and land it there.

The Roots sail on to the far side and begin their descent to discover they have not traveled far enough to clear the wall of a ravine directly beneath them. The wind has died. There is ten minutes of fuel left. They hang in the air, burning when necessary to hold their altitude, waiting. Root gambles and burns steadily now to go higher in search of a crosswind. At last the balloon begins to move westward again along the lateral axis. Clear of the ravine finally and floating down into the foothills, Root throws out the heavy tow rope, which snags between his arm and shoulder, yanking him halfway out of the basket before he can brace against its pull. Yet, as always in the past, it turns out all right.

They are awaited on the ground by Tanzanian police who arrest them on suspicion of spying. Root asks if Joan can go into the bushes for a moment and she receives their permission. She exchanges the exposed film in their cameras with fresh film. When she returns, the police demand their cameras and with great reluctance, protesting that their pictures are the only record of their flight, Root hands them over. The police take out the unexposed film and return their cameras. The Roots are obliged to spend the night and the next day in custody before charges against them are dropped. Their unexposed film is not returned. On the day following their release, word of their adventure reaches the dinner table of Dr. Michael Wood at his farm a few miles away. It is received with high amusement.

SEVEN

IAN PARKER

"Conservation is the last playground of the mind!" Ian Parker declares with some heat. "The wildlife scene is a very much bigger issue than the conservationists would have people believe, containing many opposing elements within it. Simply to demonstrate this I have tended to produce opposition to what people say—the Grzimeks of this world." Parker is the pilot who flew the weather plane for the Roots, a friend of theirs and a former business associate. He is the last of the group—I had followed the advice of others in waiting to talk with him—but the only one of them in Nairobi at the moment. He is a defensive man, protesting in the absence of challenge. He believes conservationists (among whom he includes most of the Serengeti expatriates) to be the purveyors of dangerous fictions. The African people need wildlife to eat, or to make a living from. If they choose to get rid of it altogether, that is their affair. Conservationists like Grzimek and the others are sentimentalists as opposed to Parker and his followers, who are pragmatists. "They sell a case for facts, and there is no such thing to sell. They ignore the reality of what is happening on the ground. They sell it from Europe and America, environments which have annihilated their wildlife. If Grzimek's case has validity, he should be able to sell it at home. Obviously, he can't." What is more, conservationists are a ruthless sort who don't understand their own basic drives: ". . . pacifists, proponents of peace in the world, Eden, all the rest of it. All you have to do is get up before them with a smile on your face and say, 'I saw a hell of a funny thing on the street the other day. Three kids got hold of a squirrel, stuck his tail in paraffin, and set a match to it.' Then stick around because chairs, bullets will come at you, they will threaten to hang and quarter you! What you've done is demonstrate that right beneath the surface is a very powerful sense of aggression."

Ian Parker is rather hard to take but impossible to ignore. He is the chief executive of Wildlife Services Limited, specializing in the trade of hide, hair, and ivory; agriculture; and "the science of animal production," which means the harvesting of wild animals, or cropping. Of all the controversies over how best to deal with the wild animals of East Africa, the most complex is this question of "cropping," a term which is in itself a shorthand misnomer for the larger issue. Cropping means to take the excess from an animal population; culling, to select out the inferior. Among the expatriates, cropping may mean either. Suffice to say, it is a question of harvesting animals for whatever reason—whether for their own good, to prevent them from destroying their environment, or to provide meat for human beings—and it proceeds from the assumption that principles of population regulation of domestic species may be applied to wild animals. In all cases, the argument becomes operative only after tne property rights of wild animals have tilted against them. That is, once there have become too many animals for the space provided or, as in the case of the elephant, for example, when they are biologically unsuited to stay within the space allotted them, harvesting is advanced as the way to relieve the problem.

Ian Parker apparently believes there are times when you have to be prepared to kill animals in order to conserve them and/or the parks in which they live. He believes there to be few if any instances when the priority of animals should prevail over the priorities of people—the sick and starving people of Michael Wood's Africa—and he is avowedly unsentimental about the animals' presence, even in the parks. Ian Parker stands at the intersection of the "big-business" interests the scientist had spoken of. He is a fragile-looking man: intense, and in his khaki shorts, sandals, and with briefcase underarm, rather like an aging graduate student hurrying to make up for lost time.

A problem with Parker is that he makes his living (apparently a very good one) from the cropping of wild animals of all kinds, an insistent fact underlying his aggressive attacks on the others and his righteous identification with the problems of the African people. One instinctively senses the need for an answer to his charges, and from some quarter free of commercial interest.

But like so many of the problems beginning to emerge about Serengeti, Parker's version will have to be dealt with later. It is the long side of the week now, Thursday afternoon, four days since receiving the tenuous promise from Grzimek to call. My mosaic lacks a center. I sifted my notes over and over, seeking Grzimek's elusive chronology following the events of 1959. I decided I must take the initiative and call him again. He answered the phone on the second ring. He said he would come to the hotel at five the next evening and meet me in the lounge.

It is a pleasant setting, the Norfolk lounge, with rattan sofas and chairs grouped about the room for easy conversation; I arrived half an hour early and waited. The "morass of interests" I had begun to collect seemed overwhelming. I wondered how disposed he might be to deal with them. I almost missed him again. He came through the lounge twice, taller than I had expected (he is six feet four) and slightly stooped but with a loping, athletic bounce to his stride. I had become befuddled by the inconsistency of my several impressions of him; I recognized him now finally by his gray sideburns, and introduced myself.

He sat down and ordered a pack of cigarettes from the waiter. He said he had a bet with his daughter-in-law, Michael's widow, that he would not smoke, so he did his smoking away from home. He was to my surprise extremely cordial, almost exuberantly eager to talk, but he gave the distinct impression that a single interview was all I expected from him, so I talked fast. I referred to my first correspondence with him about Pennycuick almost a year earlier. I had read everything I could find by him in translation, I said, and a month or so ago I had written him asking if I might interview him. (Too clear by his blank expression now that he had paid little attention to either letter.) I knew that Serengeti was his principal concern in Africa, I said, it was one of mine, too; and it was the reason for my interest in him. I told him I saw my story shaping roughly along the lines that he was a sort of modern Noah, and this would take some time. He nodded slightly at this last—I would later find the passage in one of his books in which he himself would draw the comparison—and, abruptly, he launched into a monologue. By the end of the first hour, he had finished off the cigarettes and switched to my cigars.

It was not always easy to follow him. His English turns careless when he wants to eliminate detail. At first, as though having discovered a convert, he rushed his account, almost breathlessly—a bright child reporting home on his progress in class. But then his story gradually turned mechanical, the telling falling away to disconnected fragments, as though he had told it so often it had lost its flavor for him. He is aware of this in himself. "I am like a missionary," he said at one point. "Stay around me long enough and I tell the same story over and over." He has no memory for

94   THE LAST PLACE ON EARTH

dates, or for many names. His humor is obvious; his favorite stories end in melodrama or sentiment; he laughs first when he feels laughter is appropriate. To my astonishment and gradual relief, he talked with few interruptions for five hours.

Grzimek began:

"At the end of the war in Ditmark, I traded my pistol to an American for a bicycle and pedaled to Frankfurt, about four hundred kilometers away. I had changed into civilian clothes. I always carried them with me toward the end so they wouldn't take me a prisoner of war. I managed to avoid the villages where most of the Americans were. I had promised one of the editors of *Frankfurter Zeitung* I would meet him in Frankfurt when Hitler was finished. He was a well-known liberal journalist named Wilhelm Hollbach, and when I came to his apartment I discovered he had been made the new Lord Mayor of Frankfurt. He was ruling the city with journalists. He made me his adjutant, and then the Americans made me president of the police. They told me I should also take over food administration. I did it for one week and doubled the rations for the animals in the zoo.

"I saw that you could make use of your experience with the stupidity of armies. Having learned about it in the German Army, I saw it was just the same with the American Army. I asked the colonel, 'Why don't streetcars run after you have occupied the city for six weeks? All the workers can't come into town. What is the reason, because in Hitler times after an air strike, they were running in three days? Can't you give me a reason for it?'

"The answer was, 'Because there are Nazis among the streetcar operators.' I answered, 'But you allow every butcher and every baker to open their shops. They were not forced to become members of the Nazi Party, but these poor chaps were city employees—they *had* to become members of the Nazi Party—and I have tried to become a member of the Nazi Party five times. They didn't take me, which was not to my merit because nobody told me that I would be fined ten years later in peacetime.'

"I said I wanted to reopen the zoo. They said, 'You are *crazy* caring for monkeys in a city that is eighty per cent in ruins.' They didn't allow me to do it, and one day I just did, and made posters and put them up all over Frankfurt. There were thirteen animals left, one hippo, two lions, two camels, and a few unimportant animals. The hippo had survived by submerging in his pool while his home burned down. I put my animals to pony carts and sent them through the streets making propaganda for the zoo. The army allowed me to open the zoo finally, so long as I didn't ask for money—it was needed for housing and other things, of course.

"The old zoo was quite small, but the surrounding blocks were totally in ruins. Since there was a new city administration, I just decided to block three roads adjoining the zoo from the traffic. I put out traffic signs and blocked the roads and everybody thought it was legal. I put brick walls across the roads, and five years later they had to abolish the old road by the laws of the country. If people had known it then—the blocked-off area was about a third larger than the zoo's grounds—they would have killed me.

"One day not so long ago, Prince Philip came to the Frankfurt Zoo. He speaks German like me. I told him that the best thing which can happen to a hundred-year-old zoo is to be flattened by the British air force, leave alone the poor animals. But the surrounding district, too, so you can enlarge it, and so on. But there was a lack of cooperation between the two air forces. The German air force should have bombed the London Zoo, which is fifty years older. It's the same thing that I told the Russians."

He laughed and paused to accept another of my cigars. "But back then, I had to get visitors into a zoo with no animals. Because I had no animals, I had to provide entertainment to make money. I learned there was a roller coaster hidden in the Black Forest, which was occupied by the French Army, but the French didn't allow *one thing* to go out from their part of Germany. I made good friends with American black officers. The black soldiers were very friendly with Germans. They always gave food to Germans. They had this slogan, 'You are slaves, *we* are slaves'—very helpful. I persuaded these chaps to go bring this roller coaster out, because the French wouldn't shoot Americans, and they did this.

"And immediately I made lots of money from these soldiers who would ride fifty or sixty times, drinking champagne, and I had to call the M.P.'s because they would raise the bars and bloody their heads. They would get drunk and try to climb in the monkey cage.

"I persuaded a circus owner to put up a tent in the zoo because there was no place for people to meet in Frankfurt. I had wrestling matches and plays. I had the condition that anybody who would go into this damn tent had to pay the entrance fee of the zoo. They had Adenauer and even Eisenhower making speeches in the tent, and anybody who wanted to come hear them had to pay. I had boxing and opera and all such things to make money. I put on fireworks and thirty thousand people came.

"But what kind of zoo is it when you have no animals? It was forbidden to go more than ten kilometers outside Frankfurt without permission from the army. I wanted to collect animals from bombed-out zoos and circuses. I asked permission to go to Neustadt, and they didn't know there were ten or twelve towns of this name all over Germany. At first I traveled all over in a wood-burning car which was formerly the lord mayor's, and then I had a truck. I got to Leipzig before the Russians and brought out most of their animals. Wherever I went I picked up animals, and when I returned I had to pick up refugees. Coming back from Bavaria once, I brought back a polar bear, a ton of cheese and twenty refugees.

"I was not permitted to use construction materials for my zoo from Frankfurt's ruins. They would be used for reconstruction of the city. When they tore down a house during the day, we would go out at night and take parts. It was not stealing because the zoo belonged to the city. One day I learned the Americans had abandoned an army camp, and that the gardeners around were stealing fences. I sent my people out to get some, and they came back with heavy steel poles, lots of them.

"That afternoon, two American officers came by and said I had stolen American property and that they would put me in jail. I was careless enough to laugh, and they said they would come back. I realized what the Germans would have done in Occupied France with French civilians who had stolen from them—they would have shot them. But in the meantime I had learned the officers had sold part of the stuff on the black market, and when they came back, I told them proudly more than half of the visitors to the zoo were American soldiers, and that I was working for the army, too, and so on. And I got back what I had stolen.

"By 1958, the zoo was more or less completed. It was the centennial of the zoo, and I invited zoo directors from all over the world. This became a good reason for the local politicians to do something about the zoo, and finish it up properly."

Grzimek went down the hall to the bathroom, and I ordered more cigars and ice from room service. When he came back, I poured him a drink and asked what his plans might be for the coming week. "I go to Uganda to see what is happening with the animals there," he said.

My earlier speech had been more effective than I had expected— either that or he had decided I might in some way be helpful to his cause; or, a third possibility, he had simply decided to accommodate me in light of the great distance I had traveled to find him. But there was no way to be sure and now, with the ill-concealed desperation of a tourist trying to cash a personal check in a foreign bank, I descended to crude flattery.

"William Conway of the Bronx Zoo says you are a genius," I said, "for the way you are able to distribute your productivity. . . ."

He sipped at his drink and looked away. "Um . . . ayah," he said. The gratuity of the compliment unsettled him.

I said I had access to a Land Rover, had camped out before in East Africa, and wondered if it might be possible to go with him into Uganda. So that we might talk more.

"Yes," he said brusquely, "that is possible," and then, returning to his story, he rushed on:

"Altogether, I have collected about eight million marks for wildlife. Most of this has gone to Africa. South and Central America are hopeless—only birds and rats are left there. I daresay I am the only person in the world who can collect money for wildlife on television. . . .

"People need animals!" Grzimek's awareness of the need in himself is obscured among his earliest memories of childhood. At fourteen he wrote his first book, a manual on bantam breeding; he took his bantams with him to the University of Leipzig. In his twenties, he published an analysis of poultry diseases that became a standard reference. He visited the United States to study American techniques of poultry raising, teaching himself English by reading Shakespeare on the ship that took him over. Soon thereafter, he devised a method of quality control of eggs which reduced spoilage from 4 per cent of total production to .25 per cent, wresting the market away from the Netherlands. He directed his studies to the biology of dogs, horses, cows, and other domestic animals, acquiring an expertise which would account throughout the war years for his movement in and out of the army (as a warrant officer) and the Ministry of Agriculture.

He had survived the war, however, not so much through his specialized knowledge as through luck and cunning. Himmler asked him to conduct experiments on dogs, an assignment he refused for reasons he does not now offer. Once he was ordered to Hitler's retreat at Berchtesgaden to see after the Führer's chickens. "He was so fond of animals that he didn't allow the servants to shoot one animal of any kind so that his housekeeper had to keep his fowls

THE LAST PLACE ON EARTH

caged in. Otherwise, they would be eaten by foxes. Every tenth tree there was a feeding place for wild birds. From that time I never believed people who were good to animals are necessarily good people. Because a dog had more rights during Nazi times than a Jew."

Grzimek was investigated during the war by the Gestapo. He was demoted on one occasion for protecting a Jew in his office. After the war, he was tried by the American military for having applied for membership in the Nazi Party; he was acquitted on the testimony of several whom he had helped. He then received certification from the Americans that he had actively fought against Hitler. "I certainly didn't deserve that," he says now. "I helped these people because they were in danger, not for political reasons. What people don't realize today is what it was like to live under a dictatorship. It was *impossible* in those times to fight against Hitler. I was one of the few Germans who knew about Auschwitz. A medical officer told me, but I didn't dare tell it to anyone else. I was no hero. It was too dangerous."

By war's end, he had become an authority on wolves, gorilla, and lions, as well as domestic species, having raised and studied them in his home and traveled the Eastern Front with a pet lion at his heels.

"People *need* animals," he said again. "What I always tell politicians and journalists is they don't realize how times have changed. In the last century eighty per cent of our population in the West lived in villages or on farms together with animals and nature. Now for the first time in human history, eighty per cent of our Western civilization live *separate and apart* from animals and nature, in big towns. What they don't realize is that what becomes rare becomes precious.

"I am always fighting about this with politicians. For instance, when they build a huge apartment house, they forbid old people to have a dog or a cat. I always used to say, 'I am not fighting for dogs, or cats, or pigeons, which are overfed, but as a social matter.' In old times on the farm, the grandchildren could go visit the grand-parents. There was contact with the family. Now we have become rich. We build the old lady an apartment or send her to a home where old people retire, where everybody speaks only from disease and every morning somebody dies. Old people want something to love and care for, even if it is only a dog or cat. Mostly it is awful for the dogs and cats. But it is not so much a matter for the S.P.C.A. It is cruelty to human beings *not* to allow an old lady to feed pigeons in the town, or to have a cat. It is a *social* need of human beings."

That it all comes down in the end to a human loss is a main argument of Grzimek, although it is an argument most often provoked by cruelty to a given species. "I am a scientist, not an S.P.C.A. person, but some things I cannot take," he says, turning to the television show I had seen last week. "To put a hen in a cage for its whole lifetime!" Problems for chickens are roughly the same as for cows—to hold down prices in the supermarkets, mass production techniques are necessary. Dye is used to strengthen the color of the yolk; the dye causes disease; the disease is treated with antibiotics which remain in the meat and are consumed by the customer. Farmers can no longer afford to raise chickens in the more natural way—on green Tyrolean farms, now empty—since the per-unit cost is not competitive. Grzimek had pictured and identified the enemy—German industrialists "who build skyscrapers and keep half a million hens"—and then concluded to his uneasy audience: "I wanted you at least to know what you are eating every day."

Africans are different. They have always lived peaceably with their animals and in natural balance with their environment. The African, Grzimek says, is in mystic contact with the animal soul; in some tribal traditions, his soul passes after death into the animal's body to survive in this form—a marked contrast to other religions that place man outside and above nature.

"You should be careful not to say so much in publications about what we Europeans and the old colonialists have done. It is only *partly* true." He repeated some of the things he had said in his first letter—how Mobutu and Kaunda had set aside new parklands. "Nyerere has even moved people away from the park at Lamai Wedge, something neither Germans nor Americans ever did. [The Lamai reference was lost to me; he made no effort to explain.] Nyerere has increased the parks of Tanzania from one at independence to *ten!*"

Even excluding the contributions of Grzimek himself, it seemed a view decidedly at odds with that held by the Europeans I had just talked with, and I said so. He rolled over my exception. "Look at the record of the colonialists! The British game department was always the newest and smallest department, with the smallest budget; the animals came under their sole jurisdiction. The game department earned money by selling ivory, by inviting down foreign hunters. They regarded the game as pests. They were not interested in conserving them. They wanted to control them.

THE LAST PLACE ON EARTH

"Look at what happened to the hippo! It was an animal that used to be found from the origins of the rivers down to the ocean. It was totally shot out—for pleasure. One of the famous explorers wrote, 'We came to a river and it was full of hippos. I sat on a rock and amused myself for three hours shooting hippos.' They *dared* to publish this at the time!

"Hemingway and his books were the main attitude of those times. Now it turns out that the hippo has six or seven stomachs and it can graze totally dry grass which no antelope can digest. The hippo was a source of meat for the African people. They never took more than they needed, so that their meat supply was in equilibrium with nature. But it was shot out in colonial times. Now you have a protein deficiency in African children, and you see them everywhere with protruding bellies. But the hippo is shot out. If you go down the Congo River now, you don't see one hippo, no crocodiles, because all the steamers going up, the people just sat there shooting at everything. *That* was the colonial tradition."

Old wars. We had moved to the porch terrace outside my room over the entranceway to the hotel; Italian motorscooters popped and spluttered interference from the street below. It was toward midnight and his exuberance had faded, the chopped accent become slurred, oddly fragile. Yet he seemed to want to go on. There was no need to press him—the Uganda safari promised me the optimum circumstances I had sought in my original plan—and while the concerns of the Serengeti expatriates would seem to weigh heavily on his own actions now (I kept waiting for him to turn to them), he was lost to his reflections, the roots of his incredible odyssey.

"What becomes rare becomes precious"—long ago that had been the only hope he could see for the animals of East Africa. Around the time of the Serengeti expedition, possibly earlier—he is no longer sure—he realized Africa's animals had become a sort of commodity in search of a market. The problem was, no one else seemed to grasp this, neither the potential buyers—the European tourists—nor the African sellers. As broker, Grzimek made it his task to bring the principals together, a challenge under the circumstances not unlike that of rebuilding his zoo with neither animals nor money. In East Africa, it would be a matter of educating the people to the scarcity value of their resources.

"Eighty per cent of the population of Tanzania have never *seen* a lion or an elephant. Even English children have seen more such animals, because they have zoos. But it is too expensive for Africans to visit the parks; it is a long journey and the accommodations too costly. Only in such places do the animals survive. So I donated money to build youth hostels for children to visit free there, and I gave color posters about wildlife in Swahili, gave cinemobiles to show wildlife films in the villages. 'Serengeti Shall Not Die' was the first film translated into Swahili. Very popular and very effective. Soon, the attitude began to change."

Next he went to work on Julius Nyerere, whom he tracked to his small office in a schoolhouse in Dar es Salaam. Nyerere was then leader of the opposition in the colonial Parliament. "What becomes rare becomes precious—that was the basis for my argument to Nyerere. I told him to look into books of famous travelers to Europe two hundred years ago, like for instance Casanova. He traveled nearly all the countries of Europe, and he described them—kings' courts, castles, big towns, famous buildings—but not one word about nature although he traveled for weeks in slow-moving coaches. The most beautiful landscapes of Europe were ignored because he had been brought up like most people then in small villages in open countries. You can't expect a farmer to appreciate a wild boar which eats his potatoes. To the farmer, it is not rare and it is not precious.

"I told Nyerere, 'Your country is a poor-looking country. I don't think people will come to see the green hills of Hemingway, which a big part of the year are not even green; they are gray. But you own elephants and lion and rhino and hippo, which don't occur elsewhere in the world. Wildlife has become very rare, and you could sell it to tourists.' I told him what tourism means for some countries—that Switzerland at that time earned forty per cent of its national revenue from tourism."

In Europe, there was a different problem—buyer resistance to East Africa as a resort destination, largely, Grzimek says, because of misleading impressions created by hunters, adventure-story writers and filmmakers. "They wanted to show themselves as heroes. They gave the impression you have to walk through wild bush for weeks; that you wake up in your tent with a cobra in your bed; that lions are sitting behind every bush. They never published that there are good hotels and roads, that it is not dangerous to travel. Even Walt Disney! I wrote him and tried to persuade him to say in his films that what he showed of Africa was only in *the national parks!* But he was just *deaf* to this. I realized tourists didn't come because of this awful picture of Africa."

Grzimek tried to persuade BOAC and Lufthansa to offer inexpensive package tours to East Africa; there was no interest. Meanwhile, independent Tanzania had committed its meager resources to an expanded tourist program (which would later result in the hotels and roads built by John Owen). Grzimek resorted to other means: "I did an ugly trick. I told one day on television, it is now possible to go to East Africa from Germany for three weeks for two thousand marks, all expenses included. It was a lie because the *air fare* was more than two thousand marks. In the next three days, people all over Germany phoned their travel agencies asking to make the trip. Who would be doing them?

"The agencies were forced to use old propeller planes—they were just then changing to jets—and to hire Yugoslavian pilots to deliver the package tours at the price I had quoted. The newspapers attacked me because I had misused state-owned television for commercial propaganda. I said, 'Yes I did. I don't do my television programs for the pleasure of old ladies loving cats. And so on. I intend to achieve something with it, and I will continue. You are right if you can prove that I earn anything through the tourist business, but you will never be able to do that!' After the first tour—sixty people went—and when they came back they told ten thousand, 'How marvelous! How wonderful!' So that I always used to say, 'Africa is like an infection. If you get it once, you can't get rid of it. You always go back!' That is how it worked, and after that, many other tours came in."

His face relaxed into a wide grin of triumph.

"Um . . . ayah," he said. "But in recent years my aim has changed. Tourism may stop because of wars—anything—and you must make people *proud* of what they have done. I don't insist so much on what we Europeans have done here but what the Africans have done. . . ." And again the brittle sermon—the contributions of Mobutu, Kaunda, Nyerere. He seemed unaware he was repeating himself.

"From the very beginning, I was different from many others," he said. "I was fighting for last pieces of wilderness, not for elephants and lions, because the main condition of having an ecological unit is that you do not place an unnatural emphasis on the question of animal survival.

"This is very difficult to sell to the public. For example, when it was published that elephants were dying from thirst in Tsavo, I got letters from people saying, 'Why don't you send trucks of water?' I can't tell a big audience in public, 'That is *nature,* that a part of the elephants *have* to die. . . .' "

I wondered why not but waited for more. I had, in fact, heard that he *had* sent water trucks once to save dying elephants, into Cameroon. Did this have to do with the cropping controversies? What for a man like this was an "unnatural" emphasis on animal survival? He had not yet slowed for details, and he did not now. Odd that he seemed so indifferent to qualification. He was both a scientist and a journalist yet he rushed past constraint indifferently; little time to bother—the far side of precision.

". . . The drought comes. It has been so for thousands of years, and if I made the animals survive, then you would have doubled the population next time, and in the next drought you have to take double the action.

"It is a similar matter, and I see no solution for it, of people starving in Ethiopia. I think they have starved there in every drought for tens of thousands of years. In this way, the human population remained in a number which could survive in this dry country. In old times, nobody cared. You didn't hear about it. You had many people dying from starvation in European countries. You had no roads, no cars, and if you had a bad harvest, people died from hunger. Even in Germany. Everywhere."

"I'm not sure I understand. . . ." Elephants and Ethiopians? But, lids drooping, Grzimek was captive to his own sermon.

"Veterinarians successfully fought rinderpest, and now you have an invasion of cattle, which is not used for food but is just for the pride of its proprietor, and so on. Cattle are *not* African animals, they are forest animals. You can see they look like skeletons just outside the parks, whereas all the game looks, even in dry times, quite well. It is because of modern developments that cattle have increased so much. At the end of it there will be a new India in Africa. The country turns to desert. And nobody will care for it. Who cares now for India?

"For instance now, at Lake Rudolf, with the Turkana tribe. They had a heavy drought and a lot of people died. In the modern state, you can't afford to let people die. It's against humanity, human dignity. They brought food and put up barracks at Lake Rudolf, and after eight years these people are still separated from their nomadic tribes. They are not related anymore. They are fed by international aid. They try to learn fishing, which does not seem to work. What is the solution of it? I do not know."

He had talked us both into exhaustion—a taxing experience. Still, whatever my confusions, he had gone to some lengths to educate me to the vast complex of problems here, and for this I was grateful, all the more curious and involved, and hopeful now that he would lead me on—but *where*, exactly, I had no notion at all. His pronouncements did not invite analysis. They were too heavily freighted with rhetoric—all part of a piece, Grzimek's position. From what I could make of it, he seemed to have worked out for himself his own sense of the order of things, a singular view of life based on the interdependence of man and animal (as yet lamentably unacknowledged by man). In idiosyncratic fashion, this view would seem to parse with Conway's back in New York; what is good for one is good for the other—"biophylaxis." There was as well what Gnosa called his Schweitzer inclinations, adding passion to the view—the explanation, called back over his shoulder, of a man rushing to avert disaster. Was the idea worthy of such an obsession? I was certainly not the one to judge. Grzimek believed so to the extent it stood as ultimate justification for whatever expedient lay open to him.

But beyond the obvious values to his cause, there was still some quality about him ajar with his too hurried generalities. For me, the personality seemed more intriguing than the propaganda—even his description of himself suggested a force stronger than his ideas. Perhaps it was because his very facility—the mechanized soliloquy, a rehearsed answer for everything—seemed somehow to reinforce his remoteness. Or perhaps it was because others here in the Nairobi community had begun to persuade me there was some unspoken force, some odd mystique, that informed his view more than anything he might say. The past was very much in attendance for Bernhard Grzimek, encouraging others to make more of it than they should. In New York, William Conway had spoken of it in terms of a disquieting coincidence. Grzimek had been invited in the mid-sixties to New York to receive the gold medal award of the New York Zoological Society, in Michael's name as well as his own. He had declined because he would be in Africa, but then he appeared after all. "He said he realized the award would fall on the evening of Michael's death," Conway said.

At George Adamson's camp in Garissa in northeastern Kenya, where he still works at rehabilitating domestic lions to the wilderness, Adamson talked softly and tentatively one evening about the problems of African animals. When the conversation turned to Grzimek, musing over the obsessions of the man, he told of passing the memorial to Michael at Ngorongoro and seeing by moonlight a lion at the base of it, as though standing sentry. A professional hunter present at the campfire waited a long minute and then said, almost with embarrassment, "Yes, and I was with some tourists who came in behind me. It was the night of the *tenth* anniversary of Michael's death, and there was a whole pride of lions out there. They took flash pictures of it. They showed me." Whatever the case, it was worth noting that Grzimek hadn't mentioned Michael tonight, or the Serengeti, or what was to become of it.

Nor for that matter had he taken any more than the most cursory note of the Serengeti expatriates, the small group I had heard so much of in the past week; on the face of it an even more striking omission, as though he had chosen deliberately to exclude them. This, too, was difficult to understand. A generation had passed since the arrival of Grzimek and his son to save Serengeti, and the expatriates surrounding him now were still deeply engaged in that same war of survival, its outcome still seriously in doubt. Grzimek hadn't dealt with them, not with Derek Bryceson, his great antagonist, nor even Alan Root, his traveling companion and surrogate friend—inconceivable that he would not see them as relevant. Most of the time he was in Frankfurt; they were here, on the ground where it mattered. Without allies he couldn't function from a command post four thousand miles away. His obsession with the ultimate fate of the last herd was for them a daily concern.

Moreover, they were as sensitive as he was to the need for more data—historical, scientific, cultural. Most of them were compiling their own records: John Owen was said to be writing a history of the Tanzanian Parks Department; Hugh Lamprey, of the Serengeti Research Institute; Mary Leakey, of her continuing discoveries in the Olduvai Gorge; Michael Wood, on practicing medicine in a primitive setting; Myles Turner, of his experiences in Serengeti as a park warden; and Ian Parker, of his controversial theories of game cropping. Alan Root was busy recording visual history with his films. Collectively they would produce work bearing directly on Grzimek's own self-appointed mission.

But Grzimek had indicated none of this. Later, as I was to move through the tiny community of Serengeti expatriates in the course of my stay, hearing from each of them his own version of events, it would become clear why Grzimek hadn't felt it necessary to spend much time with their place in the overall scheme of things—certainly not in the course of an evening's sermon to another Western reporter passing through. It had nothing to do with his remote temperament.

East Africa now, fourteen years after independence, finally belonged to the Africans, a reality that at last had come clear to both expatriate and Tanzanian. Africanization had made the fact irrevocable, had undercut the last illusions. Whatever the theories, prejudices, or commitments of the expatriates, whatever their ties to Grzimek since Serengeti days and his to them, they were all in the last analysis simply onlookers. Even the financially resourceful, brilliantly manipulative, passionately obsessive Bernhard Grzimek saw himself in such terms. He, too, now was an onlooker. Only a few years ago, they had been the quarreling carpenters of the last ark; now that task lay to others.

"In the last few years, my aim has changed"—it was his peroration tonight—"tourism may stop because of wars, anything, and you must make people *proud* of what they have done. . . ." And: "I don't insist so much on what we Europeans have done here *but what the Africans have done.* . . ."

For Grzimek now, the immediate future of the animals of Serengeti, as with the rest of the animals in Tanzania, Kenya, and Uganda, depended upon the disposition of the peoples of Tanzania, Kenya and Uganda. Or perhaps in more practical terms, given the cruel political problems of modern East Africa, upon the disposition of their leaders.

PART TWO

Into
Amin's
Hand

EIGHT

As with each of my previous trips to Africa, I was to discover more about what I had seen after returning home than I had while I was there, a curious inversion of the learning process which has often proved costly for me in several respects, no less so on this occasion. Idi Amin, the President of Uganda, had not yet become a notorious news figure, and I had scarcely heard of his country. For Grzimek, however, another trip across Uganda would seem routine if not quite unexceptional (no trip in East Africa is unexceptional). He had been there often, the first time with Michael, when they had driven an old battered truck out of the Congo and across its green hills into northern Tanzania for their first view of Serengeti. Then with Alan Root back the other way on their harrowing excursion into Kivu Province during the Lumumba uprising. In 1968, he had gone in to lobby, persuade, and pay whatever necessary to stop the construction of a power dam at Murchison Falls which would have destroyed the river life along the Nile below it. (The dam was moved to another river that runs dry three months out of the year. Grzimek was so grateful for the government's decision, he told reporters at the time, he was giving the park two thousand pounds to buy a new airplane.) His most recent trip had been the one he had made two years earlier, when Idi Amin had closed the borders to tourists. Grzimek had flown into the capital of Kampala to warn against the implications of his policy: without tourists, the parks would not be able to pay their way. Amin had reversed the restriction but too late—the tourists had been frightened off.

Now Grzimek would be going back again. He had said Friday night only that he wanted to see how the animals were faring. The journey would have to be typical of his annual surveys here, doubtless including some missionary work with Ugandan politicians—a long detour from Serengeti, more than a thousand miles, but surely instructive to the problems faced by any East African national park, Serengeti no less. Along the way, Grzimek could tell me whatever I wanted to know about Serengeti. In any case, a routine trip for Grzimek under the circumstances, and therefore, I assumed—for a full grasp of the situation lay ahead of me—routine for me as well.

From a variety of sources, General Idi Amin Dada's background would become rudely clear to me several months later. Very early in his administration, he had expelled the Western press. The American Embassy had withdrawn and the reports of his political atrocities become widespread. There was some disagreement over how many people had been killed in the first three years of his reign: some said ninety thousand; the International Council of Jurists said two hundred and fifty thousand. In August of 1972, he expelled fifty thousand Indians and Pakistanis with six weeks' notice. General Amin commanded an army of fourteen thousand. On one occasion, he announced his intention of storming the Golan Heights; on another, of marching through Tanzania to claim a seaport. He planned an invasion of South Africa. Only the Russian ambassador to Uganda could dissuade him from building a memorial to Adolf Hitler. Western newsmen stationed in Nairobi reported that no one was allowed to speak at Amin's cabinet meetings unless first spoken to by Amin. People were said to disappear in Uganda. On February 10th, in 1973, Amin declared a "Day of Death" for his enemies and held public executions in seven towns so that even the parents of the victims could be instructed by their example. The chief justice of the national court system was led from his bench and never seen again. A foreign minister's remains were found floating in the Nile. Soldiers and civilians had been slaughtered with savage indignity: some shot in the legs to cripple them and then set on fire; some thrown live into the Nile to be eaten by crocodiles; some forced to beat others with sledgehammers until the last man standing was himself hammered to death; some forced to eat the raw flesh of others; and some suffocated to death with their own mutilated genitals. One report told of an occasion when Amin drew his pistol and killed a messenger who had brought him bad news.

If these accounts were true, they suggested the strong resemblance of Amin to an earlier Ugandan ruler named Mutesa who lived a hundred years ago in the vicinity of Amin's Kampala of the mid-seventies. Mutesa, too, as Alan Moorehead described him, was almost beyond belief:

"Hardly a day went by without some victim being executed at

his command, and this was done wilfully, casually, almost as a kind of game. . . . A girl would commit some breach of etiquette by talking too loudly, a page would neglect to close or open a door, and at once, on a sign from Mutesa, they would be taken away, screaming, to have their heads lopped off. A roll of drums obliterated the cries of the death throes. Nothing that W. S. Gilbert was about to invent with his Lord High Executioner in the *Mikado*, nothing in the behavior of the raving Red Queen in *Alice's Adventures in Wonderland*, was more fantastic than the scenes that occurred whenever Mutesa held a court, the only difference being that here these scenes were hideously and monstrously real. Torture by burning alive, the mutilation of victims by cutting off their hands, ears, and feet [two policemen in Amin's Kampala cut off a butcher's hands with his meat cleaver], the burial of living wives with their dead husbands . . . all these things taken as a matter of course. This was more than a simple bloodlust: Mutesa crushed out life in the same way as a child will step on an insect, never for an instant thinking of the consequences, or experiencing a moment's pain, except his own.

". . . He had other attributes besides this inherited blood thirstiness. He was very far from being stupid: in this savage world he had the appearance and the manner of royalty, and an instinctive knowledge of politics."

So had Amin, a physical giant of a man who was Uganda's boxing champion from 1951 through 1960 and who was said to court his soldiers' favor by joining them periodically for the Ugandan equivalent of consciousness-raising sessions. By the mid-seventies, after the Israeli raid to rescue hostages held in Uganda and the internal crises following thereafter, Amin would come to be seen as monstrous even to many of his previous African supporters. It would be misleading, nevertheless, to view him, then or now, outside the context of recent African political history.

Before 1960, the British held the east coast of most of Africa, the French and Belgians most of the west and center. With independence in 1960, some three hundred million people formed into forty countries seeking self-rule and self-support almost overnight. The colonialists departing believed they were leaving behind the best of their own institutions: parliamentary rule, civil liberties, an established trade market. Yet, in fact, they had created circumstances which would lead to an epidemic of military dictators like Idi Amin

Dada. Through the hundred years of their occupancy, the colonialists had held Africa not so much by the effectiveness of their institutions as the implied presence of military power to support them. After independence, with that presence removed, Africa's new civilian leaders soon found their own authority in question. Moreover, because they could not immediately demonstrate to their constituencies that democratic self-rule was superior to authoritarian colonial rule—poverty and injustice not diminishing as promised but often spreading all the more rapidly—their hold had grown weaker. In 1964, to their mutual mortification, the new leaders of Kenya, Tanzania and Uganda were forced to call in the British to put down attempted coups; and in many other countries, civilian governments began to fall. From 1966 through 1971, in one new African nation after another, there was a military coup a year, sometimes several (in 1974 and 1975, there would be seven), and always to the even greater embarrassment of the Europeans back home. Having sought to establish the best aspects of their "civilization," they had left behind the worst—government by military force. Twenty-nine of Africa's governments are military.

Worse still, the new strong-arm rulers would come from Africans recruited to the colonial military. During the Second World War, three hundred and seventy thousand Africans had fought for the British; forty-five thousand for the French in Algeria and Indonesia. By the time of independence in 1960, many of them were in service across the continent, their leaders a tiny elite who had often fought together or, as in the case of the British Africans, trained together at Sandhurst. Whatever their home nations, they remained a strong influence upon one another. Colonel Joseph Mobutu of the Congo (now President of Zaire) in the disarray following independence demonstrated for all of them how easily power could be seized by taking Léopoldville with only a few hundred men: command a few key points in a capital city and you could control the country. "Once Mobutu had taken his army into political fields," writes the British correspondent Joseph Hatch, "it was only a matter of time before officers in other states experimented with political action. And for each officer group which did so, there were former companions of military colleges and battlefields likely to be taunted with lack of virility if they did not follow suit. The chain reaction of military politics has lengthened since."

In 1971 in Uganda, with the rise of Idi Amin Dada, there came the most convulsive, most ironic wrench of all. Amin had served the British with the King's African Rifles in Burma and against the Mau Mau uprising in Kenya. At the time the British prepared to depart Uganda, he was a sergeant major in the Uganda Army, one of two ranking seniors. Hastily the British had chosen him over the other noncom, made him second lieutenant, and placed the tiny army under his command. (By 1975, only Mobutu would be able to dissuade Amin from executing a British expatriate whose sole offense was to call him a tyrant.) A few years later, when the civilian president of Uganda was careless enough to leave the country for an international conference, Amin took over Uganda, and he has ruled it ever since.

Grzimek was awaiting registration papers for his vehicle coming in from Tanzania. If they arrived in the Monday mail, we would leave Tuesday after breakfast. In our Friday evening talk, he hadn't indicated where exactly in Uganda he would go or how long he would stay, and I had no intention of disturbing the fragility of my invitation by pressing him. For one whose sole concern was wildlife, however, there weren't many places to go in Uganda, eighty-five per cent of the game having been destroyed in the panic over tsetse some years earlier. But there were still the great parks of Murchison Falls and Queen Elizabeth, which were close by one another on the western border, while Uganda's third park, Kidepo Valley, lay to the north and somewhat out of the way. I assumed the first two would be his most likely objectives. Both are heavily populated with elephant and hippopotamus, and Murchison Falls especially is noted for a last stock of crocodile along the banks of the Nile though it was said to have suffered greatly from poaching in recent years. Both parks are near the center of equatorial Africa, separated from the eastern border of Zaire by lakes and the Ruwenzori mountain range—the Mountains of the Moon—and the road there from Nairobi is seven hundred and fifty miles, most of it tarmac but a long haul in any case.

Closer consideration now suggested this trip might not for me, after all, be quite so routine. The American Embassy in Kampala, the capital, had been shut down eighteen months earlier, and as I talked with others over the weekend preceding departure, the impression began to form that travel through Uganda was not to be taken lightly. You would be required to exchange your vehicle at the border for one of theirs; what would become of yours was unclear. You would be required to turn over your passport at the border. In Kampala it was said that Amin's men sometimes leaped from their cars and beat up whites on the sidewalks. People were said to disappear in Uganda, and so on.

Throughout East Africa, Grzimek's unusual name had great carrying power but what if we were to become separated along the way? No one could speak with certainty; the wiser course was to stay out. Someone suggested I check with the American Embassy in Nairobi, and when I did, I was sobered by an official's questioning of my purpose, anticipated length of stay, and his careful listing of my name, address, and closest of kin. Three Americans had been killed in Uganda in the last two years, a Peace Corps worker, a teacher and a journalist. The office suggested I notify it when I had come out so that it would know I had got out.

I decided to call a young friend in Nairobi, Boris Tisminiezky, and ask him along. Now in his early twenties, Boris had driven my wife and me on our first tour with the Root & Leakey Safari Company. Of Russian extraction, he had spent his childhood in Trieste, his teens in Nairobi, had been educated at the University of South Africa, and was now home on vacation awaiting assignment as a mining engineer to an obscure post in Zambia. Often he had spent such intervals as a free-lance courier, or guide, for various tourist companies. On a second trip, this time with my teenage son, I had invited him along for an impromptu excursion we were making into Kenya and Tanzania, where he proved himself even more adept than I had known him to be from our first trip. He was a facile linguist who could joke unpatronizingly with locals in Swahili; an expert driver and outdoorsman; an avid student of wildlife conservation; a varsity team rugby player; a militant competitor in word games; and, of not incidental importance which I had hoped would not be lost on my thirteen-year-old, a young man whose occasional frustrations and sense of adventure never seemed to tax his impeccable manners. Yet he had been as intuitively responsive to the fast-shifting circumstances of traveling alone in the wilderness as the occasion required. Arriving in Nairobi from Tsavo on Boxing Day, midway through our trip, the three of us had decided to go camping out in Masai Mara, the northern extension of the Serengeti ecosystem. It was noon, our parked Land Rover had been looted by thieves while we were at lunch, we were some two

116   THE LAST PLACE ON EARTH

hundred miles away from the first camp site and without equipment of any kind, and all the shops were closed. Boris borrowed two pots and a kerosene lamp from his aunt, and we sped over the dirt road and hairpin turns of the western rift escarpment to arrive at the Masai Mara gatepost after dark, where we ate a cold supper of pâté, crackers and beans and listened to hyena in the darkness beyond our campfire. It would be helpful to have him along on the trip to Uganda.

Boris knew of Grzimek, of course, and was interested in his work. Going into Uganda would mean for him a trip in the company of one of the world's experts on African wildlife to an area he had visited only once before, some years ago. Yet he hesitated. He had a friend in Kampala, and he would try to put through a radio call to find out what conditions were. When he failed at this, he thought it over for a while longer. At the last minute, he decided to come along—more out of concern for me, I suspected uneasily, than for the adventure of it.

This time we would pack more carefully. I rented a tent, sleeping bags, cots, Coleman lanterns, a portable stove, flashlights, extra jerry cans for water and gasoline, and bought enough canned foods to last us two weeks, longer if necessary. A Land Rover is considered self-supporting in nearly all conceivable situations but I had had breakdowns before along the empty dirt roads of Tanzania and wanted none in Uganda. I bought tire-repair equipment, extra fan belts, a compressor pump, a first-aid kit, and all available road maps. With the rearview blocked by our equipment, we could see behind us only through the fender mirrors. Our bulging Land Rover swayed with its load.

Grzimek's papers had come through on Tuesday; it was Wednesday now, and we would leave after breakfast from his home in Westlands. The air was cool and brilliantly clear, and the extra edge of apprehension added to our excitement as we drove to meet him. He was standing in his driveway loading a picnic hamper and three suitcases into his Volkswagen van. One was for himself, one for his daughter-in-law, Erika, and the third for Christian, his grandson. Erika, Michael's widow, was an apple-cheeked, pleasant woman in her late thirties. Christian, fifteen, was the younger of her two sons, a tall boy, reed-thin, with kinky blond hair and the same turned-down, pie grin as Michael and Bernhard. The three of them were dressed like an American family about to spend the day at Disneyland. Grzimek's Volkswagen was not a camper with foldaway cots or special equipment of any kind; it was an ordinary Volkswagen van, a minibus. Expressionless, he studied our bulging Land Rover.

"People think I go to Africa with guns and big safari lorries and tents. I used to do that but it is not necessary anymore. I go in the Volkswagen, which can go most places the Land Rover can go, and I eat and sleep in the lodges. My daughter-in-law does most of the driving. We will cross the border at Malaba and spend the night at the Rock Hotel in Tororo."

To reach the Uganda border from Nairobi is an all-day drive across the Kenyan countryside but an easy one: A104, connecting Kampala with Mombasa on the coast, is paved, the main access route into the interior of Uganda. There had been no reason for us to keep together. We would go ahead of the Grzimeks and wait for them at Kenya customs, then we would all cross into Uganda. Late in the afternoon, in the Kenyan highlands, our Land Rover broke down in the town of Eldoret, a benign misfortune so long as it had to happen since Eldoret has the only functioning Land Rover garage between Zaire and Nairobi. (Spare parts are unavailable in Uganda, the manager said, and car owners who can arrange to do so come out to Eldoret for repairs.) Our starter had burned out; replacing it would take at least two hours. I walked back to the main road, and when the Grzimeks came along, I flagged them down and told them we would catch up with them later at the hotel in Tororo, twelve miles inside Uganda. Grzimek hadn't seemed concerned about our delay but Boris was: he wanted to reach the border before dark, and preferably in the company of the Grzimeks.

Winter in the West is summertime in East Africa, but even so, here in the month of February, the sun sets early, around seven, and it was eight by the time we pulled into Kenya customs. We presented our passports and asked about the Grzimeks. None there knew about them, nor was there any indication they had been passed through. Oddly, we couldn't find their names on the ledger. We climbed back into the Land Rover and looked ahead into the darkness. About a hundred yards away was the Uganda customs house, but it was hard to see. Except for the weak light of a single bulb hanging from the porch the darkness would have swallowed the small frame house. For a moment I had the foolish impression that all electricity ended on Kenya's side of the border. As we slowly drove forward, Boris said, "Let me do the talking. Whatever

THE LAST PLACE ON EARTH

happens, don't look them in the eye. I mean it. Even if they should kick you in the stomach. Look at the ground and be polite." We parked at the edge of the porch and walked inside, where there was a short, fat man behind a counter desk with a kerosene lantern to his left, the light as impoverished inside as out. Several others lounged in the shadows behind him. While he studied our passports, Boris spoke softly to him in Swahili, something I would have been unable to do, I suddenly realized, had I come alone. The man laughed several times, either at his own questions or at Boris's answers. Boris remained quite serious, his eyes averted to the counter in front of him. The man directed us behind his desk and through a corridor on the right to another room where there was a second official. This man, too, asked Boris several questions, and then he stamped our passports and sent us back to the first man, who smiled coquettishly and asked Boris another question. In English, Boris said that if I had any Kenyan money I should give it to him. The man took my money—about forty shillings—laughed again and gave us back our passports. He pointed us toward another building on a hill across the road where there were no lights at all.

We drove to it and found several men out front with automatic rifles. It was too dark to tell how many there were but those we could see were not dressed in uniforms. One of them said something to Boris, and he said to me: "They want to see everything in the Land Rover. Let's get it out as quickly as possible." We unpacked it all, and they looked through everything including the inside of our sleeping bags, taking special interest in Boris's movie camera, the most conspicuously luxurious of our equipment. One of them tried to sight through the lens at the other. Boris ignored him and busied himself with our gear. Politely but sharply, he indicated to me that I was not moving fast enough. At length, one of the men nodded; we quickly repacked the Land Rover and moved on. Boris said they had wanted money and nothing else.

All of it had taken about an hour, and we had joined the Grzimeks at the Rock Hotel a few miles farther on, a surprisingly modern tropical resort with swimming pool and cocktail terrace on the outskirts of the small town of Tororo. The Grzimeks were the only guests in the dining room. They were seated about the end of a long table, Erika and Christian very straight and proper, Grzimek brooding, his face settled into the melancholy expression I had first noticed at the Norfolk. We joined them in their silence, rather ill at ease; Grzimek did not seem interested in conversation. A thin soup was placed before us and we began our dinner. Grzimek had not been recognized at the border, and the three of them had been subjected to similar treatment.

"It is only the second time this has happened with me," Grzimek said finally. "The other place was Cuba. These chaps hadn't had any business for a long time. They were enthusiastic." He sighed wearily. "Their policy is aimed not at the tourist but against the Kenya safari operator." It was one of Amin's minor miscalculations, he said, and by no means unreasonable. He saw that I didn't understand, and then, patiently, as though in an introductory lecture to African social studies, he began to explain the raveled circumstances following after his own manipulations in the early sixties to save animals with tourists—the packaged-tour plot—through our hostile reception by Ugandan soldiers of only a few moments ago.

Soon enough, as he had predicted to Julius Nyerere, Western city dwellers discovered East Africa as a vacation resort; by the mid-sixties, the growth rate of the tourist industry in East Africa was fifteen per cent a year, easily justifying to the independent governments increased investments in new parks, roads, and lodges. It seemed the perfect means to his special end. If you neglect the parks, he would now warn African leaders, you risk losing income from tourists, many of whom, he felt obliged to add, were attracted here by his television shows in Germany. Conservation paid. Cattle allowed in the parks, on the other hand, would overgraze the plain and starve out the wild herds that the tourists wanted to see. Human settlement would bring poaching and crowd the animals into unprotected areas. With African leaders it became an argument of great persuasion, for the evidence supported his claims. Eventually, the tourist income from an acre of national parkland accounted for four dollars, whereas the commercial income from an acre of pastureland for cattle yielded only half that. Grzimek could now demonstrate that the animals of East Africa had earned their right to the parklands. The success of such programs added to his own influence.

After the first of his letter-writing campaigns, in which he had enlisted tourists to complain of poaching at Ngorongoro, he had gone again to see Nyerere. He would later write of their meeting:

120   THE LAST PLACE ON EARTH

. . . Dr. Nyerere received me this time in a new skyscraper, in a room full of the same fresh, cool air as up above the Ngorongoro Crater. He greeted me with the words, "In the last few months I have been constantly criticized in the press because the rhinoceros are being slaughtered in Ngorongoro. You are undoubtedly at the back of it." Nyerere has a great sense of humor, and one can talk to him quite frankly. I told him that I wanted to go on working for the preservation of Tanganyika's wild animals in the Crater and in the Serengeti; that if one is neither a rich man nor a representative of some big industrial concern or political party, one can only work on politicians through public opinion, through press, radio and television. I warned him that I meant to go on doing that, particularly here in East Africa; at which he smiled and threw up his hands in a gesture of mock defense. As I went out of the air conditioned room I met a delegation of simple peasants in the sultry heat of the ante-room. I wondered what cares they would be unloading on him in a minute or two—and hoped he wouldn't forget mine, which were Tanganyika's too.

It is not clear when the unrestricted growth of tourism began to turn pernicious for conservators like Grzimek, but as early as the mid-sixties—at the peak of the boom—the community needed to serve tourists in Serengeti had grown into a self-supporting system of houses, offices, garages, and a school (today, it numbers twenty-five hundred), placing pressure on the animals from *inside* the park. And in 1967, there had been a related episode of even greater consequence involving, once again, the Minister of Agriculture, Derek Bryceson.

An American investor had applied for permission to build a resort on the floor of the Ngorongoro Crater modeled after Kenya's Treehouse (a facility presently in decline from the overgrazing of wild animals) and threatening more human traffic than the fragile crater floor could sustain. Reacting quickly, Grzimek had organized another mail barrage, waited until the letters had accumulated on Nyerere's desk, and then written his own warning of a self-defeating policy: The damaged crater floor would result in a *loss* of business. The animals would soon be gone and so would the tourists. To Julius Nyerere it must have seemed a perverse complaint from so outspoken an advocate of expanding tourism, but he rescinded the permit, Bryceson retreated, and things returned for the moment to *status quo*.

But there was an even more critical problem to emerge having to do with traditional rivalries between the three East African nations which Grzimek had not foreseen and could do little to prevent. The growth of tourism exacerbated these rivalries. Before independence, Kenya was a British colony, Tanganyika a trusteeship territory, and Uganda a protectorate. While administering all three, the British regarded only Kenya as properly British. Like a favored child, Kenya had always received more than its share—communications, commerce, and administration having been concentrated mainly in Nairobi—and neither independence nor a loose federation of the three countries has corrected the imbalance.

With the head start provided by the British, Kenya continues as the dominant nation. Nairobi, Kenya, for example, is considered by the outside world as the only practical port of entry to East Africa, for only in Nairobi has it been possible to develop a support system for international tourism to modern resort standards. It is a smoothly efficient operation. Once at the airport, the traveler, whether big-game hunter or vacationing schoolteacher, is met by his tour operator—any one of a number of specialists who will have arranged everything: lodges or tents, food, vehicles or aircraft, park entry fees, visa requests, and other miscellaneous details that would otherwise exhaust the visitor's time. Because reservations must be made in advance along a traveling circuit that crosses national borders, the tour operators demand payment for all services in Nairobi even though much of the traveler's time may be spent outside of Kenya. Thus, whereas Tanzania has more animals for the visitor to see than Kenya, Kenya's income from tourism is eight times that of Tanzania (and many times more than that of Uganda). It is. rather as though a European visiting Canada could get there only by going first to New York, hiring New York guides and vehicles, and paying all fees to New York tour operators.

The bitterness engendered by such disparities is evident in the outcome of a recent effort by Tanzania to divert the tourist flow away from Nairobi. Several years ago, the government constructed a seventeen-million-dollar international jet airport just inside the Tanzanian border near Arusha, at the foot of Mount Kilimanjaro, but only a few miles from Nairobi. According to plan, tourists bound for Serengeti would fly over Nairobi to Arusha, the last town

THE LAST PLACE ON EARTH

before entering the wilderness road to the Serengeti, and arrange their tours there. The money spent would remain in Tanzania. To support the effort, the Aga Khan agreed to build a multimillion-dollar resort hotel in Arusha providing the necessary rooms to lodge the expected visitors. The plan failed because international carriers refused to add to their schedules an airport so close to the larger facility in Nairobi. In retaliation, Tanzania threatened to shut down its airport in the capital of Dar es Salaam, but the airlines remained adamant. Then, in the week construction was to begin on the new hotel, the government nationalized all businesses with more than five thousand shillings income, which included an office building owned by the Aga Khan in Dar es Salaam. He canceled his Arusha hotel. Now the airport at Kilimanjaro stands empty, costing the hard-pressed Tanzanians a million dollars a year to keep operative. Meanwhile, the Americans, West Germans, and Japanese continue to pour into Serengeti from Nairobi, Kenya, and pour out again, prepaid, with little of their valued currency remaining behind.

From such troublesome developments had Grzimek begun to reconsider the consequences of an unrestricted tourist policy. Tourists are susceptible to faddism; they come and as quickly they may go. They avoid trouble areas (like Uganda). They may pollute natural settings, as they have today in the Caribbean, the Seychelles, and the islands of the South Pacific. Tourism is also an avenue for political greed and limitless exploitation. When expansion plans fail—as they had for Tanzania with its unused jetport— the animal market may be the first to suffer.

I remembered something one of the Europeans had told me over lunch in Nairobi. Several months ago, as rumors had gathered over the deepening involvement of the Kenyatta family in the illegal trade of ivory, Grzimek had issued a statement to *The East African Standard*. The gist of it was that he wanted to commend the African people on their conservation of wildlife in the face of the example of all other civilizations which had systematically destroyed their own. At the time it seemed an odd way to deal with the problems of elephant poaching. But it was more than this: it was reassurance against the evils of the day, but it was also an indication of how deeply his thinking had shifted from tourism toward other solutions.

"Uganda *wants* tourists," Grzimek was saying now. "They just don't want the money to go to the Kenyan operators." Apparently the best anyone here had been able to come up with was, first, to close the borders to the operators by turning back tourists, and then, when this was seen as self-defeating, to require the exchange of vehicles at the border, forcing business to the Ugandans.

"*That* is why you heard stories that you would have to change your vehicle for one of theirs," Grzimek said. "If you are going to look at their animals, they want you to rent *their* equipment, and you can't blame them. The troubles at the border are not because of the *tourist* but because of the tour operators in Nairobi." Now, from our experience this evening, even this policy had been abandoned.

"Even so," Boris said, "from the stories we heard in Nairobi, I'm surprised we got in with so little trouble."

"It is easy to exaggerate about things in Africa," Grzimek said. "Sometimes it all comes out crazy. What people say it is like and what it is really like is different. On our first trip into the Congo, Michael and I spent time with Pygmies. Because they are small and vulnerable, Pygmy families attach themselves to the ruling tribes for their protection. And there was an American anthropologist there earlier named Putnam who had moved into the Congo and taken over a tribe of Pygmies, and they were under his protection. The rest of the tribes and their Pygmy families were becoming Westernized, but Putnam kept his tribe in what he said was their original state. It was nonsense. Putnam even took in the *National Geographic*. He published stories about how these shy people would come out to the road only if salt was left for them. They just did what Putnam taught them to do. When Putnam died, his wife took over the family, then she moved away. When we got there, the Putnams' house was in ruins, but this same tribe brought us pieces of furniture, half a guest book, and other things thinking the Putnams had come back to look after them! I was through that forest again recently and I tried to find from that tribe a Pygmy couple Michael and I had known from our first trip. I wanted to photograph them. They were gone but their daughter was there. I told her I wanted to make her picture, and she started to take off her clothes. She remembered Putnam's law that a Pygmy should not wear European clothes for a photographer." He shrugged wanly. Grzimek likes Africans, and his concern for their problems seems genuine.

"I really don't believe the people are living happier in Africa today than in old times," he said. "The old village life was quite nice. Nobody could starve from hunger, the whole village had to

124

help them. And they had a kind of communal system. They worked all together in the field. Then there was a council of elders—*notables* they were called in West Africa—and they divided the whole harvest. If an old man who had worked his whole lifetime at the coast decided to come back to his village, they had to feed him because he belonged to the village. There was never an orphan in a local village in all of Africa. It is now all destroyed in slums like Nairobi, and so on. I don't believe it is a wonderful development for Africa.

"Mobutu won't let tourists take pictures of the Pygmies anymore. He drafts them into the army. He doesn't like them being treated as freaks or animals. . . ."

Then, abruptly:

"Mobutu is *very strong* for conservation. Along the Sudanese border where there is some poaching, his soldiers give one warning and then shoot to kill. Skulls of the victims are put on top of anthills. It works very well."

On the front of Grzimek's van there is a black silhouette of a hedgehog, the same imprint that appears on his stationery. I asked him what it meant.

"When I was a child, they gave me the nickname of 'Igel' in my school, which means hedgehog, because I brought one with me every day. It is easier to pronounce than my name. So I keep it for my mark.

"When I made the film after the death of my son, I came to Los Angeles and was sitting in the Chinese cinema, and when I heard the television people putting up their lamps asking one another, 'How is this name pronounced?'—then I knew I had won the American competition for documentaries. Because it is amusing, the Americans and the English people always tell me, 'No Englishman can pronounce this name,' and I always have to add, 'No *German* either. It is a Polish name.'"

He laughed. Erika and Christian smiled at him.

"Shifting the scene a moment, one day I had a cup of coffee with Martin Bormann, the Reichs Councilor. He again asked me what kind of name was that, and again I said, 'A Polish name.' For some seconds, he didn't answer. . . . Um . . . ayah. But those were Nazi times. . . ."

Now we returned to silence, Grzimek brooding over his tea. Erika and Christian spoke some English but not as fluently as the older man, and they seemed either uncomfortable with it or extremely shy. At the same time, they avoided speaking German in our presence, a concession to courtesy imposing upon themselves an interlude in Coventry which would go almost unbroken throughout the length of our trip. They seemed very close, however, and attentive to Grzimek, whose mind seemed always on other things. They waited for him to go on now, but he was staring into his teacup and said nothing more. It was difficult to see him as the man who had wrestled with his son, Christian's father, in the Serengeti fifteen years ago. We said goodnight and went to our room; camping out in Tororo was clearly out of the question. The food had been all right, the service no less attentive than one would expect in New York City, and the room was reasonably clean. Still, all night long there were to be the sounds of people walking through the halls, pounding on other doors, the barking of dogs; a noisy, unimaginable procession; and it was good to be out of there early and back on the road.

NINE

There is nothing ominous about the Ugandan countryside, rather the opposite. What we see of it consists of bush fields and subsistence farms, small tin-roofed huts zigzagging along the road, one after the next, with banana trees growing wild out front. The main axis of communication between Mombasa on the Kenyan coast and Gulu to the northwest, A104, is the main axis of community as well, and people move along it alone or in small clusters pushing bicycles laden with wood or milk cans or, most often, huge bunches of green bananas. Deep into the countryside the parade continues; all are on their way to some purposeful but unseen destination. The women wear Mother Hubbard dresses like the Amish women, though theirs are of colorful patterns, and the children of both sexes are dressed in school uniforms of electric blue. Because of its long tradition of Catholic missions, Uganda has the highest literacy rate of the three East African nations. As for motor traffic, other than an occasional Peugeot taxi packed tight with eight to ten passengers and trailing blue fumes, there are few cars along A104. But there are hitchhikers of all ages, frowning and waving imperiously; they expect you to stop, because they expect to pay. The Grzimeks picked up a woman who told them she was beginning labor and was headed for the hospital. When they dropped her off, they had trouble convincing her she owed them nothing. Otherwise, our presence is less exceptional than we had expected. People are on the move, concerned with their own affairs, and this, too, is surprising in light of the widely held assumption that Amin's recent expulsion of fifty thousand Indians and Pakistanis would bring about the collapse of the economy. As in most of East Africa, the Indians had provided Uganda with her infrastructure, comprising not only the mercantile class but eighty per cent of the professional class as well. From the profusion of fruit and vegetables offered at roadside, however, Ugandans do not appear to be very dependent upon an infrastructure. In Mbale, where we stopped to exchange currency, the evidence would be even more telling: before their exodus, the Indians had operated the banks.

The Uganda Commercial Bank is one of several scattered about the town center (commanded still by a statue of George V), but it is the only one doing business. Inside, a large dank concrete room the size of a small barn, a number of townspeople are gathered in small groups, murmuring softly; others lounge on wooden benches by the walls, but no money changes hands. The bank is a gathering place. The officer who will conduct my transaction is courteous and pleasant, concerned to see that I am comfortably seated by his desk, and he moves quickly as though there is great urgency to it all and he must prove himself equal to the task. As it turns out, however, he is obliged to fill out six different forms, using three times over the same worn sheet of carbon paper; stamp each copy, which he does vigorously; and make separate entries by hand. These he renders in a tiny, meticulous script, circling his pen in the air between phrases, then jabbing at the paper with ferocious precision. Into a drawer bulging tight with similar forms, he crams the duplicate copies and then, finally, turns the money over to me with a cordial grin. The picture on the currency is that of Amin, the same as a huge portrait over his desk: three-quarter view, uniformed, slight smile. The procedure has taken forty-five minutes, but he has managed. "I am very impressed that the system works at all," Grzimek said later, having had a similar experience in another town. "Before, when you went into the banks, there was not *one* black face. Now there are no Indians and the banks are still going. It is a good sign."

In East Africa, the Indian has replaced the European as the modern black man's race problem. Brought here by the British as immigrant labor to build the East African railroad at the turn of the century, he has been suffered because of his industry in knitting together a business community through a complex of shops and small stores in all three countries and under the most adverse circumstances. In the deepest bush are such stores to be found, Fanta orange sign out front and canned goods on the shelves, Indian children playing about the stoop. Unlike the presence of the white man, imposed by force on black Africa, his was not at the time of independence to be so abruptly disengaged; he also had been a servant, and he, too, had a claim.

Amin's abrupt expulsion of the Indians, causing outrage in the West and more embarrassment to the British (who felt responsible, for many held British citizenship, but not responsible enough to accommodate them all), was not an unpopular move in Uganda, nor with many in Kenya and Tanzania who share resentment at the hold of the Indians over property they feel to be rightfully their own. The effect of it was to buttress Amin's claim as Africa's most intransigent populist; and in this light could his ceaseless jeers at non-African nations best be understood.

Apart from the ejection of the Indians, however, his policies had had little effect on the quality of life within Uganda, except primarily as a disruptive factor spreading terror in an otherwise bucolic setting. While the country might exist indefinitely without imports or the trade credits from exports, Uganda was not a safe place to be, either for visitors or residents. Amin's problem, as was true for other African dictators, lay more with ambitious soldiers like himself than with affairs of state. Some had already attempted coups against him (on one occasion arranging as signal for attack the broadcast over Uganda Radio of Tennessee Ernie Ford's "Onward Christian Soldiers"). In Amin's Uganda, the danger was not so much from the repressions of a tightly controlled police state as from the rabble authority of undisciplined troops wherever they might turn up. The General wasn't running his country, we were to learn; the privates were, and no one was safe from them.

But if Amin lacked control over his army, driving from the eastern border to the western on A104, we had seen no evidence of it—no sign of military activity of any kind if you didn't count our experience at the border—nor would we until the end of our trip. For that matter, we had traveled the near-width of Uganda without seeing evidence of Amin's wild animals until around four in the afternoon when the people began to thin out and we entered the hill country. Then, suddenly, like a tiny family running to avoid traffic, a group of colobus monkeys scurried across the road ahead of us. Their fur is as silky as an Angora cat's, streaked black and white and in the brilliant sunlight an ambiguous chiaroscuro. The colobus is endangered—the skins make attractive rugs—and we were awakened to the fact farther up the road when we came to a family that had been run over. Grzimek stopped his van to take pictures. It would point a moral to his television audience: African animals were being killed now by cars on open highways, like stray dogs and cats back home.

As we drew closer to the western parklands we would stop often for Grzimek to take pictures; after the fourth or fifth time, a tedious business. He was like a first-time tourist shooting too often and too much, wasting film. Once, passing along pastureland, he had Erika stop so that he could get out and take pictures of an English breeding bull. ("Why did you want pictures of a *bull?*" Boris asked that night. "Good specimen," Grzimek replied.) Now, closer to Paraa, it was becoming increasingly apparent that the distance back along A104 to Frankfurt, Germany, was not so great as it had at first seemed—by minibus and airline, no more than a day and a half—and that the gray-haired, slightly stooped man in sports shirt, slacks and sandals, ever squinting into his range finder, was first and last a zookeeper. If the Uganda countryside had seemed to us no more exotic than endless acres of small crops and banana trees and the subject matter of his films routine and uninteresting, it would be a mistake, nevertheless, to assume that even on this empty road in Uganda Bernhard Grzimek was, as tourists in strange places are often obliged to do, moving aimlessly and without plan.

Grzimek's zoo is situated in the Bornheim section of Frankfurt in such a way as to impose itself on the flow of local traffic which, coming from any direction, can pass around it but never quite avoid it. In 1945, the acreage he had appropriated (without asking) from the bomb-ravaged neighborhood had increased the zoo's size by a third. It is still one of Europe's smaller zoos, but it is one of the most ingeniously designed: a series of quick-changing impressions of African savanna, rock mountain ledges, and rain forests, with small buildings tucked within the man-made hills.

Inside the houses are brilliant flowers and flowering plants, all brightly lighted and immaculate, and, adding to the illusion of space, trick mirrors placed at odd angles and banked glass walls which do not seem to be there. There are even peepholes in the walls to reveal the innards of the displays—the backstage tanks, pipes, heating rods, and hoses (also immaculate)—because Grzimek, who is an admirer of Walt Disney and the naturalist-designer Carl Akeley, wants the visitor to see how the artifice is constructed and how neatly the animals' quarters are maintained. Reminders of man's responsibilities to his fellow creatures are frequent and heavily underlined. A plaque on the wall of one animal house reads: "If you cure a sick dog, he will never bite you afterwards; that is the main difference between animal and man.—*Mark Twain.*" Of all Germany's zoos, Grzimek's was the first to forbid visitors to feed the animals anything at all, even specially prepared foods. In the Bird

Bushes and the Forest Flying Hall, where there are no guards, walls, or fences, it is possible to walk within touching distance of the most exotic of species—crowned pigeon, kagu, capecaillie, picathartes. It is not what one expects from a zoo. Usually, either the animals are shut in by cages or the visitor is shut out by fences or moats. In the Forest Flying Hall, however, the crowned pigeon may stroll across the visitor's path, pluck a twig, and fly past him to its nest. The week before I arrived in Frankfurt, a teenager had broken into a grazing area at the Central Park Zoo in New York and beaten a deer unconscious. As I walked freely through the Forest Flying Hall, the memory had obtruded as an unpleasant contrast impossible to shut out. In Grzimek's zoo, the principal feeling is one of open access within a tightly confined area, and it leads the most obtuse spectator to register, however fleetingly, the impression Grzimek seeks from him—the visitor's place in the chain of animal existence. Grzimek's success with his illusions is due partly to his great sense of theatricality, partly to his eclecticism: "To be a good zoo director you must travel widely to find the ideas to steal. I told them in Moscow, if they built a new zoo it wouldn't be a modern zoo because they don't go anywhere to see what others are doing." And partly, as well, to recent developments in the science of zookeeping.

Until the end of the nineteenth century, the only concession made to progress on behalf of either the animals or the viewers was to increase the size of the cage. Early in the twentieth century, however, a German named Hagenbeck developed a new zoo near Hamburg with concealed moats allowing the impression that the animals were roaming free on islands of their natural habitat, an innovation that quickly spread to zoos around the world. Today, zoo directors pursue through technological ingenuity the illusion that man and the other mammalian species are inseparable, either through the invisible presence of the former (as the visitor glides silently near wandering herds aboard San Diego's monorail) or by his actual presence—carefully controlled—in their midst, as had been my experience walking with the crowned pigeon in Frankfurt. For the masses of Western city dwellers, it is an illusion teaching a lesson that can be learned only in zoos: by physical proximity one is made to feel the relationship between animals of the wilderness and man in the heart of his own self-made environment—at the least, a hint of the sharp epiphany to be found among the wildebeest of Serengeti. Zoos thus may now be seen to function at a higher level of the culture, no longer as just a reflection of man's vanity and dominance (the bear that rides a bicycle like a man, the elephant that stands on his head like a man), for the zoo is one of the last ways to sense the connection between man and his swiftly disappearing, obscure biological past. The zoo is the passage back. Moreover, to capture and sustain the illusion, many zoo directors feel, it is essential to study the animals *in situ*, teaching us not only of our kindredship but as well how to preserve animals from extinction.

Having himself arrived at these conclusions some twenty-five years ago, Grzimek had seized the first opportunity to leave behind the chaotic circumstances of his past and travel straight to Africa to study how animals were living in the places where they belonged. Most zoo directors at the time were content to stay home. Grzimek went to learn, and from his expeditions would come his wide experience with animals in their natural settings, a process of self-education that would soon establish him as one of the most knowledgable in his field. In his thirteen-volume encyclopedia of classifications and descriptions from two hundred and thirty-six international scientists, an impressive number of entries are from Grzimek himself, either singly or in collaboration, and on subjects ranging from the feeding habits of tapirs to the digestive system of the camel. From the first, he put his direct observations to work at the zoo. Unable to breed hippos, he noticed at Queen Victoria Park in Uganda they left the water where the embankment was steepest; when he eliminated the gradual slope in his hippo basin, allaying their anxieties, his hippos began to breed. (He has since sold some of the excess to African zoos.)

In most municipalities throughout the West, zoos are administered by the local department of recreation. *"Wrong!"* Grzimek says. "Zoos should be under the department of *education*. The tendency is to regard them as children's playgrounds, which is why it is so hard to get foundation money behind them." In recent years, however, they have come to add to their stature in a few spectacular instances as "zoo banks," breeding facilities for the last-minute rescue of disappearing species. The Arabian oryx, Père David deer, and Mongolian wild horses were saved by zoos (the latter exist today *only* in zoos). The best-known example is that of the European bison of Poland's Bialowieza Forest which had been reduced by the devastation of the First World War to two males and a few cows. Through sixteen generations of careful inbreeding within zoos, some seventeen hundred are back now in the forests of Poland.

Where the zoo quickly reaches its limitation as the preserver of species, however, is in the risk of erasing their genetic characteristics—their wildness. David Ehrenfeld, the biological conservationist, observes:

> There is the possibility that the complex behavioral adaptations appropriate to the wild may disappear through genetic change combined with lack of selective pressure in zoos. Cave animals frequently show a loss or reduction of eyes and pigment, not necessarily because these features would be disadvantageous in caves but because random, normally deleterious mutations that affect the pigment and eye-forming systems go unchallenged by natural selection.

In the United States, systematic steps toward breeding endangered animals are being taken at Maryland's Patuxent National Wildlife Center with the masked quail and other species. Grzimek has been at the process in his own fashion, devising his techniques as he goes. From orphaned animals rescued by park rangers and from surplus zoo stock—rhinos, chimpanzees, gorilla, and a variety of plains game—he has for the past nine years stocked Rubondo Island in Lake Victoria by returning his emigrant menagerie to a setting that, surrounded by water, will encourage their wildness. It is one of his purposes on this present trip to Africa to persuade Derek Bryceson and the government of Tanzania to declare Rubondo Island a national park and take it off his hands.

"The *main* purpose of zoos is still to acquire animals and show them to people," Grzimek says. "There are better ways to breed. You need bigger numbers to have better chances. And there are some species we will never be able to breed—orangutan, for example, which are almost gone. The best way to reproduce animals is in their own environment. If we breed some animals for more than one or two generations they change. They are no longer the animals produced by nature. They are not wild, they are domestic. So we must have a natural environment to send them back to, which is why I tell Africans the importance of their national parks."

This, of course, was why Grzimek's great energies in the later years of his life had been drawn to the establishment and preservation of national parks in East Africa, and especially of Serengeti where there was a greater diversity of mammals left now than anywhere else.

Murchinson Falls Park in Uganda—it is now apparent this is our destination—is no longer known by that name. It is now Kabalega

Falls. It borders Lake Mobutu Sese Seke, which was formerly known as Lake Albert, and it lies to the northeast of Uganda's second principal park, Ruwenzori National Park, which was formerly Queen Elizabeth Park, bordering Lake Idi Amin Dada (formerly Lake Edward). General Amin has changed all the old colonial names, too quickly for the Shell road maps to keep up. Even without Amin's modifications, however, it is difficult enough for the Western visitor to keep one park straight from another in East Africa. Relative sizes can be a helpful measure. Serengeti, the most important park in Tanzania, is the size of Connecticut. Tsavo, in Kenya, is the size of New Jersey. Kabalega Falls is the size of Rhode Island.

There are two lodges for visitors at Kabalega Falls, Chobe and Paraa, the latter considerably deeper into the park and situated on a hill overlooking the Nile River. Going into Chobe finally, some dozen miles past the park gate along a dirt road which cuts across swelling hills that have been burned over, at a distance some fifty yards behind the Grzimeks' van, Boris and I play at an old game: the first to see a wild animal and correctly identify it is clearly the superior traveler. But we see nothing—not at all the same as at Serengeti when the plain is empty, for there it is always an interlude awaiting the next unpredictable event, the unseen animals a palpable presence. The plains of Chobe are scorched and empty, and when we pull into the lodge, we find we are the only visitors: no vehicles in the car park, no movement about the building. Inside, in the foyer of the bar, two employees are playing *bau*, African chess. They stare at us briefly and then return to their board. "The policy of Amin," Grzimek mutters. "I told him two years ago, when he stopped tourism altogether, it would take a long time to get it back. Now look at this. When he opened the border to tourism again, no one came. And it will be a long time before they do." There is no reason to linger. It is late afternoon and all the game is said to be down by the Nile around Paraa lodge, a hundred and ten kilometers away; we gulp Fanta sodas and hurry on.

There, arriving near dusk, we are greeted by the chief warden of Paraa, who is almost pathetically grateful for the presence of Grzimek. He is the first Ugandan we have seen to realize who Grzimek is. He escorts the Grzimeks to their room and dispatches a ranger to guide Boris and me to our camp site. No one has used it for five months, the ranger tells us; there are no tourists at Paraa, either. But there are plenty of animals, he promises, and we will

134   THE LAST PLACE ON EARTH

begin to see them tomorrow when we go out early on a game run by boat up the Nile. He leaves, and we sit a moment before unpacking to survey our setting—rolling plains, burned out, all still much too peaceful. It is nothing at all like our earlier trips together. In Serengeti, at the same hour on our first evening, a pride of lions had walked single file through the grass no more than fifty yards from our tents; we heard them roaring across the plain throughout the night. At Tsavo, at first light, we had come from our tents to find three elephants grazing no more than twenty yards away. On my second trip to Serengeti with Boris and my son, we had heard a racket of noises throughout the long night, like an orchestra tuning up. Before dawn, just beyond the edge of our campfire, Grant's gazelle had leaped past the shadows fleeing some invisible threat. At Paraa, there are no sounds, only emptiness.

There are two places left in the world where crocodile survive in substantial quantity: at Kenya's Lake Rudolf, where they number in the thousands, and at Kabalega Falls along a seven-mile stretch of the Victoria Nile, from the lodge at Paraa to the foot of the falls. There are some six hundred here (a year ago, there were a thousand), and they are distinguished from Rudolf's stock because Kabalega's are the last of the river crocs. They feed on fish and the river's detritus, animals drowned upstream or male hippos killed in a family dispute, or sometimes land mammals, including humans, who come too close. As we move up the river in a canopied boat, the only passengers, the park warden points them out on both shores, dry-caked and baking, some with their mouths frozen in a wide yawn (since they don't sweat, this is the only way they have of evaporating internal moistures). Left alone, they can grow to monstrous size, up to twenty feet in length, standing four feet high.

"Nobody knows for sure how long they live," Grzimek says between shots, "maybe more than a hundred years. Some of these chaps were here when Baker passed through." Their eggs are preyed upon by the monitor lizard, mongoose, baboon, vulture, marabou stork, and the African eagle owl. Occasionally we see the huge lizards loitering at the edge of croc territory, miniature dragons patiently awaiting the right moment. They can easily outdistance the crocs; once they spot the nest, the eggs will go. Infant crocodiles are easy pickings, too, until they grow large enough to eat their predators, at which point they become invincible. Like the rhino and elephant on land, they have no enemies but man. Norman Myers reports that while a hyena biting steel leaves the imprint of its teeth, the crocodile snaps so fiercely that its teeth are driven back through their sockets. They are among the world's oldest creatures, dating back more than a hundred million years, a last key to the Mesozoic Age.

Poaching of crocs for the leather industry became almost unmanageable here in the mid-sixties, causing Grzimek to give fight on two fronts. Because there are no roads along the riverbanks, poachers were able to escape by boat even when seen from ranger headquarters at the lodge. Grzimek bought and arranged for delivery to the park a bright-red amphibious car, a vehicle designed in the West for recreation, his notion being that the rangers could drive overland in it until they hit water, and then keep going. It had proved impractical—the waterway here is still the ideal route for poaching—but not before Grzimek had tested out the jaunty red water car for himself, driving to the foot of the falls between herds of startled hippo, one of which placed himself squarely beneath the machine, lifted it clear of the water, and lowered it back again—all recorded for Grzimek's color-photo files by the ubiquitous Roots motorboating along behind.

Back in Germany, Grzimek had been more effective. Offenbach was then a key European production center for the crocodile leather industry. Getting wind of a possible attack from Grzimek on his television show, industry representatives sought him out asking what they might do to prevent unfavorable publicity. Like a general imposing terms of surrender, he listed his conditions: a hundred thousand marks from the industry for scientific control of the quantity and quality of crocs to be harvested; the scientists to report to Grzimek but the industry to pay their salaries; the industry to abide by the scientists' findings. The industrialists protested that such stringent measures would cause five thousand employees to lose their jobs. "Fine," Grzimek said. "You stop now and save the species. If you don't, in five to eight years the crocodiles will be gone, anyway." The industry met his demands.

The park warden observes that the population of the crocs is coming back, the pressure now is against Kabalega's elephants. Sitting to change the film in his camera, Grzimek seems to ignore the remark. "Once I received a photograph from Indonesia of a human body in three parts taken from the inside of a crocodile. I published the picture in *Das Tier,* and I received a letter from a woman saying it was her father. The photograph had been left behind in her apartment, and the person who sent it to me said he could not reveal his identity. . . ." A mystery he does not bother to pursue.

To complete his film of the aquatic life in Mzima Springs, near Tsavo, Alan Root had first constructed a steel cage to protect himself from crocs and hippo. The cage would not stay righted, and so he and Joan had finally gone underwater with only rubber fins and snorkels, finding to their surprise that their presence was not challenged. Underwater instead of at the top of it, Root had theorized, the crocs had assumed they belonged there and left them alone.

"Don't count on it," Grzimek said when he heard the story. "All we know is that it's true at Mzima Springs. Animals behave differently in different settings." We were about a thousand yards from the foot of the falls, the three Grzimeks sitting together quietly looking out at the scenery. "It would be dangerous to go closer," the warden said. "We will go back now." Grzimek had made no mention of his lighthearted excursion to the foot of the falls in his fragile amphicar or his piggy-back ride on a hippo six years earlier, and he did not now.

Although there had been no evidence of it at the border, Grzimek's visit to the parks had been expected, and when we arrived back at the lodge now, about midday, a party of nine Ugandans led by a Mr. Omar, director of Uganda Parks, was waiting to greet him. It was an official reception of sorts—all of them were in business suits—and the moment was awkward for everyone but Grzimek, who shook hands all around, directing his perfunctory smile at Omar. Both parties were led to a large round table off the dining room, where for a long interlude we all just sat, sweating, sipping warm Fanta orange soda, flies buzzing about us. Softly and somewhat tentatively, Mr. Omar opened the conversation by referring to Ian Parker's cropping program here in the mid-sixties. For Kabalega's fifteen thousand elephants there were only fifteen hundred square miles of park; they had badly damaged the vegetation, and something had had to be done.

Parker had told me about the project back in Nairobi, had taken from his stuffed briefcase a copy of the report of the scheme, a chilling account:

The project involved 2,000 elephant and 4,000 hippo. It lasted over two years, though the actual work took 18 months. The animals were killed in the Uganda Parks to change habitat trends in specified offtakes to be removed within a specified time. Selling prices for both hippo and elephant were kept low enough not to retard production: The primary objective was reduction of the elephant and hippo populations, and it had to be accomplished within a specific time. If we had tried to sell the stuff really high we would probably have slowed production. Hippos sold for 300 shillings [about $41] a carcass, and elephants at 100 shillings [$13]. Demand was greater for the former, hence the higher price.

The gross profit—including revenue from ivory and hides—was of the order of one million six hundred thousand shillings [$223,000], against an initial investment of 1500 pounds [$4,500], of which we never drew more than half. After two weeks we were making a profit. For instance we were able to put in 10,000 pounds [$30,000], just mucking about with the skin, selling it off as a luxury leather. We had many chances to sell it for cheap leather, but we used salesmanship and put it across as a luxury leather. Once we succeeded in doing that it boosted the value of the skins so that it brought a higher value than the ivory. . . .

Omar's reference to the scheme seemed an appropriate enough opener—he spoke with approval of it—although Parker had said the program was ended because of corruption among the Ugandan officials administering it.

The heat was stifling to the extent that conversation of any sort became an effort, but Omar's remark had the effect of opening the pulpit to Grzimek, who lowered his voice to the level of Omar's and concentrated on him alone, adding to the discomfort of the rest of us, uncertain as to whether we should listen in, which was very difficult now, or try to ignore them. Still, the gist of Grzimek's remarks began to come through—now-familiar phrases falling into place—as he "made propaganda."

As Africans lead the world in conservation, it is their job to provide an example and see to it that national parks are left alone. . . . Cropping is NOT the answer. The Tsavo cropping experiment, for example, was a failure. Such policies lead to political control. This must not happen. . . . Soon, park policies will become a matter of politicians worrying about votes. And for politicians, when it comes to a choice between votes and elephants, the elephants always lose. . . . Kenneth Kaunda of Zambia is a good example of a leader who does not allow politics within his parks. He has given over a third of all Zambia to national parks. . . .

Sensing a pause in the monologue, Omar hurried an announcement:

"Only yesterday, General Idi Amin proclaimed an end to all hunting in the nation of Uganda."

It was an unexpected gain. Caught unawares, Grzimek extended his pause, turned momentarily reflective, and then responded with great solemnity:

"The great leaders of world conservation are African.

"Kaunda.

"Nyerere.

"Mobutu.

"And now . . . Amin!"

Encouraged, Omar went on. "Uganda is considering adding even more new parks, and one local tribe has offered its land for such a purpose."

Now, tactfully, Grzimek again lowered his voice:

Good. . . . Education on conservation is taking hold. But it is not the number of parks you have, but the SIZE. . . . There must be adequate room. Again there is the example of Mobutu. In Bukavu, where the gorilla is crowded in a park of only eighty-five square miles, Mobutu has made it now two hundred square miles. . . . Serengeti is even a better example. When there was trouble on the border at Lamai Wedge and much poaching, he [Grzimek] pointed out to Nyerere that the people had no other way to live, that they HAD to poach. Why couldn't Nyerere tighten the boundaries? . . . Later, Nyerere told him he had solved the problem by relocating people. He [Grzimek] was incredulous! This never could have been done under colonial times. No government would have dared to do it. But Nyerere said he gave the people there a hospital and a school, and they were content. Why not? People are moved by other governments to build bridges, dams, railroads. Why not to save the animals? . . . A tribe in Tanzania had offered land for a park, too. He [Grzimek] had put up fifty thousand pounds for the purpose, but with a deadline. If the money wasn't used by that time for the park, it couldn't be used at all. That way, he had avoided the control of the politicians. . . .

While Omar had listened attentively throughout it all, his eyes had begun to glaze slightly, as though the message was one he himself had delivered before. Omar, of course, was not the problem and both men knew it. Omar was presenting Uganda's case for wildlife to the outside European community; Grzimek was speaking indirectly to Amin. At lunch, their ritualistic exchange completed, both men became convivial, and Grzimek as informal as he had as yet allowed himself to be. Over coffee, Omar told Grzimek that Amin wished to see him in Kampala on his way out. Grzimek made a date for next Tuesday.

Not much happens at midday in East Africa. Kabalega Falls is just across the lake from Zaire, at an elevation of six hundred and nineteen feet, and the damp heat weakens all resolve; but even on the cool plateaus of the Great Rift Valley eastward, where the breeze evaporates perspiration as it forms, nothing stirs—too hot. In Kenya and Tanzania, it is a dry, leaden heat stopping action without seeming cause: one simply is disinclined to move. But in west Uganda, it is the drenching heat of the tropics, soggy and unpleasant: motion is impossible. Whether above the valley or below it, however, the heat shapes the traveler's day into two phases: the game run before breakfast when the soft Swahili call of *hodi* is heard outside his tent, about half an hour's warning before first light when the Land Rover will head out into the dark African morning; and then, after a defensive nap through midday followed by tea around four, when the air has cooled, the game run in late afternoon. It is a schedule honored even by the animals of East Africa, and now, in late afternoon when the animals have resumed feeding, the Grzimek party loads in together aboard the warden's Volks van for a game run along the northern shore of the Victoria Nile. In about two hours, the sun will set. Outside the lodge, only a few feet from the entranceway, an elephant is grazing at the side of a flame tree. Before boarding, Grzimek photographs it. "Dust Bin Nelly?" Boris asks. Grzimek grunts. "Yes . . . same problem as Lord Mayor." Their cryptic exchange is left hanging in the air as we move out.

Our host, the park warden of Paraa, is a thin man with a large Adam's apple, soft-spoken and polite, named Wyhomi Nguana. He wears dark slacks and a sports shirt, and his only sign of rank is the presence of a driver, similarly attired, behind the wheel of the van. Nguana's responsibility is the same as any park warden's in East

Africa: the watchcare of the animals within his park. As he sits to the side of his driver, turned halfway toward Grzimek and awaiting the German's judgment of Kabalega, he forces the contrasts in the relative assets of East Africa's parks.

In Kenya, at Tsavo West, Nguana's equivalent is an expatriate named Ted Goss, a strapping, red-haired man who wears bush jackets, khaki shorts, sandals, and a rakish felt safari hat folded to the side like an Australian soldier's. It is the essential macho costume which has inspired lounge suits for city men in Europe and America, although on Goss it is all quite convincing. He also wears an elephant-hair bracelet made from the tail of the creature that stepped on his leg and almost killed him. Goss has available to him an airplane and a helicopter, both of which he can fly; and he commands squads of smartly trained rangers who are uniformed like British soldiers. They snap to attention and salute his presence. At his disposal are trucks, bulldozers, backhoes, road makers, and a fleet of Land Rovers. On the terrace of Kilaguni lodge, having a Pimm's cup before lunch and looking out on the park's elephants gathering at the water hole to the front, he is a commanding figure indeed. Nguana seems to have only his Volkswagen van and driver. Yet despite the visible differences in their circumstances, the park systems of both Goss and Nguana share a common hazard, I was to learn, which is the ambivalence of the governments administering them.

Grzimek exchanges seats now with Nguana for a better view, and as we bounce over the dirt track, there being nothing yet to see other than the burned hills, he fixes his attention on the warden.

"Is there much poaching?"

"Yes, there is poaching."

"What do you do about it?"

"Not very much. We don't have the vehicles."

"How many do you have?"

"We have one Land Rover that is working. There are three others, but they are not working. We have five vehicles for the tourists."

"How many have you caught?"

"I have been here since July fifth. We have caught thirty since then. We catch half of those who poach."

"What happens to them?"

"In Gulu, to the north, they get two months. In Masindi, in the south, they get fifteen months."

"How do the poachers come?"

"By dugout across the lake."

"I have heard that the soldiers are shooting the game."

"Yes. The military police come in boats, shoot the animals, then they return."

"I asked Amin before if this was what was happening, and he said no, that they would not do it unless he gave the order. I told him, then your soldiers are different from the British, the Germans, or any other soldiers who ever held a rifle."

"Yes."

Grzimek surprised me. He had initiated the conversation, was pressing Nguana, in fact. Our road carries on over the same long, low, empty, scorched hills we had first seen at the entrance to the park, the same wasted terrain—monotonous and dispiriting.

"The poachers set fire to the grass," Nguana says. "We try to control the grass by burning, but they burn, too, to trap the game, and we lose our young trees. Some of the rangers are involved in the poaching, we think. We cannot do anything to them until we can prove it. But we know who they are, and they have been warned."

Off to the left, several miles distant, we are able to see now a row of whitewashed huts.

"What are those?" Grzimek asks.

"They are rangers' huts," the warden says.

"Why are they painted white? Look how they stand out."

"Yes," says Nguana, "it is like our new lodge." We all look across the hills to the right. Some three miles away, gleaming white, is the lodge we have come from.

"No, they *shouldn't* be white," Grzimek says. "They should be brown or green so they blend with the land. Camouflage. The way they are at Tsavo or Ngorongoro."

"Yes."

"It is the natural way"—and, more gently—"the way *African* houses were before Europeans came."

"Yes."

"You got it from us, the whitewashed buildings. It is inappropriate."

"Yes. We will change it."

Nearing the riverbank the vegetation at last begins to revive, the grass is thick and high and as we turn with a slow bend in the road the countryside opens generously into a long sloping plain bound on our left by a tree-lined stream about a hundred yards away. Between the stream and the road is a giant herd of some two hundred elephants. Nguana's driver kills the motor, and we sit and watch them—at once the most troublesome, enigmatic, and intriguing of the larger mammalian species in Africa. Because of their great visibility and gargantuan needs, they have become paradigmatic of the dilemma for all African wildlife. A hundred years ago, they roamed the continent from Ethiopia to the Cape, and there were some ten million of them. Now, according to the best estimates, there are less than a million left, with no place to go: towns and small farms contain them. Because their environment is so circum-scribed by man, the natural-selection process for them has ended. Kabalega's elephants used to migrate more than a thousand miles, from the lakes eastward past Kampala, all of which now is given over to agriculture. But within the past three years, the threat to all Africa's elephants has grown even more critical, and there is no parallel for their plight among living creatures. Inflation has escalated the value of their ivory: "white gold." While the oyster's pearl is protected by the sea, the elephant can be killed with poisoned arrows, the most primitive of weapons.

Watching them now in such abundance, I remembered the reflections of a professional hunter I once met in Kenya: "They are magnificent animals. They can communicate with one another, you know, and when one falls to the ground, others come to his assistance and try to pry him with their tusks back to his feet—some say because they know the great weight of his bulk will collapse his lungs if he stays down too long. I'm convinced they have a sense of humor. Once, I saw a herd playing about a mud slide, sitting on their buns and slipping from top to bottom, happy as pie. Another time, I came upon a big bull who obviously resented my presence. He ambled on ahead of my vehicle, uprooted a tree, and laid it across the road. Then he walked about fifty yards and tore up another one and put it down on the road. Then, I swear, he stood back and laughed at me. There's no pleasure in killing them."

The elephant's ways invite anthropomorphism. Elephants are believed to have some conception of death, and possibly even of the reasons they are hunted. They have been known to seize the tusks from a dead member of the family and smash them to pieces. Here in Uganda, during one of the cropping episodes, the ears and feet of the destroyed elephants were stored in a shed to be prepared for sale as handbags and umbrella stands. A group of elephants broke into the shed, removed the objects, and buried them. Scientists involved in the project are said to feel uncomfortable still about the incident.

Grazing peacefully here, the mighty herd is strung out loosely but in rough approximation of a straggler's column. When there is trouble, they will close ranks and move off in quick step with flank guards, rear and advance points. Once, Boris, my son, and I spotted a large herd moving at dusk across the dry lake bed at Amboseli, Mount Kilimanjaro rising in the distance behind them—a calendar photograph. Boris drove toward them from the side, my son and I standing in the roof hatch to take our pictures. As we drew closer, the left flank guards turned, ears fanning, and moved to meet us, the rest of the column keeping to its ponderous pace. We drove out to the front and around toward their right. The left flank guards returned to the column, and now the right flank guards turned toward us, giant ears waving, warning us to come no closer. It seemed a military formation of great arrogance. For a company of soldiers, the flank guard warnings would have been the signal for dispersal. For the elephants, the flank guards were protection enough; the main file held to its course. But their suggestion of security was deceptive. The larger the herd, Boris whispers to me now, the more threatened they feel; in this corner of Kabalega Falls they have collected together for safety. Very soon we would see why.

Our dirt track takes us along the shore of the Albert Nile, somewhat southwest of our boat ride earlier in the day, where the grass is tall and reedy now, banana yellow. Near the bank a male lion walks parallel to the river, observing our approach without interest. Purposefully but unhurried, his mouth open and tongue lolling, he leads us upstream to an elephant's carcass being fed upon by vulture and marabou stork. It is no more than a day old. Our driver stops and we stare like pedestrians hypnotized by a street accident.

"They came from the river and shot it," Nguana says. "Sometimes they use poison arrows, and sometimes they put sulfuric acid in bananas and follow them until they fall."

The ivory has been chopped out; the large ears, the exposed sinus cavities and the rear teeth all that are left of the head. The carcass is like ancient leather and the cavities of its body appear to be filled with rotting straw; the limbs cotton-stuffed. A large hole has been torn from its side—the vultures feed from inside it, taking turns, until we drive closer. Then they back away and slowly fly off to a point downstream to await our departure. It is a hulk, lifeless,

THE LAST PLACE ON EARTH

covered with the excrement of the scavengers. Against the blue water of the Nile, the waving yellow grass, the clean open sky, the presence of death does not seem intrusive. It is the knowledge of the poacher's presence that is unsettling, the wasted carcass evidence that he has come and gone. There is nothing to prepare one for such a sight, except perhaps the displaced associative memory of a New York apartment robbed in the owner's absence, all the drawers pulled open and their familiar contents strewn about the floor.

Grzimek has said nothing. Almost mechanically he gets out his camera and has the warden bend over the carcass as though examining where the tusks had been. He takes a picture. Then he has him point to the oral cavity and takes another picture. Neither will be very interesting graphically, the point too labored, but they will serve his purpose. There is no reason to stay longer, and we move back to the van.

"They want me to give some money for research here," Grzimek says to Nguana. "I think you need vehicles the most. . . . Yes . . . we will have to do something about that."

Someone remembers the lion that had ambled on up the shore. We drive cross country to pick up his trail and follow along behind him to a sight of the life cycle resuming. At the top of a grass hill a herd of Grant's gazelle is grazing nervously. There are perhaps fifty of them. When they see the lion approaching, they close intervals and leap away to a specified distance that seems by common consent to be prearranged. The lion ambles on toward them at the same steady pace he had set leading us to the elephant. Holding to their station, the gazelle bunch together like frightened schoolgirls and turn to watch, those in the rear crowding toward the front to get a better look. The lion draws closer and now the herd leaps wildly away again, another twenty yards, stops, wheels in place shrinking *forward* toward their indifferent pursuer. Nguana laughs. "They want to keep an eye on him so they know where he is."

In Frankfurt, one of Grzimek's associates, Dr. Dieter Backhaus, had told of his studies of the flight distance of plains game: a measurable space which, once invaded by an enemy, triggers the animal's flight. Such distances may vary within a single species like Grant's gazelle according to variable factors: whether the enemy is beast or human, and if human, whether man or woman, white, black, European, or African. Against the dying sun the lion and the gazelle leapfrog forward in silent rhythms to the top of the hill until they come to a tree in which a leopard is sleeping. The lion sinks to his haunches, gazing upward at the leopard. Except for their twitching tails, the gazelle freeze and the tableau is fixed.

Light is fading. As we come down from the hill seeking the track to the lodge, Grzimek goes back to work on the warden.

"We saw dancing at the lodge last night."

"Yes."

"It is the music of Uganda performed for tourists. Our tourists could dance with your Uganda dancers. It is possible now. The music in all of America and Europe is African music."

Nguana looks puzzled.

"No, it is *true!* The influence of African music is why the tourist can dance easily with the dancers here. It is *your* music we dance to in our countries."

The warden smiles courteously.

"All this business about changing the names of the lakes," Grzimek says, "from Edward to Mobutu, from Albert to Amin. Why *shouldn't* they? I tell people that if the Germans occupied England for eighty years and then left, the British wouldn't keep the German names. Why should they? They were there first. It is what I always tell Africans. In Germany we were a colony, *too.* We were ruled by Rome for many years."

I felt a momentary twinge for Nguana. It was the most effusive I had seen Grzimek. Whatever he had in mind, he was pushing very hard.

We were in darkness now, the last light damping the scorched hills dark brown, then shutting them out altogether. In East Africa, it is not advisable to be out after dark even within the safety of a vehicle (in Kenya, it is against the law). So little is still known about the habits of wild animals there is active disagreement between even those who live among them in the national parks. Whether light at night attracts dangerous animals or repels them is occasion for one such dispute, and as we bounce over the dirt road leading back, our headlights piercing the darkness, fragments of inconsistent wisdom come too easily to mind, the random memories of past trips forming their own logic.

When Boris had lost his race with daylight to get my son and me to the Masai Mara gate, he had kept his headlights off, a risky course, I had observed with some hesitancy, given the deep ruts and potholes in the dirt road. "The wildebeest may stampede you if you

146

leave them on," he had muttered, careening down the ravaged track, and indeed, when he flicked his lights briefly to get the road's bearing, their reflection gleamed back ghostly ringlets across the plain. Once, in Tsavo, when our game run had kept us after dark, the worried camp manager had sent another driver out for us. Leading the way back, he had kept his headlights off, too. As we descended a dry creek bed, causing him to stop briefly to gear down, I looked off to the right and saw not ten feet away the half-silhouette of an enormous elephant facing the side of our vehicle, silent black looming mass blending into the dark bush. "I would rather sleep under a mosquito net and nothing else than in a tent with a campfire burning," Gordon Harvey once remarked in connection with the dangers of lion in the Serengeti. "Animals are curious. They see a light and it draws them. They want to know what's up." If it was true that nearly all animals are peaceable unless directly threatened, as Grzimek often declared, then it would stand to reason that a car rounding a curve with headlights blazing would present to a larger animal, grazing or dozing near the road, at the very least the possibility of an unfriendly intrusion. Yet our driver now, who surely knew what he was doing, sped along with his headlights flooding the darkness. Boris and I strained forward to scan the road while Grzimek continued to exhort Nguana— "Everywhere I look I see *schools!* Uganda is a *nation* of schools. Primary schools! Secondary schools! Schools *everywhere!*" In the rear of the van, Erika and Christian observed their polite silence. We rounded a curve with our lights blazing ahead straight into the eyes of a large elephant feeding at the side of the road, her calf a few feet behind her. The driver slammed on his brakes.

A charging elephant or rhino may be bluffing, maybe not. In either case, it is a terrifying experience even when you are surrounded by the heavy welded steel of a Land Rover, which we were not. Having transgressed, one holds the terror while the animal makes up its mind. There is, too, an added danger from the innocence first-time visitors carry with them about such confrontations: since the animal looks peaceful, it is assumed to be peaceful. With animals so benignly in place and unthreatening, the visitor may too quickly accept himself as part of the setting as well, even get out of his car for a closer look—as I once saw happen with a tourist on a back road near Tsavo where he had debarked to photograph seven large elephants on both sides of the road and was leisurely setting his lens for the best light. Coming up from behind, the driver of the lead car in our party drove past him to a point of safety, then stopped and screamed at the man to get back in his vehicle. In the confusion—my son and I were in the last Land Rover, and he was standing in the hatch photographing—I was trying to move slowly through the traffic jam when I heard my son shout a warning. I glanced to the left and the view of my window was filled by a massive field of rippling gray leather, moving closer, like a camera zoom, at an alarming rate. I accelerated, as did we all, spreading out in all directions at once. Eventually everyone had disentangled themselves without damage, but the quality of the silence afterward was akin to the mood inside our van now, as we all sat waiting with great respect for the startled cow, apparently measuring the extent of her grievance, to make the first move. She remained expressionless, her ears slowly fanning forward. A minute or so passed. Even Grzimek was quiet now. The driver did not turn off his lights or back away. At length, he raced his idling motor—superbly logical, as though politely but firmly requesting passage—and the elephant and her calf turned aside.

TEN

What would he make of what he had seen today? His manner had been that of a man tightly in control of time and purpose: clinical. He had made film for his television show and still-picture file ("I always have my camera. Who knows when an elephant may stand on his head or something?"); propagandized officials; arranged a meeting with Amin; decided, apparently, how he would spend his money here. Within eight hours or so (in the heat of midday, he met with the ranger staff while the rest of us dozed), he had checked out Kabalega Falls. The fallen elephant was the first visible evidence of poaching I had seen in Africa, and we hadn't gone looking for it—a raw warning of the border problems here. Omar had mentioned the past cropping schemes of Ian Parker drawing Grzimek's strongest negative response (although as one of several quick conclusions with little amplification). There did not seem to be very much about Kabalega Falls applicable to the present-day state of Serengeti, or so I thought. Grzimek hadn't committed himself one way or the other.

After dinner at our camp site, we rejoined the Grzimeks and Nguana on the lodge terrace, where we were surprised to find some thirty Austrian tourists who had flown in on a package tour from the west coast, hopscotching across the continent and blithely unaware that Uganda, at this moment, was no place to be. They were in a manic mood, toasting and making speeches to one another, applauding, singing songs from home with great feeling. The din did not diminish until a troupe of Ugandan dancers appeared and began their performance, at which point the earnest Austrians moved to tables about the terrace and observed like advanced students on a field trip. Soon enough, as confirmation of Grzimek's lecture to Nguana, some of them moved out on the floor and began to match their Western rock steps to the Ugandan dancers: they parsed. Over the noise of the music, we heard an elephant trumpeting nearby.

"The last time I was here," Boris said, "one of the elephants got into the kitchen. They had to use water hoses to get him out."

"Yes," said Grzimek. "It was probably Dust Bin Nelly, the one we saw before we left this afternoon. Turns on water taps, gets into dust bins—that's how she got her name. Good example of a wild animal living among people, but it can be quite dangerous. She is not afraid of visitors and they think they can feed her. Tourists think all elephants are the same. African elephants are much more dangerous than Indian elephants, which can be trained for labor. This one is a relative of another famous elephant here at Paraa named Lord Mayor. He was used to being fed, and he would open the doors of cars and steal food. One time, four Germans were sleeping in a Volkswagen. They had put bananas under the car for safekeeping. He turned over the car to get at them. They had to shoot him. He had become spoiled by the tourists."

I asked if the lion we had seen in the afternoon had been stalking the leopard, and Grzimek said no. Nguana laughed. Lions don't hunt leopards. Boris said he had read an account by the hunter Sid Downey of seeing a live jackal fall from the limb of a tree, a leopard climb down to pick it up and carry it back into the tree.

"Yes," Grzimek said, he knew of the account. "Leopards carry their kill into the trees to keep them from other predators."

Boris knew this. "But the fact is," he said, "the jackal wasn't harmed, was it? 'Twasn't dead, it was still alive."

"Maybe the leopard didn't realize it," Grzimek said. "What very often happens is that when game is captured by lions it becomes immobilized, as though anesthetized. It happened with Livingston. He was taken by a lion and dragged across the ground. He wrote later, he felt nothing. It was like a stupor. Then he was saved."

Boris agreed this could be so and told about an experience of George Adamson. Once, when he had wounded a lion and gone into the bushes to finish it, the lion had charged from his cover. Adamson's gun misfired. The lion seized him by the shoulder and dragged him over the ground and for some reason dropped him. Adamson managed to reload and kill the lion with a second shot, but only afterward did he realize he had felt nothing while he was held by the lion's jaws.

Nguana, who had made no attempt to add to the animal stories, asked politely if anyone cared for a beer. There were no takers.

"People still get eaten by wild animals," Grzimek said. "In Uganda, three leopards did away with a man recently. I also read a report from one park of lions taking seven people in a truck. It is

150   THE LAST PLACE ON EARTH

surprising. Lions continue to eat humans, most often when they are walking alone at night, and drunk. The lions think they are sick." For a long time it had been assumed there was no danger from lions in the park, he said, for the present generation has no experience of preying on man. But in Serengeti a few years ago, two men had been camping out under a fly tent by an open fire. A lion had taken one of them by the head and started dragging him away. His companion's shouts caused the lion to drop the man and flee. Another camper with a light plane had flown him to the hospital in Nairobi, but he had died on the operating table. When a man-eater is caught, he is killed because he has tasted human flesh, and the assumption is he will not hesitate to try it again.

Gordon Harvey had told the story of a tourist in Serengeti who got out of his vehicle in the presence of a lion and was immediately pounced upon; and I remembered a newspaper account of a woman who was mutilated by a lion in a California drive-in zoo when she got out of her car. But there was no consistency to such experiences. In Masai Mara, Boris, my son and I had parked beside two lions at a kill and now resting over the carcass. We discovered that our car wouldn't start. The battery cable had lost contact; it had happened before but never under these circumstances. The only thing to do was to get out of the vehicle, open the hood, and adjust the cable. Boris was on the lions' side of the vehicle, so the task fell to me. An armed ranger was with us. In Swahili, Boris asked him to train his gun on the lions in case they charged while I was outside the Land Rover. The ranger replied to Boris that he would get in trouble if he should be forced to shoot the lions—an impressive lesson in the priorities governing animals' rights within the national parks. As it turned out, the event proved of more moment to us than to the stuffed lions, which hadn't budged. On another occasion, in a Land Rover directly behind a pride of lions and looking out over the Serengeti, we saw two Masai warriors armed only with spears strolling across our front perhaps a hundred yards away. Lions are accustomed to the smell of vehicles and therefore ignore them, but at the instant they spotted the Masai they turned tail and like frightened dogs they ran past us to the cover of the bush to our rear.

"You should do your best never to surprise a wild animal," Grzimek was saying. "In the case of some, when they charge, it is better to stand your ground than run. A rhino will charge and often stop short. So will an elephant." But apparently the most predictable in this respect is easily the most intimidating animal on earth, the forest gorilla. Grzimek is an authority on this species, too. The week before I met him in Nairobi, he was in Rwanda overseeing a camera crew preparing a documentary on mountain gorilla. He had raised a baby female in a crib in his bedroom, and he had collaborated with George Schaller, who lived among them for three years, on the entry in his encyclopedia. Some gorilla weigh as much as five hundred pounds, and their method of fending off trouble is to scream at you, beat their chests, and then charge you like some denizen of urban man's id. To move is to invite disaster. If you stand quietly and avert your gaze, however, the gorilla will stop short and turn away. Among the tribesmen in Cameroon, according to Grzimek's encyclopedia, it is said to be a mark of disgrace for the victim, and high humor for his fellows, when he is known to have gorilla wounds in his posterior, conclusive evidence that he broke and ran from a gorilla charge. Dian Fossey, a tall, formidable California woman currently studying mountain gorilla in Rwanda, knew all this before she arrived, Grzimek said, but on her first charge she was so unnerved she had to hold onto a tree to keep her feet from going in the opposite direction. Eventually she became so familiar to them that she was able to reach out and touch them.

I asked Grzimek about the lion he had taken with him to the Eastern Front during the war. What about its predictability? "A lion will become as domesticated as a dog so long as it is kept close by the owner instead of on a chain. Dogs kill people, too. Usually dogs that are kept on chains or at breeding centers. I know of one that killed and ate a lady. But lions and cheetahs are like dogs. If made part of a social unit, they become completely tame. So will wolves. I had one during the war for a pet, too. And once I wrestled one in the nude for Leni Riefensthal, who couldn't find anyone else to do it for her film.

"Remember the farmer when he speaks to his horse softly coming up behind it," Grzimek said. "Try never to surprise an animal. They never attack unless they feel cornered or threatened." And so on, he concluded, blithely ignoring his own stories a few minutes earlier of lions that attack drunks and leap onto truck beds to eat passengers.

Grzimek's more formal views on animal behavior are related to the German school of ethology, the recent branch of biology that seeks, among other things, evolved behavioral relationships common to several species. It is a line of inquiry that has sometimes

152   THE LAST PLACE ON EARTH

proved disquieting. A number of European scientists no longer feel that the distinction between man and other mammals (and insects) is quite so clear. Language, toolmaking, and social organization are principal delineations believed in the past to set man apart. Yet as W. H. Thorpe, a Cambridge ornithologist, now points out, several species "talk" (a chimpanzee has learned a hundred and eighty-four words of our own language, in sign gestures, and can use them syntactically); the bowerbird builds a complex architectural structure for a house and then paints it; ants, termites, and other insects organize themselves for the common good of their communities. Moreover, there are certain things many species can do that man cannot, nor even yet understand. The golden plover can navigate from Nova Scotia to Argentina, nonstop, much of the way over open sea. Horses can sense earthquakes before they occur. The return of a salmon to its breeding ground may be seen as the equivalent of a man's learning to run a gigantic maze in reverse as a result of one experience of that maze two to six years earlier.

There is much interest in such matters presently, and the animal-loving Germans lead the field of inquiry. Karl von Frisch, Konrad Lorenz, and the Dutchman Niko Tinbergen received the Nobel Prize for their studies in ethology (Tinbergen has extrapolated his observations of communication between sea gulls to seek contact with autistic children). Both Lorenz and Tinbergen were associated with Grzimek in organizing support for the Serengeti Research Institute.

"Konrad Lorenz's ideas will give us an insight into the future," Grzimek says. "Behavior is intuitive and inherited. The day will come when these ideas will trickle down into politics." Grzimek believes the next step for humankind is the recognition of its biological disposition, the time when politicians will see that no matter the ideology of human systems, the key to man's actions will be the understanding of human behavior—in his shorthand, "human nature."

Some of these views, echoing turn-of-the-century eugenics and social Darwinism, have raised strong controversy in the West; most especially the suggestion that aspects of behavior in man may be, as in other species, innate rather than acquired. Lorenz's gloomy views on aggression, for example, suggest that man is genetically destined to destroy himself. To his critics, Lorenz's ideas would provide an intellectual rationalization for such ugly phenomena as Nazism. Grzimek's own ideas are even more far-reaching in some respects, and now, against the occasional trumpetings of Uganda's unhappy elephants, and in response to my question about his remark Friday night equating the problems of elephants and starving Ethiopians to the north, he moves into unfamiliar territory:

"It is all a problem of the population explosion," he says. "Now there is a competition throughout the world between the Russians, the Chinese, and the Americans over their political systems. But the real problem is *population!* In Africa, the large families are a tradition against times when half the children would die. But now they do not die any longer in such numbers because of modern medicine, which is the humane way the rest of the world helps. So there is the problem of too many people, and too much cattle, for the same reasons. All African ministers agree, but what to do politically?

"Maybe Red China is able to solve these problems. I do not know. In my first discussions with Russian Communists, I told them, 'You will wonder what has come out of communism after a hundred years. It is very similar to Christianity. Nobody could have believed that after four thousand years there would be such fighting and killing each other ... hundreds of thousands! The French Revolution ... liberty, fraternity, and equality ... all our constitutions have these things. But what has changed? You are a young agrarian nation,' I told them. 'Very intelligent. You may win. The world may become Communist, but what will change? *Nothing* will change, because *you can't change human nature.* One day, Communists will be fighting Communists.' Look now at the Chinese Communists and the Russian Communists. It is a question of human nature.

"All great human civilizations went down for biological reasons. American scientists won't see this because, like the Communists, they derive from philosophical systems that believe human intelligence is not inherited.

"But it is an experience of human nature that the most efficient people become the rich families which produce less children because they learn that to have many children means to degrade your standard of living. The old families who develop the high culture die out. Which means most of the Egyptians now are descendants from workers in the field. The Spaniards of today are not the Spaniards when they ruled the world. The same is true for the Greeks and will be true of the Germans, and so on.

"The one exception is the Chinese, who have remained a high

154

culture for four thousand years, equal to us in arts, philosophy—only not in the last developments of technology. A different system. Until recent times, the father in the old Chinese family collected the money the sons earned and distributed it for the family's use. He built the courts, and so on. Which means that even for the rich man it was interesting to produce many children. It was true of their religion, too, that in the corner of the court there was the little idol for the soul of the ancestor.

"And it is why I am interested now in the modern development of Red China, whether they will destroy their traditions, which is dangerous, for their present system again derives from philosophy. If so, they may rule the world, but then they will go the same way.

"Neither the Americans nor the Communists will allow this argument. Well . . . the problems of mankind. I hope that when mankind finishes itself that at least some elephants have survived."

Nguana again offered to stand the table to beers. He was a likable man, and I was curious about his background. Through competitive examinations, he had won the opportunity to attend the wildlife college at Mweka, Tanzania. He had studied animal behavior there, soil characteristics, vegetation, mechanics of Land Rover repair, and had learned to fly. Initially, the school had been run by the Game Department, a division of wildlife that historically has been at odds with the Parks Department. The Game Department protects man's property from the encroachment of animals, while the Parks Department protects animals from man. Grzimek had been influential in changing the orientation of the Mweka school, and now he took over from Nguana.

"I am on the board of the college, and I had provided the money for its first building. Eighty per cent of the emphasis was on the Game Department then, and I had had to fight. I said, Why train Africans for that? The Game Department is a losing field. In settled country, elephants and lions *have to go*. I personally wouldn't let elephants come into my fields. *I* wouldn't be happy with lions threatening my children or my cattle. It is the same development as in Europe. Elephants and lions will disappear outside of national parks, whether in ten years or fifty is not important. What we have to stress is the importance of *national parks*."

Boris was waiting for a pause. "Are you going to participate in the Botswana problem?" he asked. He had recently been on safari to the Okovanggo delta, a little-known corner of southwestern Africa, to find an unusual abundance of game. But now the delta had become threatened by the construction of a new diamond mine in the area. It was a subject of concern to him.

"We are paying a biologist to work in the swamps to get data on its drainage," Grzimek said, "just to have some facts to fight the mining company. Because if they come in with their own experts, the poor government doesn't know what to say about it. That is the only hope, and the only reason we do it."

"I think I know more or less what the situation is there," Boris said politely. "Because I worked in the gold mines in South Africa. If any action could be taken against those big interests involved . . . the fact is, these people throw a *lot* of the water away. They don't really need all that water they reckon they need. . . ."

"That is what I think we have to find out," Grzimek said crisply, not waiting for him to finish. "Because all you can get is the opinion of the mining companies. They are not neutral. If they say there is a surplus of water, I'm inclined not to believe it. That's why we pay a chap there to get the facts. The danger is, they take a little water first, then they expand, and you can never stop them."

Boris said, "If someone could just tell them, 'Okay, you've got to run that mine'—it would be too difficult to stop them, it's a *very* rich mine—'but you can have just so much water and no more,' I think that would be the only line of attack. . . ."

"Yes. That is why we have the man there. To get those facts. Because who else knows or cares about Okovanggo swamp?"

There was more to it than that, but Grzimek showed no interest in pursuing Boris's view. Anyway, it was late. Tomorrow, he said, we would head out for Ruwenzori two hundred and thirty-five miles to the southeast, a long day's drive, for much of it would be over dirt track. Then to Kampala for the meeting with Amin. We said goodnight.

THE LAST PLACE ON EARTH

ELEVEN

As Omar had observed to Grzimek yesterday, General Idi Amin considers himself a dedicated conservationist, a claim that would later be demonstrated in a documentary made by a French film team and distributed throughout Europe showing Amin in several moods, among them the holidaying Amin on that same boat trip up the Albert Nile at Kabalega, smiling genially, clapping and whistling at the crocodiles, and explaining their habits to the camera. (The film also showed a street-side execution, causing shock throughout Europe and ridicule of his pretensions; Amin demanded the film be recalled and the execution scene deleted.) Nor could his claim be directly disputed. Even though hunters hardly cared to come into Uganda, he had nevertheless declared an end to all hunting within his nation—for Grzimek, an important indication of intent. Whether he was a "great" conservator, as Grzimek had so emphatically declared to Omar, however, was less certain.

As we drove out the gate heading south, his pronouncement seemed now even more questionable. For a distance of some five miles adjacent to the park border, small huts were packed together as tightly as in a suburban tract. There were no signs of cattle or cultivation, and the conclusion seemed apparent: the people here lived by poaching. Boris said he had read that the settlements extended about two-thirds the circumference of the entire border. In 1968, the leaders of African states with national parks had agreed at an international conference to surround their park borders with buffer zones, areas of limited access, to separate the borders from human encroachment. The Kabalega Falls buffer zones were not effective. Boris had also heard from a ranger that there was even now a move under way to degazette one buffer zone in the north—to return the land to the local people by revoking the law providing it. (Grzimek had made a note of this for his meeting with Amin.) To Omar, Grzimek had come down quite heavily on the example of Julius Nyerere in Tanzania moving people away from Serengeti's borders at the Lamai Wedge. Perhaps this was why. Whatever his reason, the policies of Amin the conservationist, whose soldiers were invading the park and whose park rangers themselves were poaching the animals, hardly seemed exemplary.

And yet, whatever Amin's intentions toward the animals he owned or the people he ruled, the conditions forcing the issue of the animals' right to their parkland were as stringent here as elsewhere, more so. In Uganda, the population expansion rate was 5.2 per cent—higher than any other East African nation and projecting to a doubled population in fourteen years. The people of Uganda were not so poor as the people of Tanzania but that was not saying much. International agreements regarding conservation practices—on the ground where they apply—seem increasingly remote. Grzimek had said, "It can be easier to work with a dictatorship on these matters of conservation than with a democracy—you don't have to deal with parliaments." Most likely that was why he saw some potential to Amin that others had thus far overlooked.

We made an improbable safari—a family of Germans, a Russian/Italian, and an American—and if there was no reason for all of us to feel especially familiar with one another, we had at least become slightly more comfortable traveling together. At first, the Grzimeks had gone their own way at their own convenience with little information to us about when they would stop and where; I was constantly at Boris not to get too far out front for fear they would take a different route and lose us. Now, at least, we had an indication of their intention. Erika had said they might stop at Fort Portal in midafternoon to break the long trip to Ruwenzori, and if they did I wanted to be with them. While it had seemed the most practical course to trail behind them on the tarmac road from Mbale, once we hit the dirt track it had become a different matter. The trailing car loses the advantage to the lead car, any sense of virgin country lost to the passengers within the trailing car, which moves along enveloped by a suffocating cloud of fine dust. Boris didn't like coming up from behind; he was a good driver on dirt roads and a fast one, and Erika, who was driving the Grzimeks, was too slow. It became impossible for Boris to avoid creeping ever closer.

Late in the morning on a downhill run, he suddenly shifted into third, pulled out to the side of the van, accelerated and moved past them, holding his speed until he had left them a mile or so behind. "Now they won't have to eat our dirt and we can wait on them in Fort Portal." We had known each other for four years, but during that time only at brief intervals of ten days or so. He had been indispensable, acting as driver, interpreter, and cool head in a strange hostile country; despite the difference in our ages—we were a generation apart—it had been easy to defer to his judgment on most matters at hand. Nearly always he had been proved right, and our relationship had become comfortable and easy. But I had come a long way in pursuit of the elusive Grzimek, and I had no intention of losing him now—or risking the loss by causing him inconvenience, which would include tailing behind in our dust. It was possible to be too cautious about such matters, even slightly paranoid, but, in light of Grzimek's unbending reserve, imprudent to take too much for granted.

I asked Boris to stop at the side of the road; as casually as possible I told him how I felt and stated my intentions. So long as we were in Uganda, we would drive behind the Grzimeks and keep their van within our line of sight. Expressionless, Boris studied the dashboard as I said this. I realized our informal relationship had now been perhaps too sharply defined and that I must seem to him almost as obsessive as Grzimek now seemed to me. We sat in silence, hot and uncomfortable, awaiting the Grzimeks' van, working at having the awkward moment between us pass. "Just a minute," Boris said. He got out of the Land Rover, crossed the road, and walked to a small hut near the bush. When he came back he had a ripe pineapple which he proceeded to cut into large dripping chunks. We were tired and thirsty and it was delicious. The Grzimeks' van came over the hill. I flagged them down (they wouldn't have stopped otherwise) and invited them to have some of Boris's pineapple. Erika and Bernhard declined but Christian looked interested. Boris said nothing. I suggested Christian ride with us into Fort Portal. Grzimek and Erika looked at each other and then at Christian who, half shrugging and with a timid smile, climbed down to join us. Boris gave him a chunk of pineapple, and as the Grzimeks moved back into the lead, I felt some reassurance now, whatever it had cost me in other respects, that the Grzimeks would be watching out for us in Fort Portal.

What to make of this man? Watching him is almost more instructive than listening to him. He is a willing but impatient conversationalist, a one-way street: the monologuist tailoring words to his convenience. All conclusions and pronouncements and no connectives. What bores or strikes him as self-evident, or serves solely as transition ("and so on" is often his only concession), he simply leaves out, moving on according to the program fixed in his mind. "Ask questions," he had said to me once during a rare pause. "*What?*" I had said, unsure of what he had meant. "Ask *questions.*" And it had come through to me that you didn't interview Grzimek. He worked out of a set piece. You prompted him.

Chronology is not very important, either. After the Serengeti adventure—events having progressed consistently up through that climactic experience—his progress by his own account turns random: hurrying across the African continent from Mozambique to Cameroon, then on to New Guinea, Moscow, Australia (the Roots went along), India, and Hong Kong, buying water tanks or airplanes or subsidizing park staffs—he doesn't seem quite sure now where he was when; an elusive trail. His facts are imprisoned by his program and sometimes, like his lion stories, contradictory. He is clearly not the best witness to the mechanics of his own techniques. He doesn't have to be. What is of consequence to him are measurable results.

Our host is napping now, his daughter-in-law driving at a moderate speed over the dirt track along the road from Paraa to Ruwenzori, their van stirring dust clouds just ahead of my piqued driver. It will be an all-day trip. But the weather is brilliantly clear—we have not yet come into the day's heat—and the journey promises to be uneventful. With his young grandson our unknowing hostage, munching on the last of our pineapple, the lull in our hectic excursion encourages speculations on the methods and present intentions of Bernhard Grzimek in independent East Africa.

Grzimek is a man in a hurry. He acts alone. His effectiveness now in East Africa rests in large part with the response to his programs by key politicians; this last a complex, tricky business.

Because of the growth of the population and the spread of agriculture, the national parks have become the last line of resistance. He does not, therefore, worry so much any longer about all the animals of East Africa, only those left in the parks. Nothing there should be touched. The inviolability of park borders—the political guarantee of the animals' property rights—has become his major concern; the legislated preservation of them established within his lifetime, an obsession.

Among the extensive complex of conservation agencies in East Africa, some are more visible than Grzimek's sources and some have more money. He willingly enters into joint projects with many of

160

them, but nearly all of them, to his mind, are inflexible, hampered by bureaucracy and abstruse political restrictions—too slow to respond. The largest and best known are the International Union for the Conservation of Nature, an independent organization established by, and affiliated with, the United Nations, and its funding source, the World Wildlife Fund. "Both are *too* large," says Dr. Richard Faust, Grzimek's successor as zoo director and assistant administrator of his funding organizations. "Recently, two girls rehabilitating orangutan in Indonesia urgently requested funds for a car and other operating expenses. First they came to us. We channeled money to World Wildlife, and still, after eight months, they had not received a penny. The Swiss didn't return our money. We sent the money directly to them, and they received it in seven days." The London and New York Zoological Societies are responsive, as are the East African Wildlife Society (British/Kenyan) and the African Wildlife Leadership Foundation (American), but none can move quite so swiftly and effectively as Grzimek because none is so much the reflection of a leader like Grzimek who goes to the field himself and there decides what needs to be done.

On the occasion of the Congo uprising, representatives of the Gazinga government came directly to Grzimek at the Frankfurt Zoo asking money to pay park employees stationed in the eastern Congo and cut off from the central government. Otherwise they would be forced to kill their own animals in order to survive. Grzimek went first to the German minister for international cooperation and then to Robert MacNamara of the World Bank. Both refused assistance because the Gazinga government was believed to be under Communist influence. Grzimek asked the petitioners to sign an agreement that the funds he raised would go directly to the park employees (and not through the government). Then, to be sure, he sent the money to a Belgian biologist named Jacques Verschuren stationed at Serengeti, bought him a Land Rover, and dispatched him directly into the eastern Congo to pay the employees himself, which he did for two years until the political situation had stabilized. (When Grzimek visits that park today, rangers and children parade in his honor.)

"That's one of the main difficulties with international organizations," Grzimek says. "They are nice people but they will say they can't persuade the American or German government to do anything for a chap like Amin. He's killed too many people, and so on. That is a situation where chaps like me have to go in, because we can't help it if you have a Communist Party or Uganda has a dictatorship. That has nothing to do with conservation or of natural ecology."

The rate of wildlife attrition is too great to waste time: the "Red Data Books" of endangered species indicate one species of plant life and one species of mammal are becoming extinct each year. Other agencies are too timid or they waste time. In the end, they may not come through. So Grzimek prefers to act on his own.

Except for the early days in Tanganyika when he and Nyerere were getting the measure of the other, a time now well in the past, Grzimek does not talk much about his influence with African leaders. In this respect alone, as the Frankfurt cameraman had supposed, he is very much a different man from the one he is at home. "His methods in Africa *have* to be different from his methods in Europe," Hugh Lamprey would later remark. "You see, he knows in a European community it is accepted that you hammer your political opponents. In West Germany, you can get away with it. But, by Jove, you do it here and you're through, you're finished. They won't listen to you. You can be effective only by being very subtle indeed."

Dissension is unwelcome, especially from former oppressors. This is no less true in Kenya, where elephant poaching has been traced to officials high in the government, than in Uganda, where a British citizen named Denis Hill would almost lose his life for criticizing Idi Amin. Even in Tanzania, of the three nations the least inclined toward racial discrimination, it is considered mis-chievous to criticize openly the policies of government. ("Those of you who don't like the way we do things should get out," Derek Bryceson said before the Tanzania Parliament several years ago.) The most flagrant abuses of natural resources here do not, therefore, easily come to light. Kenya's elephant population, according to one estimate, is being reduced at the rate of three a day. The export of charcoal out of Kenya, causing the devastation of an acre of scrub bush to produce a ton of fuel, is destroying the countryside. Yet European conservationists here force themselves to look the other way—"a conspiracy of silence," *The London Sunday Times* would comment in breaking the story—to maintain their tenuous position within the community. While Grzimek's past contributions and considerable financial resources set him apart from all the others, he is as cautious as the rest. "I never say to Europeans what I say to Africans here," he once observed in an *East African Standard* interview. "It is because I am from the outside and share your

THE LAST PLACE ON EARTH

concerns that I can say what I do." It is sufficient to his purpose to point out that African leaders are proving themselves leaders in conservation whereas other world leaders are faltering, and that they have received far less credit than they deserve ("It is only partly true that old colonialists like myself and John Owen have done so much for national parks. It is mainly *black* politicians, and they certainly don't want to hear otherwise"). While Grzimek goes no further in this regard, others do.

Conway tells of reading a speech by a West African leader on the subject of conservation that drew, almost to the eccentric phrasing, from an earlier address by Grzimek to representatives of Third World nations.

John McDougall, the Nairobi newsman, tells of an occasion when Grzimek urged another West African leader to set aside a park free of human traffic for a period beyond his own lifetime. " 'Fine idea,' the official had said. He would think about it. Then Grzimek went on television back home and congratulated the man on his magnificent gesture. As praise rolled in, the leader had said, 'Yes, I did think it was a good idea.' "

"X—— is Grzimek down the line," says Philip Thresher, a former assistant to John Owen. "Grzimek would say to him, 'You want to be the first in Africa? How can you do this with no national parks? Your soldiers are where your parks should be.' In ten minutes' time, you would have seven or eight parks."

Grzimek seeks to discourage such tales. For many modern African leaders the white culture, which imposed its own standards so insensitively, still holds the measure of their progress, or lack of it. Thus, the acknowledgment of white influence from any quarter often means for Africans the loss of pride. Unquestionably, African pride is the one intangible Grzimek now sees as more important than any other in assuring the preservation of Africa's animals. It is at this point that his words take over from his actions, and he will talk at great length, and from personal experience, about the proper way to regard such matters.

"Africans mostly have inferiority complexes. What nobody tells an African but speaks of among themselves is that an African is less intelligent, less courageous; yet everybody believes Red Indians of North America are heroes. It comes from our literature whereas we can see from African history, which is not so well known, that in many tribes the young man could marry and become a full member of his society *after* he had killed a lion or an elephant with poor weapons in the open field. I do not know an example of such personal courage in another culture in the last thousand years.

"And they really *can* be proud. They spend so much of their national income for conservation—in a poor country like Tanzania more than eight times proportionately than America spends. And they fine new African poachers, not as it was done in colonial times. British judges would fine poachers only twenty shillings because they were poor natives. Now poaching is seen by African governments as an offense against national pride and national property, and they get one to two years in prison. And so on.

"When I went into the Congo during the civil uprising, I learned that Africans had *not* destroyed their animals as Europeans had during their wars, when they shot the last European bisons. Where two armies had crossed the main road through Albert National Park, the buffalo were still standing by the side of the road, totally tame. There were posters of both parties saying that wildlife was a common heritage of the Congolese people and that soldiers shooting the animals would receive two years in prison. It was a totally new experience. . . ."

Thus, moving quickly and alone, and for these reasons, does he continue on at great length, making his present "propaganda."

Would such methods work for his purposes here in Uganda now, I wondered, against the disheartening conditions we had just witnessed at Kabalega Falls?

Boris was chatting with Christian, gently drawing him out on his school in Frankfurt, the animals he had seen, the earlier trips to Africa. Erika and Christian traveled regularly now with Grzimek. As had been the case for Christian's father, the field expeditions with Grzimek counted as credit against the more pedestrian schoolwork missed. (The Serengeti film was to serve as Michael's thesis for his doctorate in zoology.) Erika and Christian enjoyed each other. While they were always solicitous of the older man, they seemed to find his preoccupied air a source of constant amusement—the absent-minded professor. In Tororo, Erika had put two spoonfuls of sugar in Grzimek's tea for him, and as he talked on, he put two spoonfuls in himself. They giggled to each other and said nothing.

Boris was closer to Christian's age than mine; he had a good way with boys, involving Christian now, as he had my son on past trips, in the countryside we were traveling through. He had an endless source of lore about the animals and plants of East Africa, the region's various tribes, and many of its problems. He chatted easily, but he didn't offer his information until he was asked.

When it came to Grzimek, however, there was clearly something that bothered him, although this, too, he seemed hesitant to speak of. What he knew about Grzimek was through Grzimek's reputation within the Nairobi community and what he had seen in the past few days. Driving back to our camp site last night (with headlights off), I had chatted about Grzimek's reactions to the game run, drawing little from Boris other than a skeptical grin. It was enough. Boris was like Root, Turner, and the other British expatriates who did what they did and seldom spoke of it (Grzimek talked of very little else). Or perhaps it was Grzimek's tendency to overstate things. Boris leaned toward qualification. He found Ian Parker's position on cropping the game to save it more persuasive on scientific grounds than anything he had heard thus far from Grzimek. Also, Grzimek's very healthy ego had become a bit hard to take. There were few stories Grzimek had told us, or the African officials, to which he was not central, ending with his getting the best of the opposition, man or beast. (On the other hand, there were many stories Grzimek *could* have told us but hadn't—McDougall, Thresher, and Conway all had their own versions—and the fact was, they were even more impressive.)

It was more than just a question of temperament. If Grzimek's accounts weren't self-aggrandizing, they were certainly oracular, often too simplistic, and nearly always didactic. That's the way it was; Grzimek knew, he had been there. His self-effacing protests hinted of a heavy disingenuousness: "You mustn't credit old colonials and Europeans like me. It is really the African leaders who save animals for all mankind," and so on; and yet, in almost the same breath: "I provided the money for the Mweka college building," or, "I daresay I am the only person in the world who can collect money for wildlife on television." There was, too, his Prussian manner, almost a caricature of style in prewar Germany. He said he would have become a member of the Nazi Party had he been accepted—remarkable candor from one point of view, appalling from another. Touring the front lines with a lion at his boot heel, wrestling wolves in the nude—the image was today surrealistic, unconsciously parodic of the pantheistic *Wandervogel* strain that had so suited the Nazi ideal. His biological views of human history seemed at first hearing to conform to the mode. Yet it would prove to be the case that they were closely allied to those of E. O. Wilson, the American biologist whose own theories are now viewed by all but the most radical biologists as moderate and deserving of reflection.

Grzimek tells such stories about himself and advances his views without self-consciousness or apology—rather as part of the mechanical recital of the past leading to his present position. As quickly and with no change in emphasis, he would relate his exposure to the various horrors of wartime Germany. In veterinarian school at Berlin, he was shown the decapitated cadavers of zoologists whose only offense had been to make jokes about the Hitler regime. As though his selfless involvement with black Africa were not evidence enough of his sentiments, his views on race are supported by personal involvements at home. His third son, Thomas, is an adopted child. "He was the only black child in a school of six hundred. The papers said he was my illegitimate son from Africa. I didn't bother to correct it. I thought it would help his position in school." Then the triumphant laugh. But it would be his only reference to the child. The persona of Bernhard Grzimek was a bewilderment. "A difficult man," William Conway in New York had sighed, "but a necessary one."

It was easy enough to see how all this would bother Boris, a younger man of another culture, a different temperament. By now, it had long ceased to bother me. So much of Grzimek's world was new for me, his lifelong obsession so different from my own interests that I had become an eager audience of one, all disbelief suspended, as though in attendance at some bizarre theatrical event in which this cold and distant actor was forcing me to reckon beyond the boundaries of curiosity to a quality of existence wholly in biological terms, something I had never really thought much about until now—and only to discover how frighteningly constricted that existence had become.

While I was uncertain where Grzimek was taking me, however, I found I could trust him implicitly on two counts that I *could* measure—the discipline of his passion and the extravagance of his hope. I admired the way he had learned to temper the passion with cunning, waiting for the right moment to release it and then acting, boldly, when its force would prove most effective. Grzimek had said the Serengeti shall (or must) not die, and even though many in the East African community considered the case terminal, he was personally prepared to back it up. But increasingly now, as others like Lamprey and Conway would say of him, his purpose was of an order higher than this, higher than the conservation of all African parks and their animals. In his own manipulative, idiosyncratic way, Bernhard Grzimek had declared a one-man war against the diminution of nature. Biophylaxis. It seemed absurd on the face of it in this day and age, the extreme in posturing. Yet nothing I had seen of him, read or heard of him, indicated otherwise. *He wasn't bluffing!* That he often strutted, exaggerated, manipulated, and exploited seemed now, in the action of being, perfectly consistent. A showman of pity; it was part of the act. Who else today so deeply shared such remote concerns, who would so completely commit himself?

What still remained enigmatic about him, from my vantage, was the reserve he had constructed about his inner life for whatever reasons, conscious or otherwise. Grzimek was a public man, trading heavily in sentiment; *that* part was an inconsistency. I remembered the uncomfortable expression of his colleagues in Frankfurt when I asked who were his friends—he had none. Erika and Christian lived within that reserve, and there would be nothing said between them or us during the course of our trip that would invite more than the most formal acknowledgment of our circumstantial relationship. (I didn't understand exactly why all this should have concerned me. If Grzimek's actions so clearly spoke his intentions, what business of it was mine? Perhaps the need to see some human connection to his profoundly humane concerns—or perhaps simply a worn professional reflex? In any case, little progress here—I was becoming diverted by the reservations expressed about him in Frankfurt, not in Africa.) If anything, with my constant questions, I was concerned that I might inadvertently push too far: the cameraman in Frankfurt had given fair warning. Grzimek considered himself a former journalist but when he now dealt with the press, it was mainly to "make propaganda." I could expect an edge on no other basis—I was as essential to him as my account might be toward serving his purpose—and I realized I would have to be very careful about that.

Earlier in the evening before, when he had seemed at one point to be loosening up, I *had* gone too far. During the performance of the dancers, one of them had knelt before Boris, the custom for inviting a man to join her. Grzimek pointed to me and said to her with a wicked grin, "Ask him instead." It had seemed a relaxation of his formality and as good a time as any to ask him about anything. I tried to swing the conversation back to the Serengeti of the fifties, to which he responded mechanically, and then—seeking an unprogrammed emotion from the man—specifically to the circumstances surrounding the plane crash that killed Michael. His mouth turned down and he looked at me coldly. "That is all in the book. You can get it there."

Boris had dropped back now—we could just see the Grzimek van cresting a far hill, a tiny dust puff in the distance. Christian was napping. Time was passing very swiftly; soon we would be heading back the other way. So entangled had we become in the hapless circumstances of Uganda's animals, all relevance to Serengeti and its future was fading. I was quite wrong about this, although I hadn't known so at the time. Grzimek understood my concerns, however, and he had said he, too, wanted to deal with Serengeti before we parted. If not tomorrow night, the next; he would make a point of it.

TWELVE

Fort Portal, three-forty P.M.: a rock band is playing in the dart room of the Mountains of the Moon Hotel. The dart room is off to the right of the bar which is, in turn, next to the dining room, empty but ready, with linen on the tables and straight severe oak chairs in place. To the far right, the dart room opens onto a cool stone terrace where we rest now, in wicker chairs with piled cushions. From a combination of things—the hard day's travel, the long talk of the night before, and from our separate tensions—we are played out, unable to deal with the anomalies of the Mountains of the Moon Hotel. To our front is a soft playing field bounded by giant eucalyptus and beyond, in their shade, English stone houses with orange tile roofs and perfect lawns, miniatures of the hotel that at one time must have been the social center of Fort Portal—all of it slightly off register, like a bad color print. Behind the hotel is a formal garden whose bursting hibiscus work back to the front climbing toward the green canvas awning above the terrace, further distancing the view. The colonialists' preferences have been meticulously preserved including even the sterling tea service. But as the waiter pours, someone inside the dart room is at an amplifier tuning a splitting electronic whistle into the polyphonics of a Fender guitar: too noisy here for ghosts.

In the business district, only blocks away, the Indians had controlled the town, had built most of it, and this, too, was a familiar sight but set in another frame—a frontier town misplaced by a continent. On either side of the street, wood-roofed porches connected one store to the next, each structure a single story but all of irregular heights, all of them opening onto the rambling porches. You could see inside them the rows of open shelves, with only a few wares. There were Indian signs still over the entrances but always, facing the door, General Amin peering from the same giant photograph we had seen in the bank, same three-quarter view, slight smile. The suburbs had belonged to the British, the town to the Indians; now all of it belonged to the Ugandans, who did not seem quite yet ready to let their impress go.

It is growing late, the noise out of the dart room is overbearing, and we hurry back onto Route A109 to Ruwenzori where the road at last slips into character. At the side, a man has rested his bicycle and is clipping back weeds from the road edge with a hand scythe. Shortly after Amin came to power, two Americans were killed along here, one a teacher named Siedle and the other a journalist named Stroh. They had come this way to investigate the report of a massacre by Amin's troops of hundreds of soldiers belonging to the Acholi and Langi tribes. Why the teacher accompanied the journalist isn't known. Amin says they were from the C.I.A. In Tanzania, a deserter from the Ugandan Army said the two men had been killed because they were "proud." Along this road leading to the hills beneath the Mountains of the Moon, which separate Uganda from the immense rain forests of Zaire to the west, and then along the sides of the hills themselves, there are rows of fires burning, in horizontal lines but at odd angles and irregular intervals. They seem to be fed by the *greenness* of the hills, not by dead dry grass, and though not attended so far as we can tell, their advance is restrained and orderly, unhurried. Creeping fires. The sight is rather what one expects to find in an industrialized area, like the controlled natural-gas flames burning off through metal scaffolding along the New Jersey Turnpike. Off to the right somewhere, obscured by haze, are the Mountains of the Moon—Mount Stanley, Mount Speke, Mount Baker. Light is weak and there is a steel gray cast to the air, the late sun enormous but dulled by the gray haze to a weak reflection of the orange fires crawling the hills. This is as close as we will come to the heart of Africa. At the edge of Ruwenzori Park is a cement factory: the steel cast to the dying evening proves to be a pollution haze.

A pollution haze! Grzimek later says we should not be surprised, that the smoke from industrial furnaces is not the half of it. While "civilized" nations have prohibited the sale of harmful pesticides within their own boundaries, some of them now are exporting DDT and other dangerous chemicals at a rate six times greater than when the bans were imposed; they export them to "underdeveloped" areas like Africa. It was another quick pronouncement, almost too patently ironical, yet easily confirmed later. During this year of our travels, the State Department's Agency for International Development funded for export to underdeveloped tropical countries a

170   THE LAST PLACE ON EARTH

million pounds of DDT and three-quarters of a million pounds of aldrin, a pesticide whose use was to be discontinued in America for its harmful effects on humans. Our humans.

Across from the cement factory are the first *Euphorbia candelabrum*, occasional small clusters of elephant, and telephone poles carrying cables over their heads.

Ruwenzori is important as a reference point for the cropping argument here in East Africa because of its hippopotamus population, which is seldom in balance with its food supply. There are more here than anywhere else on earth, some fourteen thousand. They breed too fast for the existing vegetation to keep up with their needs—a hundred and fifty pounds of forage each at a single feeding. This causes the erosion of the lakeshores, and in turn destroys the food supply of other species. Their tusk ivory is more desired than the elephant's because it is harder. Their hide, when cured, is tough enough to cut diamonds. They make excellent eating, with less fat and more protein per pound than cattle.

Norman Myers cites a persuasive example of the advantages of cropping hippo at Ruwenzori: An analysis of one specific area, "a small peninsula less than two square miles at Mweya close by the park lodge, showed that almost 100 hippo had been causing what looked like critical erosion. After they were reduced [by cropping], the vegetation quickly recovered. And after a few more years . . . the elephant population had doubled, the waterbuck population had trebled, and the buffalo had increased sixfold. . . . If the hippos had not been shot out, there might soon have been few animals of any sort left." Eleven thousand hippo have been cropped at Ruwenzori since the late fifties.

There are many who favor this argument, Boris says. Besides Ian Parker, its best-known exponent in East Africa, and a variety of scientists and ecologists, a number of conservation and governmental institutions as well, including the United Nation's Food and Agriculture Organization, which is currently conducting a multi-million-dollar program of cropping plains game in southeast Kenya. Boris says this faction, because it advocates the use of modern technology to solve such problems, is known out here as "Man's Way." The other side, as "Nature's Way."

One must have a strong feeling for animals of all sorts to have much of an affinity for the hippo. They are water pigs, vast, rubbery creatures with pink underbellies, both slothful and belligerent, like sulking, overweight bullies. At Ruwenzori they seem to be every-where, floating offshore, grazing far inland during the dark hours, grunting and huckling, primeval hogs. (The genius of Disney's perverse casting of them in *Fantasia*—in tutus for the water ballet!)

A saltworks, a fish factory, several fishing villages, and the cement factory at Kasese are located either on the borders of Ruwenzori Park or inside them. People live within the park in such numbers that they must now be considered part of the environment. Worry over buffer zones here is pointless. This afternoon, Grzimek took pictures of a hippo grazing within yards of a group of women at the lakeshore doing their wash. The political question of the hippo's rights to the parkland of Ruwenzori is closed: the hippo lost.

Late in the afternoon, we visited a mud bog listed on the map as a hippo pool; it was a thick primordial ooze. On Grzimek's visit here several years ago, it had been a shallow lake, but since then it has been choked off by the spread of water cabbage into an ugly brown sump which appeared at first glance to be without life. Then we saw on the far bank a herd of elephants, grazing about some bushes. Coming closer, we saw a buffalo out near the center, its legs sucked under by the mud. A hundred yards or so to the right, there were some thirty to forty hippo, only the soft arcs of their backs protruding from the sludge. Except for the slow browsing of the elephants in the background, it was a scene without movement until the buffalo began to struggle convulsively to get free. Then it lay back again, exhausted. Three vultures wheeled overhead, about a hundred feet up. "They are not quite sure he is dead," the warden of Ruwenzori said. Grzimek took pictures. Next morning on our way out, we came by again and the buffalo was dead. Nature's Way.

Little to note about Ruwenzori for us, but much, we assume, for Grzimek. Earlier this morning, only two days after happening over the dead elephant at Paraa, and with a day of travel in between, Boris and I had gone out at first light to find another elephant carcass, the ivory cut out of its head. Ivory grows with age. This was a young elephant, not much of a take, suggesting that the poachers were settling for whatever they could find. In the moist haze, the same as held over Kasese the evening before, there were the same vulture and stork ringing the carcass but now a hyena as well, tugging at a skein of a hoof. A pack of them came out of the bush, sniffed about and looked impassively at our Land Rover, then trotted on leaving the one there still tugging at the hoof. We were by the shore about three miles from our camp. On the way, we had

THE LAST PLACE ON EARTH

seen two dugouts and a powerboat nearby; most likely the poachers had come and gone by the water. In each of the two parks, a dead elephant within two hours of random driving: one wondered what might be the statistical projection of poaching as against Amin's total elephant population. A partial answer would come several months later in a report by John Eames, the editor of *Africana:*

At Kabalega Falls the elephant population dropped from fifteen thousand to seven thousand within the year.

Coming back from Serengeti several years ago, we had been hurried by the gathering darkness to set up camp off the dirt track in a grove of acacia trees some miles beyond the park borders. Although we would be sleeping in the Land Rover—impregnable to nearly everything but an angry elephant—Boris had gone to great lengths to situate the vehicle so that we would be protected by trees to the left and thorn bushes to our right. He took similar precautions here, siting our tent directly alongside a large baobab tree, backing up the Land Rover behind and improvising a half-perimeter of jerry cans, two on each side about six feet apart. To the front, the embankment fell away sharply to the lake's edge. If Grzimek were right, that animals become dangerous only when threatened, it seemed an unnecessary precaution. Maybe so, Boris said, but he had his own reasons. Once, camping out in a small pup tent with a schoolmate, he had awakened in the middle of the night for no discernible reason. He looked out the opening and saw by the light of the moon a rhinoceros ten yards away, his head lowered, staring into the tent, staring straight at him. It was about three o'clock in the morning, and the rhino remained there, silent, for a long time. Abruptly it snorted, turned, and trotted away. Ever since on safari, Boris has awakened at three and spent a terrible few minutes before getting back to sleep. Further, Grzimek had remarked casually today that the hippopotamus accounts for more human deaths in East Africa than any other species. Most of them occur from the offender's unwitting presence in the path the hippo follows from his grazing grounds during the night back to the water. Rather than change course, the hippo attacks whatever happens in its way. They are surprisingly fast and agile in such circumstances, as fast as rhino, faster than man. The art of avoiding them is in knowing where the hippo's path is not.

Some of this had begun to restore for us the fine, sharp-edged sense of the savanna wilderness. The Grzimeks would join us here later. We had a good dinner of stew, bean sprouts and chocolate pudding, and set a small bar for the Grzimeks with ice from the lodge and Pepsi's for Christian. Then we flipped to see who would wash the dishes while the other drove to get the Grzimeks— necessarily, of course, exposing the access route from our rear. I lost. Unlike the quiet of Paraa, there were plenty of sounds now out in the darkness, the most ominous the heavy grunts of hippo moving inland to their grazing grounds. As Grzimek had first observed many years ago, they prefer steep embankments. With Boris slowly moving the darkened Land Rover out toward the road back to the lodge, I realized it would be the first time I had been completely alone in the open at night since I had first come to Africa. Grzimek had quoted an epigraph at the head of his chapter on the night he spent out in Ngorongoro: "Every man should spend at least one night a month in the open, so as to shed all vain airs for a time." The porcine grunts rolled through the darkness from several directions and at varying distances. I turned the Coleman lanterns as high as they would go—to hell with stories about bright lights attracting lion—and rattled my soaking pots and pans with great vigor.

Slumped in his camp chair, worn down by the cumulative travel, Grzimek sipped at his whiskey without much enthusiasm. He spoke in a metallic, reedy pitch, his accent almost too thick to follow. He was not especially surprised by our discovery of another slain elephant, but his indignation took an unexpected turn.

"How can you blame them? They see young scientists come and kill their animals, or rich hunters. Yet if the people hunt, they may receive two years in jail. They see the scientists and the hunters kill the animals and throw away the meat. They can't be blamed for not understanding. These young scientists who come here for a year or two, they think they have the right to do what they want for research. I know one who killed three hundred wildebeest, another who killed wild dog—they soon face extinction. They are *blind*," he said, covering his eyes. "They do any damn thing for their thesis.

"I asked the scientist in charge at one of these places, 'Did the researcher find out if there were other studies that could benefit? Did he try to find a way to use the dead animals for any purpose other than his own?' I am against scientists doing this sort of thing unless strictly supervised. They shouldn't be left to do it on their own. They need someone of judgment to say when they can and when they can't shoot the animals. Who says the scientist is an

THE LAST PLACE ON EARTH

expert? We don't know enough yet for experts. There can be no experts. Let a scientist spend his life out here and *then* he becomes an expert."

Apparently his resentments carried over from a meeting earlier at the lodge with a tall, dignified man who had joined the warden to greet our arrival last evening. He was the director of ecology for Uganda, and his precise diction and graceful idioms suggested a London education. He was one of the reasons Grzimek had come into Uganda, for he had requested a two-hundred-thousand-dollar grant to set up scientific studies of conditions within the park. His problems had been compounded by the destruction of his small office/laboratory by fire. He said he suspected arson. At one point Grzimek spoke of the falls at Kabalega. "Do you know who Murchison was?" he said to the director.

"No."

"He was director of the London Geographical Society who paid for Baker's expedition that discovered the falls."

"That is the value of old age," the director said smoothly.

Grzimek had not seemed sympathetic to the request. Besides, the director and the chief warden had been feuding, apparently over administrative problems at Ruwenzori, and he wasn't sympathetic about this, either. "They will be at each other's throats until it is made clear that only one man is in charge. The scientist is seeking prestige."

"Normal, understandable," I'd said.

"Not in business," Grzimek said. "It is the way they think out here, that a chap educated in London is suited to run things. Not at all. The chap on the scene who knows what he is doing is what they need." The director's request was not specific, and Grzimek had not seen himself the proper source of assistance. "He should decide what his problems are and then ask universities in America and Europe to send scientists to solve these problems. They will realize there is no money here and then will fund the scientists with the necessary amount to do the work."

But it was his impatience with the scientific approach that was surprising, a sort of sideswipe. I was beginning to see that it was part of Grzimek's method to pass lightly over those problems which were the more severe out here—political problems of the encroachment against park borders, or scientific problems, like cropping. Grzimek knew where he stood on such matters: When people got in the way, you moved them, as Nyerere had in Serengeti, at the place called Lamai Wedge. In national parks, you didn't crop animals. He had stated his position without qualification to Omar, had mentioned "the Tsavo episode," and had gone no further. It was sufficient for Grzimek that he had declared himself. Yet in the past three days the magnitude of both issues was becoming evident. It was as though he didn't want too much attention drawn to these matters. Now it was Grzimek who had brought up the efficacy of science out here—how did he feel about cropping?

"The first scientists coming out here, not excluding me, were very quick in giving advice—what should be done and what not. But the more you learn of the interaction of the different parts of nature, the more cautious you become in giving advice. Mainly the thing is, you shouldn't try to *manage* things. Leave it to nature to do it. Because *we don't know enough about it!* It is not only game interacting with vegetation, it is a lot of small animals living in tons per acre, underground, which *nobody* knows about. It is the chemicals in the soil, it is humidity, it is fire, it is infectious diseases, it is parasites of the game. Here in Uganda the advice of research committees was to shoot out big parts of the game, and so on. I think people would be very careful to do that now, and particularly after what we have learned in the meantime. At the Serengeti Research Institute you have a place where for the first time—not only in Africa but taking in the *whole world*—there is the combined work of different biologists from different branches interlinking their research so that there is put together a mosaic of knowledge which is only half done. A *quarter* done!

"Michael and I very soon learned that the wildebeest migration must have its reasons, that is why we collected samples of plants to find the nutritional value, investigated the fertility of soil, and so on. It showed that when you investigated these things, you had to go on investigating *other* things. That was why botanists came to explore the different species and others to investigate the interaction of plants and soil, and then to make ultraviolet photographs from planes, which were financed by us, to show the change of vegetation in the Serengeti. And in fifty years' time, when you can compare the reaction of the vegetation to the amount of rain to the animals grazing there and so on, you may get the answer."

Ask questions.

Tomorrow we would head out for Kampala. To Boris and me, amateur bystanders, the list of problems we ourselves had observed or heard of seemed endless. Amin's soldiers were appropriating park equipment. Soldiers, local residents, even rangers were poaching the game. You could shoot it from the road or the lake. Buffer zones had disintegrated, and in Ruwenzori people were living inside the park. There was inadequate equipment and no money to replace it. In Ruwenzori the warden had told us there was only one running vehicle—Grzimek had used his own van to make the afternoon game run. There were no arms, no ammunition. At Ruwenzori the hippopotamus had been cropped so often it had learned now, once the shooting started, to migrate across the lake to Zaire's adjacent park where it is still protected. There were the random incidents of two dead elephants. Only a year ago Kabalega Falls was, after Nairobi, the most frequently visited park in East Africa. Now there were few tourists and little hope for more. Under such circumstances what would Grzimek hope to accomplish with Amin? What would he say?

Wearily and deeply guttural, his English becoming ensnarled by reverse phrases: "They sent me a request for two hundred thousand dollars for research. Looking into it, I would give the answer, '*Not one penny.*' What is needed here—I talked with Mr. Omano, who is a friend of the President—what he would tell me as a foreigner is he has certain needs, that certain things don't work. But speaking with the lower people, I get a stronger impression. I would try to tell the President at first that '*Yours . . . will . . . be . . . the . . . first . . . African . . . country . . . to . . . abolish . . . nature . . . reserves . . . after . . . independence!*' That other African countries have *added* national parks after independence because it is for African prestige to protect its culture. And that the judge at one province doesn't cooperate because he fines poachers only two months, which is not the case with other judges near the parks. That the problem is that the army still does a bit of poaching but in general it is true that the army *is* cooperating with the national parks [he had heard Nguana differently] . . . and that the parks will be poached out if they don't get transportation and guns, ammunition and trained pilots, one more plane and radio communication. But what I mainly want to tell him is what Mobutu has done in Zaire, what Kaunda has done in Zambia. When these presidents get together, they don't have a chance to talk about animals. I tell them what the others have done. I will tell him also what he would like to hear—that Kenya earns lots of money, and you hear everywhere that lots of politicians are bribed, they do business with ivory, and so on. Those are the main things."

The Grzimeks returned to the lodge. Boris said the cropping issue, the main scientific controversy out here, was more complicated than Grzimek had indicated. While it was true that the hippo population had come out of balance in the fifties, there was active disagreement among the expatriates as to whether the corrective methods had been effective. A thousand hippo a year had been cropped. The reproduction cycle for a mature female is a calf every three years. But when the number of the animal exceeded the food supply, the hippo population slowed its reproduction rate almost to a dead stop, moving collectively as a species to correct its own imbalance. One view (the Grzimek view) had it that everything else—vegetation, soil, other ungulates—would adjust their processes accordingly and the situation would ultimately right itself. By man's interference in their reproductive cycles through cropping, however, the animals would continue to overproduce, with the result that self-regulation down the line would be hopelessly altered. The objection to cropping was (as Grzimek had concluded) that there was insufficient data to know what would happen when man interfered with the natural process—Nature's Way.

"Were these questions at issue in Serengeti?"

"Yes," he said. "Certainly. In fact they are more hotly argued there than anywhere else."

I should try to talk with Parker and Hugh Lamprey, if possible, for both sides of it, he said. As to the political question—the problem of border violations—the key men were John Owen, who had set up Serengeti's park system; Myles Turner, who was there throughout the period; and Derek Bryceson, who ran it now. Assuming I could find them.

Meanwhile there was Grzimek, now heading for his audience with General Amin. Under these quite desperate circumstances, it would be instructive to see how he made out.

From *Time* magazine, two months later:

In Kampala, the capital, much of the terror is committed by Big Daddy's personal goon squad, the 3,000 man Public Safety Unit. Like Haiti's feared Tonton Macoute, members of the squad are almost always dressed in sports shirts and wear dark glasses even at night. They are given to cruising Kampala's streets in their Peugeots, stopping occasionally to pick up a suspect. The unlucky victim is pushed into the car, driven off and seldom seen again.

Coming out of Ruwenzori next morning on the road to Kampala along a narrow dirt track that did not allow room for passing in either direction, I was driving at a comfortable interval behind the Grzimeks when I happened to notice through my right fender mirror a white car trying to get by, darting out and back impatiently, very close to our tail and almost lost in our dust cloud. I faded as far left as I could and slowed down. The car pulled around us—it was a European make, unusual in any case for it appeared in very good condition—and through the rear window we saw angry faces glaring back at us. The car stopped in the middle of the track, forcing us to stop. Two men got out of the back seat and walked toward me; their driver remained behind the wheel. They were wearing sports shirts and dark glasses. "What is the trouble with you?" one of them said to me. "Why would you not move over?" I said I hadn't known they were behind me until I had seen them in the mirror. "We hooted and we hooted and we *hooted!*" the one said. I said I was terribly sorry, I really hadn't heard them. He looked from me to Boris who was looking at the floorboard. "It's all right," the one said abruptly. "Okay." They got back in their car, and as their driver pulled away, they looked back through the rear window, smiled, and waved.

From the front page of the Tuesday edition of *The Voice of Uganda:*

Asked whether it was true that the Israelis wanted to poison the Nile, President Amin agreed that it was true when the Israelis were still in Uganda. The president added that the Israelis heard that Sudan might join the war, so they wanted to poison the Nile in order to weaken the Egyptians and the Sudanese. . . .

. . . When told that other leaders such as De Gaulle, Mao, Gadaffi, and Napoleon also had dreams like him, he said that his dreams were always true . . . when he was still young, he dreamt that he would be Commander of the Army and Head of State and both dreams had come true. . . .

. . . President Amin . . . knows when he will die, and how, and . . . he works only according to God's instruction. He revealed . . . that he has the machines that the Americans were using to spy on the Soviet and Chinese embassies here, adding that President Nixon wanted to bring the Watergate business here. He said that the Americans ran away because they were afraid and embarrassed. He wondered how over 200 million Americans would be scared of him when he has nothing. . . .

And from the same edition:

ANIMAL PAINTING COMPETITION
TO BE ORGANIZED SOON

President Amin has received the Frankfurt Zoological Society West Germany Professor Grzimek who called on him at Parliament Buildings. The President and the professor discussed a number of issues related to the Uganda national parks.

The professor proposed that there should be a painting competition of wild animals in Uganda schools. The winners of which will be awarded different prizes.

The best could even be awarded a free ticket to visit countries like France. Others could be given watches, radios, and various gifts. He said even teachers should be supplied with pictures of all wild animals found in the parks, so that they can find it easy to educate their students. Game rangers who arrest poachers, he added, must be given special gifts. Teachers and their students must visit the parks occasionally, he concluded. He called for preservation of the different animal species found in the Uganda Parks. . . .

An animal-painting competition!
Grzimek had left for his meeting with Amin in a neat seersucker, very much the professor of Giessen I had first seen on the television screen in Frankfurt. At the sidewalk terrace of the Speke Hotel where we waited, he had returned to our table several hours later, now in shirtsleeves, his coat over his shoulder, slightly drawn but his mood unchanged.

"You are not supposed to be here," he said to me, brightening briefly. "We saw John Owen at Parliament House. He is here in Kampala. Journalists are forbidden. He told us so. You may have to go to jail. Yes. I am sure you can tell them you are only a tourist."

The meeting with Amin had been fruitful. There was no time to go into it. The Grzimek family was expected within the hour for a reception at the German Embassy, and they would return to the hotel around nine. Owen was staying at the Grant Hotel. He was waiting to see Amin, too. Grzimek knew how anxious I was to see

180 THE LAST PLACE ON EARTH

him. I would probably find him there now. If so, I might want to bring him back to the hotel later, and the Grzimeks would join us for a nightcap. . . .

The Grzimeks moved on. Boris went inside the lobby to seek directions to the Grant Hotel. I sat at the sidewalk table, more puzzled than ever. If the past five days were to serve as a cautionary example of what possible fate awaited the Serengeti Plain in Julius Nyerere's Tanzania, then our detour through Amin's parks had indeed been instructive. Otherwise we were only witnesses to the exhaustion of a natural resource within a difficult political setting. Perhaps, as Grzimek claimed, conservation policies could be more easily maintained under a dictatorship. But not under this one. Since *The Voice of Uganda* printed only what Amin wanted to hear, the plan of an art competition for schoolchildren was apparently all Grzimek had brought that Amin found useful. In light of Grzimek's greater response to lesser problems (he had been more exercised over the whitewashed ranger huts at Paraa than at Amin's apparent indifference to his Uganda proposals), what seemed astonishing now was his equanimity in the face of the calamity we had all observed over the past week: an attrition of wildlife resources which—if Amin's official reaction to this intractable old man was in any way indicative—could be viewed only as irreversible.

Amin's animals were doomed.

A half-shrug from Grzimek. He would now turn his attention elsewhere. The Uganda safari was over. We would head back for Nairobi tomorrow.

PART THREE

Into Tanzania's Hand

THIRTEEN

Idi Amin Dada of Uganda was a source of acute embarrassment to his neighbor, Dr. Julius Nyerere, the President of Tanzania, and frequently one of considerable anxiety. To Dr. Nyerere, General Amin stood for values that were corruptive and self-destructive in the modern African state. Amin was a military dictator, Nyerere a socialist and philosopher. Amin's military forces (supplied by the Russians) were superior to Nyerere's (supplied by the Chinese). Nyerere had given refuge to the man Amin had overthrown, Milton Obote, and a group of Obote's followers had sought unsuccessfully to unseat Amin by attacking his borders from within Tanzania, just beyond the Serengeti. In turn, Amin had tried to persuade the Israelis to support him in a drive across Tanzania to seize a seaport for himself, and he had added insult to injury by directing crude jibes at Nyerere in the press ("I want to assure you that I love you very much, and if you had been a woman, I would have considered marrying you"). Nyerere had called Amin a murderer. Amin believed in the infallibility of himself, as directed through dreams from heaven; Nyerere believed the future of Tanzania lay in the modification of socialism to African rural traditions. As Amin had added to his power, Nyerere had sought to diminish his. Amin of Uganda held his office through fear; Nyerere of Tanzania, through veneration.

However, there was less marked a distinction between them in the way the two men felt about the preservation of their wild animals. While Amin had declared himself an ardent conservationist, his parks were rotting through neglect, like his unserviced command cars. Julius Nyerere's position toward wild animals was, at best, ambiguous. His greater concern was for the social progress of the people. Shortly after independence, he had said: "From now on we are fighting not man but nature and we are seeking to wrest from nature a better and fuller life for ourselves." Nature posed problems in Tanzania far exceeding those in Uganda. There are fifteen million people in Tanzania, four times the land size of

Uganda. But only ten per cent of the land is arable, and ninety-six per cent of the people live from that ten per cent. (Serengeti and all the acreage surrounding it lie within that ten per cent.) The competition wild animals pose for human existence is more critical in Tanzania than anywhere else in East Africa, holding back the farmers and the increasingly restricted nomadic peoples, like the Masai, on the eastern edge of Serengeti. In fact, Julius Nyerere himself had been raised in one such tribe on the edges of Serengeti where game was looked on as food, and government employees, who even then policed against poaching, as the enemy. Together, these circumstances would weigh more heavily against Nyerere's feeling for the wildlife of Tanzania.

Nevertheless, although Nyerere sought to hold himself aloof from the seemingly irreconcilable conflicts over the borders of his parks, which had grown in frequency throughout the sixties, his actions ultimately spoke louder than his few words on the subject. Since the Serengeti was the last great reserve for Africa's wild herds, the animals there were treated by the government with great deference. Serengeti (indeed, the whole Tanzanian park system) was a model for all of Africa (Grzimek claimed, for the whole world). In times of crisis, when the last desperate appeal had come from Bernhard Grzimek, Nyerere would shift his support from his own Minister of Agriculture, Derek Bryceson, to the side of the parks.

Yet the man himself remained an enigma on the subject. Some expatriates, Grzimek among them, took hope from Nyerere's increasing interest in Serengeti through his own newfound hobby as amateur botanist, and they often cited this as an indication of Nyerere's increasing sensitivity to the need for conservation. Yet no one of them felt with certainty that Nyerere's position was absolutely clear, nor that if it should be today, whether it might not change again tomorrow. There were many pressures on Dr. Nyerere. Moreover, the progress of Nyerere's own philosophy— ujamaa ("familyhood" in Swahili), the concept that the local communities of Tanzania should govern and provide for themselves—inevitably would diminish Nyerere's influence in such matters, whatever his own preferences.

In Tanzania since independence, however, there had been one man in Nyerere's government whose position toward wildlife was resolutely and exuberantly clear, and almost as relentless as Bernhard Grzimek's. This was the former district commissioner in Sudan, the tall, deceptively avuncular, pipe-puffing, high-spirited

186   THE LAST PLACE ON EARTH

expatriate named John Owen, who was now, by coincidence, in Kampala, Uganda.

If today Idi Amin's animal parks offered a case study of how to squander wild-animal resources, John Owen's program for Tanzania formed at the time of independence could as well serve as the school solution of how to save them. "You mustn't credit old colonials like John Owen and me," Grzimek kept reminding himself and others, "it is really the work of the African people," and this was so: the ultimate decisions in Tanzania were Parliament's and Julius Nyerere's. But what John Owen had managed to achieve in ten years acting as the agent of a country desperately poor and torn by conflicting priorities—of the need to feed its people and of the stubborn pride born of independence—was extraordinary.

By the time he took office as director of parks, Owen was well advanced into middle age (older than Grzimek when he had learned with Michael to fly in order to survey Serengeti). From the beginning, the independent government had been favorable to wildlife and had so committed itself in the Arusha Manifesto of 1961:

> The survival of our wildlife is a matter of grave concern to all of us in Africa. These wild creatures amid the wild places they inhabit are not only important as a source of wonder and inspiration but are an integral part of our natural resources and of our future livelihood and well being.
>
> In accepting the trusteeship of our wildlife we solemnly declare that we will do everything in our power to make sure that our children's grandchildren will be able to enjoy this rich and precious inheritance.
>
> The conservation of wildlife and wild places calls for specialist knowledge, trained manpower and money, and we look to other nations to co-operate in this important task—the success or failure of which not only affects the Continent of Africa, but the rest of the world as well.

That was enough for John Owen. He realized that a country just forming would never again have the unchallenged freedom of designating wilderness areas as national parks; that land so contaminated by tsetse and parched from aridity offered little immediate possibility for commercial development; and that funding for park purposes to supplement the impecunious government's resources might well be found outside the country. To this latter end, he set out for Europe and America already in a position to show that the new government had allotted a hundred thousand dollars toward the creation of new parks, even though the money was critically needed elsewhere.

By 1971, when John Owen left the Parks Department, there were seven national parks in Tanzania and two more soon to come. The Tanzanian government had continued to contribute what it could, but most of the money needed to establish these parks had been found in the West by John Owen, who never seemed to rest, adding one new project to the next, from procuring binoculars for schoolchildren visiting Serengeti to a fleet of five airplanes for his various wardens.

At one point around the mid-sixties, when he decided he needed an assistant, the scheme he concocted for finding his man bears special note as typical of his resourceful imagination even though isolated in one of the most remote corners of the world, and as well of the strong feelings with which he viewed his mission. The custom was to advertise such an opening in *The Times* of London or perhaps *The New Statesman,* in one of those classified sections for bizarre jobs in obscure corners of the realm. But for some reason, Owen decided his assistant should be an American, and he set about writing an advertisement which would attract one. In New York City, Owen went to Howard Stein, the President of the Dreyfus Fund, whose commercial symbol is a lion strolling about Wall Street. "The lion's done a lot for you," Owen said. "What have you done for the lion?" Stein agreed to pay the cost of running Owen's ad in *The New York Times,* and when John Oakes, the head of the editorial page, read it, he wrote an editorial directing his readers to the page upon which the ad appeared. This is what the ad said:

THE NATIONAL PARKS OF TANZANIA
WANTED: AN ASSISTANT TO THE DIRECTOR

The Serengeti and other national parks of Tanzania cover an area larger than Belgium. They are the finest wildlife sanctuaries in the world. The fight to save them unimpaired for posterity presents a challenge worth any man's life.

The African leaders in the Tanzanian government wholeheartedly support this effort and have urged me to secure now all areas worthy of park status before it is too late. This concern is matched by international support on an unprecedented scale. No comparable opportunity for conservation exists anywhere else in the world.

I wish to recruit a resolute man prepared to help me grasp this opportunity. He will serve for some years as my assistant, and although previous experience in conservation is not essential, he must have every one of the following qualifications:

Age: about 35–40.

A longing to do something worthwhile with his life.

Proved administrative ability in a business, academic, financial, legal, or governmental career.

A sophisticated, friendly, and mature personality.

A genuinely liberal outlook and in particular the capacity to like and work with African colleagues.

A sensitivity to the aesthetic qualities of the natural environment.

Some independent means which will enable him to give his services for as long as he is needed in Africa on a relatively modest salary.

Ability to fly (or learn to fly) a light airplane.

If married, a like-minded strength-giving and stoical wife.

(*Note:* The education of children presents difficult but not insoluble problems.)

Although I am British, my successor as director, in the foreseeable but still indeterminate future, will certainly be an African. This will provide a continuing and challenging opportunity for service of the greatest value but my assistant must be able by nature to find his fulfillment in the role of a Number Two—never a Number One.

Those who have the above qualifications and who wish to apply for this post should write to me care of Natural History Magazine, Central Park West and 79th Street, New York, N.Y. 10024, enclosing their curriculum vitae. This is not a job for an escapist.

John Owen
Director, Tanzania
National Parks

Owen persuaded the editors of *Natural History* to screen the answers, of which there were some eight hundred, including one from the producer of a television news show that had carried an account of his appeal, and another from an assistant editor of a national magazine, who proved the most likely candidate. "I was forty then," the editor has said since, "and I didn't think I was going anywhere in my job. I knew how to fly, and it seemed an interesting proposal. As it turned out, my wife and I decided against it for family reasons, but do you know, when the man asked me to fly over and see the park system—*at my own expense*—he suggested I see if I couldn't find someone to *donate* to the parks the airplane I came in?"

Before reporting to his new job, having gone to Frankfurt for the advice of Bernhard Grzimek, John Owen had established a relationship that would soon grow stronger through their shared concerns. By the end of the sixties, as the complex interdependent structure of the Tanzania Parks Department had evolved, each had become indispensable to the other, Owen working from the inside and Grzimek raising money and pulling strings on the outside. Owen's admiration today for Grzimek is unqualified: "He is the most important man in the world in selling wildlife to African leaders."

Grzimek's admiration for Owen is returned, although slightly tempered: It was Owen's plan to build the road from Serengeti back into Kenya completing the circuit that drew away from Tanzania the tourists' dollars; and it was Owen's decision to build the service complex in Serengeti that would grow to its present population of twenty-five hundred. Also, whatever credit is due for the present state of the parks should go to the Africans instead of to people like himself and Owen. Nevertheless, Owen was indeed an exceptional man.

So far as the expatriates were concerned, however, while all the defenders of Serengeti were deeply committed men, none would come so close as John Owen to matching the German's own near-metaphysical passion for their joint mission. Myles Turner keeps also among his voluminous files an early memorandum Owen wrote to his expatriate park wardens:

> This may sound pompous, so it probably is. But I think at this time there are certain facts, as I see them, that are worth putting down in black and white.
>
> We in the Tanzania National Parks have the great good

fortune to be working for a cause much greater than ourselves—doing what we can to give the parks the best possible chance of survival and perpetuity.

Very many people all over the world—people whose respect we can value—envy us the privilege of having this task and regard us as dedicated men.

To deserve their respect—and our own—we must always put this cause before our own interest and make a conscious effort to allow nothing to interfere with our ultimate aim.

I know from my own experience that this is a counsel of perfection. But I am sure it is worth keeping ever in mind. And, although crucial times lie ahead, I think we have a good chance of being able to do something of which we shall always be proud.

J. S. Owen
Director

Of all his projects, John Owen's decision to establish a scientific observation center in the midst of the Serengeti Plain was his most inspired. Even before the Grzimeks, there had been some awareness of the need for systematic study of the animals and their habitat. The head of the colonial game department, a man named Swynnerton, had resisted the attempt to convert the country to a beef-stock center for the Commonwealth, a policy which would have seen the elimination of most of the remaining wildlife; and it was Swynnerton also who had transferred Hugh Lamprey from pest control to conservation in the late fifties. Lee and Martha Talbot, American ecologists, were early pioneers in game surveys of the Serengeti. Pearsall, the British botanist, had urged further scientific inquiry, and the departing colonials had helped in the establishment of the Michael Grzimek laboratory. But left to the most ingeniously manipulative outsiders, even the redoubtable Grzimek, it is unlikely such an institution would exist today had not the impulse come from within the new independent government. The boldness and magic belonged to John Owen, the new director of parks.

Owen's first tentative moves in this direction were prompted by a curious fact he could not understand. In 1961, the wildebeest appeared to be overgrazing the grasslands of the Serengeti. Owen felt he ought to find out if this were so, and if it was, what should be done about it. The question quite properly, he felt, should be directed to qualified scientists. In characteristic fashion, starting with the small Michael Grzimek laboratory on hand and soon finding he would need much more, he virtually backed the new government into the establishment of an observatory station. "Owen was miles ahead of anyone else in national parks at this time," Hugh Lamprey would later remark. "He was the only man in the *world* to recognize the need for environmental studies covering the whole scope of the ecosystem. He went for the best people in the field." Through the influence of a sympathetic U.N. official, Owen obtained seed money from F.A.O. to fund the fieldwork of three biologists: the Belgian Jacques Verschuren (the same man Grzimek had sent into the Congo to pay the stranded rangers), the German Hans Klingel, and the Englishman Murray Watson. They would tell Owen what the problem was and how best he should deal with it.

Next, Owen managed to find some prefabricated wood houses discarded by a road construction company, moving these into the Banagi area to serve as living quarters and laboratories. Predictably, one line of research led the scientists backward to the next: the study of animal behavior led to the study of vegetation; vegetation to soil; soil to fire and rain; and so on. More scientists were needed. Grzimek quickly responded to Owen's call for help and together with Niko Tinbergen and Konrad Lorenz raised a substantial sum from the Fritz Thyssen and Max Planck Foundations in Germany. Next, Owen went to work on the Ford Foundation, and soon the Serengeti Research Institute was a going concern with an international staff of zoologists, botanists, veterinarians, parasitologists, geologists and, by 1966, with Hugh Lamprey, the former pest control officer of colonial days, as the administrative chief. Grzimek, Tinbergen, and other distinguished scientists served on the advisory council. In a very short time, a new complex would be established at Seronera with office buildings, laboratories, a library, hangars for the staff aircraft and glider, Land Rovers and trucks, and comfortable housing for the scientists and their families. "Stewart Udall came out once," Owen recalls, "and he was surprised to see we had more resident research scientists in the Serengeti National Park than in all the United States parks."

The function of the Institute was to advise the park on proper management of the wildlife population—essentially the same challenge Molloy had posed to Grzimek in 1957. For example, if the wildebeest were to overgraze the park, what, if anything, should be done about it? In order to answer Owen's early question of whether the wildebeest *were* overgrazing Serengeti—the original occasion for

192   THE LAST PLACE ON EARTH

organizing the effort—the scientists had first to establish the relationship of the wildebeest to their food supply. This, in turn, led to the question: How many wildebeest are there? In 1958, the Grzimeks had counted ninety-nine thousand. In 1963, Lee and Martha Talbot counted two hundred and forty thousand. Shortly thereafter, John Owen persuaded the R.A.F. to fly a Canberra bomber over the park to make aerial photographs that raised the count to two hundred and fifty thousand. By 1969, there would be more than half a million (and by the early seventies, a million). Evidently the wildebeest were not overgrazing the Serengeti, and by the mid-sixties some of the reasons for this would come clear. There had been a severe drought in 1960–61 that had now ended. Moreover, the plague of rinderpest, which had limited the growth of both wild animals and cattle, was arrested in the late fifties by the development of a serum inoculation; and since cattle had previously infected the wildebeest, which was no longer the case, the wildebeest population had grown.

But these reasons were not enough, for the land surrounding Serengeti, which fed cattle, *was* overgrazed, while the same grasses feeding the wildebeest within the park remained thick and healthy. Inexplicably, as the cattle outside the park were starving, the wildebeest inside were flourishing. And all the more perplexing, the restricted grasslands of the wildebeest within the park remained healthy, while those on the vast cattlelands outside the park's buffer zones deteriorated. For its wildebeest, Serengeti was like the sorcerer's apprentice; it was a trick of nature providing bounty to its favored few. What forces set the process of collaboration between the wildebeest and the benevolent land so otherwise forbidding to man's domestic stock? The scientists believed the answer lay in factors controlling the death rate of the herd.

Hugh Lamprey had by now joined the staff, and he tells of the next stage of the adventure:

"The question remained: What regulates the wildebeest population so that it does not overgraze its food supply? What are the mortality factors? The scientists looked first at the most obvious control mechanism, and that was predation—the various animals that feed on the wildebeest herds. The two predator biologists— George Schaller studying lion, and Hans Kruuk studying hyena— covered together practically the whole spectrum simultaneously, leopard, wild dog, and cheetah as well. Both of them came to the same conclusion: predation was an important factor in *selection*—

the predators tended to take the lame, old, sick, the infants and the weak. They probably also had the effect of damping down the oscillations in numbers frequently occurring in animal populations—but they were not the *principal* regulating mechanism. The wildebeest were being regulated by something else, something that effectively held down their numbers to a level at which they were *not* damaging their habitat.

"More zoologists were brought in. A man named Tony Sinclair— Dr. A.R.E. Sinclair, one of the most productive of all our biologists— produced the best answer. It was one we had all been expecting but were unable to demonstrate. The animals are regulated very closely indeed by their food supply."

Despite the apparent abundance of food, and even though the grassland production of the plain is never fully utilized, Lamprey says, starvation strikes the weaker of the animals at certain critical times when the food value of the dried vegetation is low, probably at the height of the dry season. "Undernutrition" is Sinclair's term for it.

"In effect," Lamprey continues, "starvation, combining with the increased susceptibility to disease which accompanies it, regulates the population at a level which is below that at which the wildebeest would destroy their habitat. Previously, there had existed an ecological dogma which held that if a population were regulated by starvation, the animals would reach numbers at which they would destroy their habitat first. In the case of the wildebeest populations of Serengeti, it seemed the other way round." Surprisingly, a limitation of food at times of population crowding apparently does not affect fertility. Lamprey continues:

"Sinclair showed that not only were the populations of ungulates being regulated by their food supplies, but that there was an equilibrium level for each herbivorous species to which it would return if it was disturbed by certain factors, such as a reduction in grass productivity due to an unusually low rainfall. But given a moderately stable climate such as exists in the Serengeti—you don't get the extreme drought conditions that you do on the other side of the rift—the large mammal populations tend to reach this equilibrium level at which they are not damaging their food supply. They are maintained at this level by a rate of mortality which is directly related to the density of the herd itself and balances the recruitment to the adult population."

The fact that the wildebeest were increasing through the sixties,

194   THE LAST PLACE ON EARTH

says Lamprey, is significant only in that this principal regulating mechanism tended to limit their number at levels *below* those at which they would have otherwise damaged their habitat. In other words, the high rainfall through the sixties produced more grass than before, food for more and more animals but never too many animals for the grass that was there. Thus, the size of the wildebeest population was determined at equilibrium by a symmetrical relationship between the wildebeests' birth and death rates, the number of animals being adjusted by the death rate—starvation as a form of control even in a time of abundance!

What had by now become apparent to the scientists of the Research Institute was a matter of even greater importance than the welfare of the wildebeest. They had discovered that the grasslands of Serengeti formed a self-sustaining ecological system, a vast and unique complex of higher mammalian life interacting responsively with its environment. Everything, they found, was interdependent, everything worked—fire, rain, soil, grass, the host of animals. Each living thing depended on the other, each flourished because of the other. Serengeti, with its extraordinary residents—from tiny, nearly blind mole rats to majestic giraffe—was at a stage, still undisturbed, of an evolutionary process that had been going on for hundreds of thousands of years.

"It is a failure of the imagination that science is unable to articulate for the rest of us exactly what a sight like this means," says the American zoologist Archie Carr. "What you're talking about is the state of order created by nature out of disorder. We can manage only the faintest perception of the beauty in this, the skill and natural selection of nature. Man's closest concept of such processes is his own creation of great art." In ways I had scarcely understood when I had first seen it, Serengeti with its ark of animals drifting the grass sea to the cycled rhythms of earth and weather was truly the last such place on earth.

Now the Serengeti Research Institute could tell John Owen and the Parks Department that to sustain Serengeti's wild herds it would be necessary to sustain the Serengeti ecosystem, all of it, since each part depended upon all others. This should be the park's purpose. Purely from a scientific perspective, and with luck, there might still be time as well for a last glimpse into the natural state of animal life in its most complex workings before the degradation of the grasslands through man's presence set in (what Grzimek called "the political problem"). How much time, however, was a serious question.

Outside of Africa it might all seem quite exaggerated and remote but not from within Serengeti where degradation surrounded the ecosystem like a pool of acid, its backwash extending throughout the savannalands which occupy more than a third of the continent. In settlements within sight of the borders were the Wasukuma, the Wakuria, and the Masai, and it was by now known that their population swell matched the nation's and would double within twenty years. (A three per cent increase in population generates a three per cent increase in the demand for food.) Ian Parker claimed that more than a million people—a fifteenth of Tanzania's total population—were hemmed in between Lake Victoria to the west and the northwest boundary of Serengeti to the east, a straight-line distance of only sixty miles. Because of the controls on rinderpest, the tribesmen's cattle herds had similarly increased; and the presence of more people and more land had served all the more quickly to overgraze the grasslands right up to the borders. You could see it flying over: the park began where the desert ended. Because there was still so much left here to lose, Serengeti had come to dramatize the nation's problems, and the continent's.

Africa's grasses are weaker than those in the Northern Hemisphere; cattle herded to the water holes trample them to dust, creating the need for more grass, more land. As the land runs out, people begin to perish—in the Sahel drought during this year of 1974, a hundred and fifty thousand of them. The wasteland grows: from Senegal to northern Ethiopia, a wound line of some thirty-five hundred miles in distance, the Sahara moves southward at rates of up to twenty miles a year. Meanwhile, the fertility of African soil remains an unsolved riddle. During the war, attempts to grow wheat in East Africa failed so disastrously that two shiploads of grain had to be sent down to avert starvation among the tenders of the grain fields; the effort to grow peanuts, for which many animals were slaughtered, lost the British government thirty-six million pounds. Within the immediate past, the overgrazing of the grasslands has become a further perversion of the natural processes of supply and demand, mocking the attempts of America and Europe to provide assistance.

Most Western agronomists still see cattle raising as the most efficient food source for Africa, despite the shocking empirical evidence to the contrary, and the conventional response to African

196   THE LAST PLACE ON EARTH

drought has been to provide money for more bore holes—ever more water to sustain the ever-increasing cattle. Paradoxically, bore holes and cattle—the two major symbols of wealth and security for rural Africans—have become the great scourge of the continent, more responsible than any other factor, save population growth, for the destruction of the African environment. Cattle will return to water long after the grass is gone, even as they go on starving; the damage comes from the impact of their hoofs, and the grass never recovers. It is a vicious circle. Even in the midst of famine, many pastoralists are unwilling to eat their animals or trade them for food. Eventually, the cattle do die from starvation, and so do their herdsmen, a grisly form of control for them both—and an irreversible destruction of the environment.

Further to the paradox, cattle are far less efficient in the productivity of meat on African land than certain species of wild ungulates. Uganda Parks studies have shown that a square kilometer of land yields between twenty-four and thirty-seven tons of wild ungulate meat as against three to five tons for cattle within a square kilometer of the best pastureland in highlands Kenya. As Grzimek had pointed out—it was at the heart of the mysteries of Serengeti—cattle destroy the fragile grasslands of the savanna while wild animals restore it. As man is so painfully discovering throughout his sphere of influence, his reversal of the natural order of things causes troubles beyond his imagination, and this is nowhere more visible today than on the borders of the Serengeti Plain. "If human beings are to remain in tropical Africa," says the Swedish zoologist Kai Curry-Lindahl, "the savannas must be kept in, or restored to, productivity, which on marginal lands—that is, about ninety per cent of the savannas—can only be accomplished with the help of wild hoofed animals."

No one is quite certain how the grasslands of Serengeti came about. "The most obvious explanation lies in the soil," observes Dr. Leslie Brown, former chief agriculturist for Kenya. "The Kapiti Plains, and those of Laikipia, which are typical of much East African grassland, are flat or gently rolling volcanic plateaus. These were first formed by fluid lavas that welled out of many fissures and solidified as a nearly flat sheet of rock. Often the soil overlying these lava flows is very shallow, and where there is little depth of soil, big trees will not normally grow. And if the trees are not large or adapted to fire, it is self-evident that they will not survive the periodic fires that sweep through natural grassland. Shallow soil, or a layer of gravel close to the surface, is thus one of the many causes of grasslands. . . ."

From Pleistocene times, the presence of these shallow grasslands permitted the evolution of the social ungulates, and it is why they are still at Serengeti within the space left them. That so many mammals of such diversity of species could live together in harmony has been explained by several biologists, notably the late Desmond Vesey-Fitzgerald and Richard Bell, through their observations of the varied nourishment provided by the limited plains vegetation. Wildebeest, zebra, hartebeest, and gazelle eat from the same grasses but at different heights of the stalks. Topis coming behind take the dried stubble of the older grass. The impala, oryx, and eland are browsers, nibbling nettles and bushes; so are rhinos, giraffe, and elephants, which move up the vegetation scale from bushes to trees (elephants tend to knock them down as well, further opening the plains to grass). The wildebeest are the hub of this moving wheel. When they roll over the plain following the rain to greener pastures, the effect is as though the grass behind has been evenly mowed, a lawn to the horizon. Certain of the species can make do with very little water, primarily that which they ingest from grasses and bushes. The destruction of the Serengeti grasslands by man's domestic herds of goats and cattle, which require limitless sources of water and hardier grasses than grow here, underlies the present-day assumption of a growing number of authorities that the most sensible use of the land is to keep it clear of cattle and harvest the ungulate population instead. Their belief is that so long as the ungulates adjust their populations to known factors, the harvesting of the herds could be manipulated in such a way as to cause the loss of their number to be offset by a compensatory acceleration of their birthrate. The population of a species, so the theory goes, is a predictable measure which can be adjusted for various purposes: take away a specified number of wildebeest—for food, say—and the wildebeest will put them back for you. These theories, too, of course, are related to the death rate.

But the wildebeest of Serengeti die at random and in a variety of ways, some of them already imposed by man. Poachers take tens of thousands a year—precisely how many is unknown—for their tails are valued as fly whisks. Man sets fires that limit the grass, and there is the persistent political question as to whether cattlemen will or will not use part of the park for wet-season range. But man's intrusion has not yet proved critical to the natural phenomenon, which goes on to the order of its own mysteries. When the rivers are flooded, the wildebeest rush in like lemmings and many are drowned. When a calf is separated from its mother—a mishap occurring in the thousands during migration—it is lost forever, for no other female will accept it. The orphan seeking maternal protection will follow a Land Rover or rush eagerly toward a lion or hyena. At the height of the calving season, when the wildebeest are most vulnerable, they smother their enemies with food. Eighty per cent of the new births occur within three weeks on the open plain. "The predators and scavengers can for once eat to satiation," observes George Schaller. "Hyenas waddle along with their bellies almost touching the ground, lions stand panting, unable to recline comfortably on the monstrous bulge of their abdomen, and vultures flap awkwardly near carcasses, too full of offal to ride the currents into the air."

It is a natural process which defies generalization. In good weather, the predators alone are unequal to the task of reducing significantly the size of the herd. After the food supply, disease is apparently the secondary limiting factor. When the rate of predation goes down, the amount of disease goes up. All of it is made even more complex, according to Schaller, "by the fact that the animals may [the *may* here is an important qualification] compensate for their losses by increasing the birth rate." However, during the drought of 1961 when a full calf crop was lost, Leslie Brown reports, the subsequent rains bringing forth bountiful grasses did not see the calving rhythms of the wildebeest restored for several seasons. How, then, to predict the process with any degree of accuracy?

Still, whatever the arguments forming for or against cropping the herds, the most haunting observation of the life and death of the wildebeest was Lamprey's: the death rate of the wildebeest was almost precisely offset by its birthrate. Whatever the interaction of the elements—of fire, rainfall, and the soil; whatever the number of hysterical animals to drown in the flooded streams; the lame, young, and old to fall to lion and hyena; the diseased and the weak to starve—however seemingly random these varieties of death, reaching even into the hundreds of thousands, the wonder was that the herds of Serengeti wildebeest would always return to a state of equilibrium safely within the carrying capacity of the grassland plains.

But what would happen if man should try to intrude systematically upon this process, his presence as harvester reaching a critical level—no matter how benign or compelling his reasons? Even with the extraordinary perceptions unfolding among the scientists at the Serengeti Research Institute, could the adjustment mechanisms of the wildebeest herds be safely caused to yield to a measurable formula? Biologically, the herd may not "know" it is being cropped. How subtle is the balance of reproduction, mortality, and environmental constraints? Could a miscalculation cause an increase of the wildebeest population above the carrying capacity of its habitat, inevitably a destruction of habitat (and not only for the wildebeest but other species as well)? Conversely, could a miscalculation cause a steady, uncompensated loss of population? The decline of the wildebeest?

Such were the troublesome concerns beginning to emerge from the studies at the Serengeti Research Institute that would preoccupy Bernhard Grzimek and John Owen and eventually align them against the "pragmatists," like Ian Parker and now many others, in the growing dispute over the ultimate wisdom of cropping wild animals—whether to make them pay for the grasslands they held to preserve the habitat, or for the more profound need of supporting a hungry continent. Such questions remain unanswered today although their implications move far beyond the secrets of the wildebeest of the Serengeti to the mystery of life itself.

FOURTEEN

John Owen had been in Kampala before we got there; he, too, was waiting to see General Amin. Grzimek's sudden appearance in Uganda and last-minute stop in Kampala had preempted Owen's place in line, which meant he would have to stay on a day or so following our departure tomorrow. Owen now was a representative of the International Union for the Conservation of Nature, which meant he was lobbying with African leaders on rather a more discrete level than Grzimek. Like Grzimek, he had proposals for Amin's parks both high-flown and modest, and, like Grzimek, he was prepared to settle for what he could get. But his funding sources were constricted. He hoped to offer diplomatic or self-help solutions to problems affecting wildlife. While Grzimek preferred Amin to improve the parks he had rather than add new ones, Owen wanted to see one established along the northern border across from a park in the Sudan so that the animals on both sides would be protected by buffer zones (as Masai Mara extends the Serengeti ecosystem into Kenya). But in Owen's other pocket was a makeshift solution to the poaching problem and the parks' declining inventory of working vehicles. For antipoaching patrols, John Owen, who had once arranged a visit to Yellowstone National Park for Tanzania's entire park board of trustees (to see, among other things, what not to do), was prepared to suggest Uganda's rangers be issued bicycles.

Back in Nairobi, no one had been exactly sure where Owen was these days or what he had been up to as he had virtually dropped from sight after leaving Tanzania. That was two years ago. Since then, he had worked for a time as a fellow at the Smithsonian in Washington; had received an honorary degree from Oxford (Grzimek had helped arrange for this), where he had studied chemistry as an undergraduate; had tried to write a book about the parks system and apparently blocked on it; and occasionally, some said, had succumbed to melancholy over his self-imposed severance from the parks of Tanzania. It was definitely a severance self-imposed—all the expatriates, even Derek Bryceson, would agree on that. Owen had been offered a five-year extension to his contract, but believing the time had come for the Tanzanians to manage their own property and affairs, he had simply resigned—had Africanized himself. From what others had said of him, the gesture seemed at the time very much a part of the man.

Now by coincidence he was in Kampala, and so far as I was concerned, not a minute too soon. Grzimek's conclusions, which brooked no interruptions and allowed for few details, were not advancing my understanding of the factual circumstances of Serengeti. There had been enough from others in Nairobi and by the contrasting example of Uganda's parks to point the issues—the political issue of border integrity and the scientific issue of cropping. But for an outsider, still murky going. Owen, however, so far as I had been able to piece it together, stood at the intersection of both these issues as a result of two episodes occurring between the summers of 1967 and 1968, which at the time had seemed unrelated, both issues centering on the Lamai Wedge, in the northwestern corner of Serengeti.

The political issue was this: By 1967, the pressure of people about the Serengeti borders had become more intense than ever. Farm settlements were coming into the Maswa area to the southwest and along the Grumeti River parallel to the western corridor. But to the northwest of the park, along the two-hundred-square-mile salient known as the Lamai Wedge, matters were clearly out of hand. Some twenty-seven families of the Wakuria tribe had moved into this isolated triangle and were grazing their cattle directly within the path of the wildebeest migration. Poaching was rampant. The fragile Serengeti ecosystem was directly affected by their presence. John Owen had complained through channels and the government had swiftly responded. Within the next few months the park's borders were extended in the west to include the Grumeti, and to the south much of the Maswa was declared a game reserve, a bona fide buffer zone. And the Wakuria were moved out of the Lamai Wedge—the episode Grzimek had so strongly commended to Omar at Kabalega. (But later, I'd also heard, the Wakuria had moved back in.)

In 1967, the map looked as shown on the facing page.

The scientific issue: In 1968, Derek Bryceson, the Minister of Agriculture, had let a contract to Ian Parker's Wildlife Service Limited to crop plains game in the Loliondo range immediately to

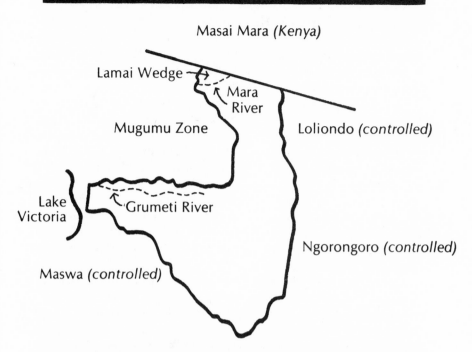

Masai Mara (Kenya)

Lamai Wedge

Mara River

Mugumu Zone

Loliondo (controlled)

Lake Victoria

Grumeti River

Ngorongoro (controlled)

Maswa (controlled)

the northeast of Serengeti and within the unprotected path of the wildebeest migration during the dry season. While the cropping would not take place within park borders, it would nevertheless draw from Serengeti's herds. Owen refused to allow Parker to move the meat across the park to the west. Parker blamed the government. "They didn't keep to their word," Ian Parker says now. "And so we moved out. The project aborted." (But now, I had heard, S.R.I. was studying the feasibility of cropping wildebeest.)

Thus, if there could be said to be a beginning point to the present problems of Serengeti—or rather more accurately, a resumption of the various pressures that have threatened the animals there since long before the Grzimeks arrived, anticipating the present cruel circumstances in Uganda's parks—these two separate challenges, each successfully for the moment repelled by John Owen, framed the dialogue that continues there now. John Owen ought to be very helpful.

Boris and I had tea with John Owen and talked on through the evening. He was an amiable man but reticent, muted, hardly what one had been prepared for. He seemed reluctant to acknowledge his contributions to Serengeti, although what he did say began by indirection to shape the difficult circumstances of the present. What he most enjoyed discussing were the strategies of his fund-foraging expeditions to the West:

". . . It's as much work to get a check for twenty-five hundred as twenty-five thousand dollars, so you might as well go for the larger amount. . . .

". . . When you go after money, you have to have a gimmick. You can't come with a hungry look in your eye. I used to have a new one every year. . . .

". . . I went to Texas looking for help, and I thought the most influential person I should see would be Lady Bird Johnson. But some wealthy people there told me I was wrong. I should look up two sisters, and their names turned out to be—Ima Hogg and Ura Hogg! Can you imagine that? . . ."

Owen confirmed the few references I'd heard to the Lamai Wedge—and Grzimek's cryptic remark to Omar. After Owen had complained about the presence of the Wakuria, Nyerere's quick response by moving them out had established an important precedent. But Owen had left Tanzania in 1972, and a year later the Wakuria had apparently moved back in, testing the precedent. He was not certain of what had followed. He thought the Wakuria had moved out again but he didn't know for sure. He had flown over recently and had seen some cattle grazing within the Lamai Wedge, but that was all. In any case, he didn't think the grasslands could support cattle. The grass was too fragile, and the water was alkaline. Owen was emphatically clear about the growing controversy of cropping as against Nature's Way, however, and somewhat more detailed now than Grzimek had been.

"I started out believing there was something to this cropping business, but I don't now and I'll tell you why. Animals live by cycles which we do not yet fully understand. Left to themselves, they will take care of their needs, even overpopulation. They don't need us to help them. Beyond that, cropping to be effective means eventually killing in large numbers—a quarter of a million animals, for example, in the Serengeti. There is no way a new African country could manage this neatly, effectively or humanely. Selling off all that meat invites corruption. And what are they to tell their own people after insisting the national park is to *preserve* animals? Conservation is a mystique. With such practices, you would destroy it in a second. Also, you know, it is rather nice to have someplace left on earth where man is not dominant.''

With Grzimek and Owen on one side—the Nature's Way faction—the dispute with Parker and his allies on the other had narrowed to the question of managing natural processes within a specified environment, whether Serengeti or anywhere else. Owen and Grzimek insisted nature at Serengeti was still capable of managing itself. Ian Parker argued that nowhere was this any longer so, and he would often cite the elephants as the most visible example of a destructive natural force that, unmanaged by man, would destroy not only crops and villages but the parklands as well, Serengeti included. It had been a telling point, for the presence of elephant had forced the question inside Serengeti in 1968—at virtually the same time Owen was protesting Parker's negotiations with Bryceson to crop in the northeast. It was a question, in fact, which had even set the wardens of Serengeti against the scientists of the Serengeti Research Institute. Elephants had been absent from Serengeti for at least forty years prior to 1955 but then had entered from both the north and the south, some two thousand of them, damaging the woodlands and even coming onto the plains to knock down acacias, of which there were all too few. The wardens wanted to shoot them—management in the crudest terms. The scientists wanted them left alone. "When I would come down from Arusha," Owen says, "the wardens would take me around and show me the trampled acacias. Next day, the scientists would take me out and show me the new acacia shoots blooming in another part of the park. Acacia seeds are carried and fertilized by elephant dung.''

I remembered what Gordon Harvey had said about George Schaller and the lion cubs: "He sat in his Land Rover and watched them starve to death! Can you believe it? All he had to do was throw them meat. He said they shouldn't be interfered with, and Owen backed him up.''

"But the larger point is," Owen was saying now, "by shooting the game you magnify the problem. Once you start it you must carry on. Otherwise the dynamics of reproduction are such that the production rate is increased to compensate for their diminution. If you can continue, you can hold it, but once you stop, you get an overshoot. This is what is happening right now with the hippo in Ruwenzori. By shooting, you lose the chance to see what will happen in the cycles—which is what S.R.I. is all about.

"We just don't know enough about the animals or their habitat.

In my first year, we had an international conference of ecologists gather at Ngorongoro—Peter Scott, Sir Julian Huxley, top people from all over the world. It happened to coincide with the drought of nineteen sixty to nineteen sixty-one. I remember they all went down into the crater and they all agreed the area was badly overgrazed. The animals should be cropped to save it, they said. Before the dust from the Land Rovers had settled, there was a downpour and the floor of the crater was suddenly covered everywhere with clover. I was astonished at the rejuvenation resources of the African soil, and so were they."

It was nearing nine now, and as we walked together to the Speke Hotel, Owen wandered back to his favorite theme:

"Once I read about a painting that sold at Sotheby's for six hundred thousand dollars. It was about the size of a playing card, a version of Saint George and the dragon, believed to be by Hubert van Eyck. I got an idea. I arranged to have reproductions made of the painting, same size. . . ."

The lobby of the Speke was cavernous and dank, pools of shadows separated by weak table lights: Arabic—a setting hard to relax in. So were the streets of Kampala with their mixture of influences: Catholic, Muslim, tourist/modern, the vestiges of colonialism and savagery (the paper today reported the conviction of a man for forcing another to eat his own severed ear). Crossing the street yesterday evening, Boris and I had nearly been run down by a car swerving purposely out of its path directly toward us. Earlier this afternoon, while Grzimek was seeing Amin, Boris, Erika, Christian and I had gone to the palace of the Baganda kings, carefully preserved, an incredible structure of thatched straw three stories high. In this setting, during his search for the source of the Nile, John Speke was received by Mutesa, the King, who had, upon assuming the throne, burned alive sixty of his brothers. Mutesa had sat facing Speke for an hour before acknowledging his presence. An unhappy country. It was in Uganda somewhere to the north that the present-day tribe called the Ik had been moved to make room for a national park—Kidepo, I now assumed. Traditional hunters, they had been moved like the Wakuria to another part of the country and had been forced to seek subsistence by foraging after berries and roots. The anthropologist Colin Turnbull had then lived among them to report on the social disintegration of a primitive people as they systematically starved. At the museum, because I knew nothing of this strange country, I took down an inscription just inside the

THE LAST PLACE ON EARTH

entrance: *"Defined by no natural or traditional boundaries, Uganda which evolved during the years which followed [followed what?] and which was constituted the Uganda protectorate by the Uganda Order in Council 1402 constantly expanded and contracted its limits in accordance with political expediency. At varying times its claims expanded from Ruwenzori to Ethiopia, Ethiopia to Naivasha, and from Lake Kibut to the Sobat River. These boundary adjustments were influenced by the colonial powers."*

". . . and I sent these reproductions," Owen was saying, "exactly the same size as the original—really no larger than a playing card—to selected donors, pointing out that the price of a square inch of this card could buy two hundred and fifty square miles to add to the Serengeti. I wrote a note saying, 'If you want to sustain culture, why don't you come on over and have yourself some fun by seeing what you can do here?' "

It was close to ten when the Grzimeks arrived.

Owen's presence refreshed Grzimek, bringing the first pro-nounced change in his mood since we had left Nairobi. With exuberance—the same high-spirited enthusiasm that had attended our first meeting—he told Owen what he had said to Nyerere when he first met him sixteen years ago; how he had bet Kenneth Kaunda, the President of Zambia, a bottle of champagne that Zambia's schoolbooks probably had pictures of blond, blue-eyed children but no pictures of elephants or giraffe, and had won; and that he would have sat down with Hitler or Stalin, whoever had won the war, to advance the cause of animals—very little, it was certain, that Owen hadn't heard many times before. The Englishman listened with unforced enthusiasm, however, puffing his pipe and chuckling appropriately at the rare intervals.

"In Italy," Grzimek said, "millions of birds were being shot by the hunters. So I went to the E.E.C. and told them the shooting of the birds would affect all of Europe. They don't belong to Italy alone—the migration brought them there—they belong to Europe. I told them the scarcity of these birds would allow an increase in the insect population, and this would then necessitate an increased dependence on those damn insecticides. It happened with the Chinese. They killed all the sparrows because they were eating the rice, and then they had an insect explosion.

"So I had five thousand members of the Frankfurt Zoological Society write the officials in Brussels responsible for such decisions. Then they came back to me offering sixty thousand marks for a study to be made by ornithologists and biologists so evidence could be presented to the Italian government. They wanted me to be responsible for the scientific program, so I had posters put up in Rome. 'When you shoot the birds, you poison your children.' But you know, it is a problem how Germans are shown in such matters. The Italian papers write how Germans love animals: 'They never eat a singing bird, anything larger they put in zoos.' They tell about Germans guarding a concentration camp and a dying Jew reaching for a bird's nest to eat the little ones, and the German guard shoots him. And so on.''

Owen nodded sympathetically.

"The rhinos are being poached out because the Asians think the rhino's horn makes a powder which is an aphrodisiac, which is not true, of course. To counter the myth, I would tell them it causes cancer." Grzimek laughed and Owen chuckled.

Owen asked Grzimek what had happened in his meeting this afternoon with Amin.

"I offered a prize of a trip to Frankfurt for the schoolchild and his parents who draw the best picture of a wild animal in Uganda. I told him I would provide a mobile film unit to travel local schools and show nature films. He became excited about this. He said the films should be shown in the fishing villages inside Ruwenzori. 'Why?' I said. 'That would be futile. The people there must live as they can. It is the children unaffected by the park who will make the difference.' I told him the army was coming into the parks and taking away their vehicles. Amin said this would happen whenever there is a revolution, naturally, and when they returned them the soldiers naturally would replace them with bad vehicles. I told him I would provide vehicles for the parks, ammunition, and radio communication. Amin said he would do this, too. Amin said he was unhappy that the Nairobi press had made no mention of his ban on hunting. I see this ban of his as an indication he has been thinking about the problem since I was last here. I told him that when I came into the country I was searched at the border three times. Amin said the reason was the competition with Nairobi. He said people should fly into Uganda. I told him I had heard of people being searched when they flew in, too. I asked him about his move to degazette the reserve at Kabalega Falls. I told him this would be the first African country since independence to do this. He listened but he said nothing.''

"Well," Owen said, "do you think you accomplished much?''

THE LAST PLACE ON EARTH

"Oh yes," Grzimek said. "I am happiest that he agreed to the art contest. It will force all the teachers, even the missionaries, to spend an hour on wildlife."

We left the Grzimeks in the highlands of Kenya. In the uncertain role of emissary, Boris had said to me, "They've held a family council and they have decided to spend one day more here in Molo so you can finish your interviews." Yesterday we had crossed the border in daylight and without incident. (A soldier had walked me aside and said in English, "I think you should give me one of your jerry cans." I said that I couldn't, it wasn't mine, and he let it go at that. We were searched again and waved on, a peaceful aftermath to our night crossing a week ago.) In the late afternoon, still some two hundred miles from Nairobi, we had broken the trip here at the Highlands Hotel, an old colonial club with polo field, golf course, hunting grounds, and croquet court, all now going to seed, a Kenyan version of the Mountains of the Moon Hotel but more cheering perhaps because of the surrounding countryside— fertile pasturelands which the British so much preferred, like the hills of Wales. And, too, we are out of Uganda, out of the tropic heat and back on the eastern side of the rift, eight thousand feet high. Day after tomorrow we would go on to Nairobi, stopping off briefly perhaps to see the Alan Roots in Naivasha, if they were there, and then Grzimek would meet his sister coming down from Germany to drive her through Serengeti. Boris had to get ready for Zambia, and I would begin my search for the key expatriates of Serengeti—the more certain way, I was now sure, to deal with the fate of the Serengeti Plain. While another day here would be welcome (but not quite so desirable as going with him into Serengeti), a further extension of our strained safari seemed unlikely—Grzimek was about talked out. And so we meet now around four in the empty dining room of the inn for our last session. Erika and Christian are sitting in, a vaguely repressive presence, and I expect them to snicker like Katzenjammer Kids when the old man repeats himself, as he most certainly will do, and Boris is here, too, still weighing judgment. Away from the fireplace in our quiet corner, it is chilly; and Grzimek, quite visibly tired again, is polite and careful in his answers—both of us expect this to be a summation—but tired.

"Yes. The Lamai Wedge . . . ayah," he begins. "You see, that decision was made due to the unbelievable reaction of Julius Nyerere. I told him about the increase of illegal immigrants coming from Kenya into the Lamai Wedge. I told him it is poor country. 'People come there only for poaching. Can't you stop this?' To my great astonishment, Nyerere answered me, 'No. We will move the people.'

"And I was *astonished,* because if I would have dared to propose in colonial times to move a human village in favor of game, the administration would have replied, 'You're *crazy!'* My answer to Nyerere was 'I really can't believe it.'

"He said, 'Of course it is a political matter, we have to give them a school and a new place to settle, maybe a little hospital or something.'

"And I answered him, 'I don't have the money, Mr. President, but I promise you I raise this money because that is a model for all of Africa, that a new independent government dares to move human population in favor of nature.' We raised about fifty thousand pounds."

We had scarcely begun, and he was hovering dangerously close to his standard rhetoric, as though he were dealing with me for the first time. "But hadn't the Wakuria moved back in?" I asked. It was *his* Serengeti. Border incursions moved directly to the point of Serengeti's present problems. I found myself in the awkward position of trying to help him update his own position.

"Yes, it came a little bit later, after John Owen had left. It happened as it has happened several times since in Tanzania—an area commissioner in a meeting told this tribe, 'I give you the permission to go back into this corner of the Serengeti which was added only five years before. I allow you to go in grazing,' and they immediately built huts. And so on. And then nobody at Parks dared protest. It was a political decision. And somebody informed me.

"The day before I left for Frankfurt, I called this chap—he was a newspaperman in Nairobi—and I told him, 'Please put it in the paper because nobody knows what the area commissioner has done.' I was leaving Sunday and I spent all Saturday afternoon calling people to come meet with me. I told them, 'It's an important political meeting. We must do something because no chief park warden, nobody in the parks, can dare to go against politicians.' The paper sent somebody to investigate from Nairobi, and then they published a story about it. And then Nyerere decided again the people had to retreat. And immediately after the decision of the central government, the warden went in and destroyed all the huts."

Only two nights before in Kampala, John Owen had said cattle were still grazing the Wedge, and if this was so, the issue was certainly beyond the resolution Grzimek seemed to want me now to accept. Erika and Christian were seated on either side of him, all three of them watching me, measuring me now, I was certain—but against what defense? His manner was a warning, but there seemed nothing to be gained by fencing with him.

"What do you think will come of the Serengeti?"

"You never know. It is a political matter. If you find uranium there one day, then it will be gone. It is why I always say you should shoot every mining prospector doing research in soil in a national park. If they find gold or diamonds or uranium, it will be lost." He worked at a smile. Whatever his reason, Grzimek was shutting down on me.

"Should the boundaries be extended?"—foolish prompting from me, getting desperate, like asking if he believed the government should stop drilling bore holes. . . .

"The area between Lamai and the lake should be added. And the Maswa game reserve, too. The Maswa settlement is coming in and it may be impossible to drive them out." He marked his boundary lines on the map:

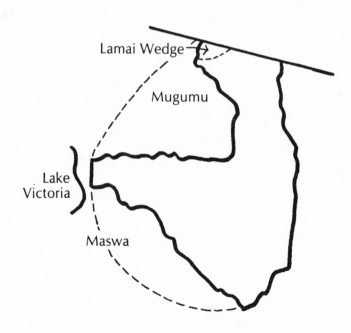

It was the same solution he and Michael had recommended to the British in 1959, except in one contradictory respect: Grzimek, too, now excluded Ngorongoro, the partitioning of which had caused the two of them to fly down to the rescue fifteen years ago. Why?

"I exclude it now because of its totally different approach," he said. "Ngorongoro is the last stronghold of the Masai. To enforce park restrictions you would have to move them out. I never was in favor of that. They are human beings and they live mostly now in dry desert country, and in dry years they will starve if they can't go up into those mountains. Their cows would die. And so on. Their presence is limited. If you keep strong measures against agriculture, it will be all right. Bryceson as Minister of Agriculture decided they should move in. As director of national parks, he helped to decide they should move out."

In our first long evening together, my few questions had been random, directionless; but it hadn't mattered for they had been unnecessary to the flow of his monologue. He had wanted very much to talk then, but—and this was the principal difference now, I realized—only so long as he directed the course of his remarks. He was, of course, a television personality, and experience had taught him that the subject of an interview has more control over its direction than the interrogator. Waiting now through the awkward silence, we both understood he would sit here politely (he had agreed to the session) as long as necessary before he would say what he had no intention of saying. I wondered now why he had troubled himself to stay over in Molo. Was he awaiting some question I hadn't thought to ask? Was he himself or his program in some jeopardy I had failed to perceive? The brave, dispirited picture of John Owen, the leader of the lost patrol, suddenly occurred to me.

"Can the Tanzanians be expected to manage now without men like Owen, Hugh Lamprey, Myles Turner—even yourself—to help them?"

He sighed and started all over again.

"That is mainly a political and ethical question. I told you about the colonial development of wildlife resources in these countries of Africa, of my fear that the animals would be doomed in the new independent states because of the prejudices against nature. That's the main reason I did propaganda all over the world against big-game hunting, not because of game the hunters shoot but because of the psychological reaction of the local people.

THE LAST PLACE ON EARTH

"And I promised these new leaders that game would be a big source of income from tourism. I told them that urban people were very fond of wildlife and wilderness, that it was not like that two hundred years ago in Europe and the United States because the population was mostly farmers. . . ."

Back to the program: how he had come to realize the false image of Africa held by tourists; how he had worked against these impressions with his television show; how he had formed the first package tours by tricking the airlines and tourist agencies. . . .

"Have I told you these stories?"

"Yes."

"You must tell me if I have told them before," he said, genuinely embarrassed.

"And then I told you," he said, more to remind me, apparently, than to tell me again, "that I think we conservationists have achieved more for the human population of these countries than international aid from outside. . . ." The income from tourism enabled them to build hospitals and schools. But now it was the pride of the people which was important, not what the colonials had done, the men like Owen and Turner—even himself. African people had done more. He enumerated his examples—the same examples cited in his first letter to me, three years ago. "All this requires a certain courage for politicians because in Africa, too, people can vote in the next election—but *elephants* can't vote, and *lions* can't vote!

"It is very different from the attitude in the rest of the world!" Although the tone of his voice had not altered appreciably, had become even softer and less distinct, he began to speak now with urgency. He was no longer talking to me, or to Boris, or to his family. It was as though he were talking aloud, sorrowfully, to himself.

"The U.N., for example, it is hopeless! Until recent times, they didn't care for ecology or the preservation of nature. They left it mostly to associations raising private funds. If you consider the past twenty years and you think of what has happened to the ecology and the economy of mankind by not going into the conservation of nature—what money, what possibilities of survival have been lost!— you may realize what a mistake that they have created F.A.O. and built an agricultural organization with *millions* of dollars and didn't make a similar unit from the beginning for the conservation of nature. All this must now be done by the I.U.C.N., which is mostly supported by private money. But it is now a matter which has become survival for this planet, for *mankind!* It is really *unbelievable* that this should depend upon private fundings. It should be one of the *first* responsibilities of the United Nations."

"But Serengeti," I insisted now, trying to bring him back. "Everyone seems to agree that the game must somehow pay its way, whatever help may or may not come from outside agencies. You have said you are against cropping. Tanzania distrusts tourism, and Tanzania has no money. How do you expect Serengeti, or any of the other parks, to survive such circumstances?"

"The problem of tourism is mainly a nationalistic competition between African countries, which I have explained to you," he said, softly still. "Even in Tanzania they have *increased* the budget for parks, and even with the main politicians who say, 'We do not want these damn Europeans,' and things like that, even these politicians say, '*But we want to have our national parks. They are important.*' In Tanzania, the main reason the most recent national park was gazetted was because the people didn't like to see European or American hunters shooting *their* game in *their* country. They even agreed to move six villages out of this district and sacrifice their district to a park, and to build a new bridge to this national park. But that shows again tourism is not the reason for their policy, but even if it is, why shouldn't it be?"

"But the Serengeti Plain, Dr. Grzimek—you say that the ultimate survival of African wildlife will come down to this one place. Do you honestly believe the animals can survive there indefinitely?"

"Yes. Our main aim must be to put European and white pride aside and tell what Africans are doing in conservation, and help to make the people proud of it. You see, that was what I stressed in Uganda—to make youth hostels in the parks, make school competitions, bring cinema units into the local villages to the local populations which have never *seen* an elephant, never *seen* a lion in Africa, because these animals exist in only the most remote districts—to make them aware and *proud* of it. It is my experience that if you achieve that, then they *have* to defend it.

"If it becomes the common conscience of all mankind that these herds are so valuable as the common *property* of mankind—the pride of mankind—and are held for research in ecology, which is becoming more and more important for all mankind, and if we make Africans proud of this property because they are leading in the conservation of it, I don't see a big danger for them. Because if

THE LAST PLACE ON EARTH

you raise such a lot of money to preserve ancient symbols, to dig up antiquities, as they have in Athens with the Acropolis, which is now sacred to all peoples, then there will never be a scarcity of such things in this world. But if the elephants are gone or the tigers, which are close to extinction, then they are *gone* and we will never discover them again on another planet. They belong to our planet and the planet belongs to the animals, too. *They* are part of nature and *we* are part of nature. We must realize we are animals, too. We eat the same food and breathe the same air and live from the same soil. Every species dying out is an indicator to the death of mankind."

We had moved into a lounge off the dining room and were seated about the open hearth. The fire had died away, and the room had grown cold. It was over. We sat in silence for a while, and then for some reason Boris began to talk about the gold mines of South Africa, what it was like to work in them; the relationship of management to the black laborers; the Zulu tribes, their language. Interesting but irrelevant to our discussion, yet apparently of some future use to Grzimek. For the first time since I had met him, Grzimek listened carefully.

Perhaps it is appropriate at this point now for Bernhard Grzimek (in the pew for once instead of the pulpit) to return within this account to his place in the distance beyond my experience when I first had heard of him in Africa five years ago—to the more suitable role of a presence, really, rather than that of an exotic personality. In these eight days he had turned around again on me. What I had seen, what little I had heard, had caused my own views to fall victim. His program *was* in fact more compelling than his exotic personality, although in marked ways as obscured—and almost as though deliberately—as was his own inner reckoning. Perhaps it was not that he distrusted connectives so much as he did the use that might be made of them by others. Whatever the case—whether from convenience, apprehension, oversight or impatience—the fact was, Grzimek left out too much. The interstitial stuff would have to come from the others, as Boris had said: Turner, who was on the ground of Serengeti for eighteen years; Parker, who would speak for cropping; Lamprey, for the scientific community; Bryceson, for Tanzania (and the legal status now of Lamai). What was left was the passion. "I am like a missionary," he had said. "I tell the same story over and over." But now it was over with Grzimek. I was sure he had told me all he was going to (all he would have told Omar, Nguana, Owen, Amin—anyone else). The man *was* a conclusion—more, an imperative—and he carried himself forward to the heathen wherever he found them, like a Bible-belt Fundamentalist thumping out the last terms for salvation. Near the end of *Serengeti Shall Not Die,* he had written:

> Millions feared Hitler and millions were enthralled by him. Millions laid down their lives for him and other millions died fighting against him. Today when German school children are asked questions about Hitler most of them know very little about him and cannot even name his henchmen. . . . Men are easily inspired by human ideas, but they forget them just as quickly. Only nature is eternal, unless we senselessly destroy it. In fifty years time nobody will be interested in the results of the conferences which fill today's headlines.
>
> But when fifty years from now a lion walks into the red dawn and roars resoundingly, it will mean something to people and quicken their hearts whether they are bolsheviks or democrats, or whether they speak English, German, Russian or Swahili. They will stand in quiet awe as, for the first time in their lives, they watch twenty thousand zebras wander across the endless plains.

It was the same impulse leading him today, fourteen years later. Whatever his future actions might be, they would grow out of the privacy of his own counsel and be carried out through methods he alone would see as the most appropriate. Bystanders were welcome so long as they stood clear. But the impulse as stated so many years earlier—the principal beginning connective for me with the Bernhard Grzimek of another age—was unchanged. Through two days on either side of this moment, beginning with the peaceful crossing of the border yesterday to the interlude here at Molo and on through tomorrow noon when we would part company at Alan Root's house, Grzimek would commence to recede gradually into the somehow more believable perspective of local apocrypha where his omissions and contradictions didn't so much matter. Grzimek was more believable as a force out here, anyway, than in person. A *zeitgeist.* In my few remaining days in Africa, the conviction would grow; I would find him in absentia never very far from the subsequent events to affect modern Serengeti in the accounts I was

to hear from others, and always—precariously, superbly skillfully—
pivotal to their outcome. But fading now. Driving his aging sister
with Erika and Christian in their minibus through Serengeti (the
extended silence!), flying with his old enemy and new ally, Derek
Bryceson, into Rubondo to lobby for a new park.

And so on.

Grzimek was slipping back into place, an irrepressible reminder
(whatever his programmatic protests to the contrary) of the
lingering expatriate impulse to consign Serengeti safely into the
custody of its own people.

FIFTEEN

"Let's look a bit closer at the Lamai Wedge," said Myles Turner, turning to the map:

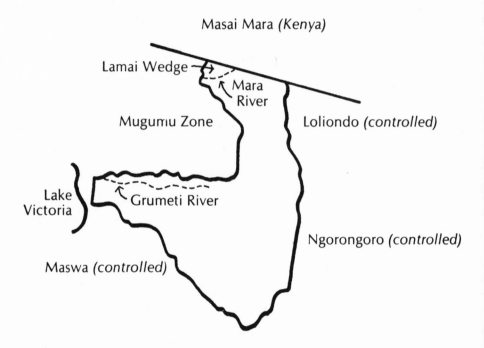

"To understand the Lamai episode, you have to know something about the Wakuria tribe settled about it. It's one of the most difficult tribes in Tanzania. You know, don't you, that the army mutinied in this country just after independence and *damn* nearly took the country over? The British happened to have an aircraft carrier offshore. The Royal Air Force was up in Kenya at the time and they sent a few planes down, and the marines came in, fired one bazooka through the army barracks, and that did it. Saved Tanzania. *Anyhow* . . .

"The people who *started* this mutiny down there in Dar es Salaam were the Wakuria battalion. Now, they're people from northwestwards of the Serengeti, from north of the Mara River, which is the long side of the triangular wedge. They're fierce chaps. You get a good one and they make wonderful rangers. But by God, you know, they're a tough, *tough* tribe. . . ."

Heading east from George Dove's camp in Serengeti, past Mary Leakey's digs and about four hours more along the dirt road leading up and over the crater, you go through Arusha and then up the steep climb of Mount Meru to find the former Serengeti warden Myles Turner. An essential witness. "It is impossible not to become emotionally involved with the Serengeti," Hugh Lamprey would later remark, "and many of us would gladly have dedicated our lives' work to it. Myles Turner came near to doing that." It is a long way now from Amin's Kampala and our evening with Turner's and Lamprey's old boss and beloved friend, John Owen—some four hundred miles to the northwest—but it is a dimensional distance as well. Turner and his wife live on the outer crescent of mountains rimming the Serengeti, in the Arusha park warden's quarters, a house dating back to 1906, a year before Fritz Jaeger walked off the boundaries of the Serengeti for the first time. "It was built by a German family named Trappe," Turner says, "and they were a pretty tough bunch. They lived in this smoky old house with three Alsatian dogs. The old woman was the leader of the family, the only woman in East Africa ever to be a professional hunter."

The portico of the Turner house is recessed, and it looks out on what surely must be one of the most stunning views in the country. At the far edge of the lawn are loitering buffalo, and beyond, for the yard abruptly slides away down the side of the mountain, is the southwestern face of Mount Kilimanjaro rising into the clouds. Unlike Serengeti, the park of Mount Meru is a miniature, only the very peak of the mountain reserved for the dwindling animals there, rising farmlands forming the floodline that has left them stranded on their small, snow-capped island.

Myles Turner now is like a combat officer transferred behind the lines while the battle rages on without him. Facing out on Kilimanjaro turned orange-granite in the late sun, his old Trappe house reinforces the impression; it is as though sited by design to René Dubos's specifications for the right cave, Pleistocene man's early command post: "on the one hand the need for an enclosed area which gives a sense of protection, on the other hand the need for an unobstructed view of the distant horizon." Yet because there are fewer animals here than at Serengeti, there are fewer poachers, and thus little of the action he experienced for so many years as deputy warden of Serengeti, almost always in pursuit of intruders about its borders, including, prominently, members of the Wakuria tribe.

Turner is an enthusiastic raconteur, a meticulous diarist with packrat files, and for two nights he pours forth the lore of Serengeti, turning occasionally for confirmation from his attractive wife, Kay, who sits with us hemming the edge of a new skirt, varying Bach recordings occasionally with Vivaldi on their generator-powered turntable. First hosts to the Grzimeks in the Serengeti, the Turners had named a child after Michael, and when the younger Grzimek failed to return on schedule one evening from the southwest, they had bundled their baby, first-aid kit, and a bottle of brandy in their Land Rover and sped to his rescue. (Michael had damaged the undercarriage of his plane taxiing across the uneven plain.)

Both Turners are writing their own accounts of life in the Serengeti, important records of its most critical years. "You must believe me when I say that *nobody* knows Serengeti better than Myles Turner," George Dove had remarked yesterday, "every warthog hole of it. He really, really knows it." It is a judgment Turner now methodically confirms. From his files he brings out the original Pearsall report of 1957, old memoranda from John Owen, a bibliography of the plains (books now long out of print), and he adds to it from his own experiences. He tells how the lions are disappearing from Serengeti (the Wasukuma believe their skins nurture virility, and rental of a skin to a tribesman to sleep upon for a single evening will bring twenty shillings); why predators disappear first in poached areas (they are killed to keep them from robbing the snares); how cattle did, in fact, graze Serengeti many years ago; and at great length, with awe turning lyrical, of the peregrinations of the wildebeest herd.

Then Myles Turner turned to that which concerned him most, the integrity of the borders about Serengeti:

We must back up another step, for it is important that I understand, he says, the nature of Julius Nyerere's *ujamaa* concept of governing Tanzania. It is idealistic, extremely risky, and much of Nyerere's great prestige across the continent rests on its success, which is by no means assured. As Grzimek had pointed out, the African family formed the governing center of tribal communities before the colonials arrived. *Ujamaa,* which translates as "familyhood," is Nyerere's attempt to reaffirm rural African communal life by borrowing from the West only those principles of socialism which apply to local problems—self-help, the dignity of the individual, a collective effort to assure the survival of all. The practical effect of his philosophy has been the creation of *ujamaa* villages, small rural collectives scattered across the country. It is Nyerere's desire to see the gradual transfer of power from the central government downward to these small, local communities of Tanzania.

Tanzania has a single-party parliamentary government, but the highest authority in the land is the party itself, T.A.N.U. (Tanganyika African National Union), for it is intended to express the direct will of the people. Governmental administration is managed through various levels of commissioners, but it is T.A.N.U. which fuels the system. One should bear in mind that now, more than ever, the people of Tanzania feel that all the land is rightfully theirs. Because Serengeti is situated in the small portion of Tanzania that is considered habitable, and because the population of the nation has grown so rapidly, especially here, the pressures about Serengeti's borders have become as intense as those encircling the parks in Uganda. There are buffer zones surrounding Serengeti, of course—here Turner referred me back to his map—but there is heavy human traffic within some of them.

Thus, the key to all the border problems in Serengeti over recent years, ever since 1967 when it first emerged as a crisis, continuing through the present day and symptomatic of future problems certain to arise, is the political episode of the Lamai Wedge, involving not only the question of animal rights vs. human rights, and the pressure from the human population swelling about the borders, but as well the developing political attitudes of the Tanzanian government since independence. For whatever reason, Bernhard Grzimek may not have cared to discuss it in detail, but Turner is willing. And to understand *Lamai's* significance, Myles Turner was saying, you had to know something about the Wakuria.

". . . *Any*how, we got this Lamai country in nineteen sixty-seven when Julius Nyerere and the government extended the park boundaries to protect the wildebeest migration which moved through there. There were twenty-seven Wakuria houses within the Wedge. The money was found to compensate the people, they were moved out, and the border was extended to include the Wedge. It was *vital* to the migration but there was no way to get across the

Mara River unless you went two hundred and fifty miles out along the Musoma road, right to the edge of Lake Victoria, to get around it. But the distance across the river was only three hundred and thirty feet. Royal Little, an American, raised the money, and I built a causeway across the Mara, and now I could be over and patrolling in no time. And *then* we got into that Wakuria country.

"You've no idea of the battles we had with those poachers—they were quite out of control, prepared to fight every time. They regarded Lamai as their own hunting area, and we national parks people were enemies of law and order. National parks patrols were not permitted to fire first, but in the course of their attacks, five or six of the poachers were shot. And finally the area was cleared up."

At first the Wakuria had come down from the north, but soon pressure developed along the western border as well, Turner says. Settlement had increased swiftly in the land between the park and Lake Victoria, and cattlemen were requesting the permission of their regional commissioner to graze their herds within the park.

"We had endless meetings up there on this question, and always we held firm. 'There was no *question* of anybody coming into the park,' we said. 'This was *national parkland,* by the laws of Tanzania.' In my opinion, they just wanted to get back in there as an excuse to poach. As well as cattle grazing and crop raising, a main occupation of these fellows was poaching. They were *terrific* poachers. And they were right there on the Kenya border, so you can imagine the zebra skins and stuff going off across there to the market in Nairobi.

"These meetings with the Wakuria were always quite the thing. You'd have two or three hundred of these really tough fellows all gathered under a tree there. You'd sit down and they'd come along with their bows and arrows, spears, odd muzzle loader, odd shotgun. And they'd sit around with these faces looking at you. At times, at some of the earlier meetings before we got through as a park, I've seen them all stand up after the area commissioner had addressed them—two hundred of them—stand up, *grab* their guns, and shout at him, 'We're not *listening* to this rubbish, we're not wasting our time. We don't *want* this bloody game or national park *anywhere near us!*' And the whole lot disappear into the bush, leaving me and the area commissioner just sitting there, with four or five rangers behind us.

"*Anyway,* about five years later, after we had got the new border, we were called to yet another meeting, Stephenson and I—

Stephenson being the administrative warden of Serengeti, an ex-D.C. There was no warning at all. The regional commissioner had sent us a wire, and we flew to a landing strip nearby and then motored up to this big meeting.

"Now the head of T.A.N.U. in Masoma, the whole lake province, comes from that area. You know, don't you, that the head of T.A.N.U. in the area is more powerful than the regional commissioner? He's *really* powerful. This man was a gigantic Wakuria called Chacha, a huge fellow—they're all quite tall, well over six feet. The Wakuria had got onto him, and once again there was this same pressure—they wanted to go back, they wanted more grazing, they wanted the boundaries realigned with a large part of the park given back, they had never been consulted properly—*all* this sort of thing. But we'd done the gazetting absolutely legally, right down to the government passing special legislation. We had it all in writing. I've got every bit of it in the files here.

"The regional commissioner greeted Stephenson and me very pleasantly—this is so typical of Africa, you know. We thought it was just another argument and we were there to placate these fellows, to tell them again: '*This is a national park, and the boundaries are going to stay*'—just as we had done many times.

"But this time, without any warning, Chacha suddenly got up and said to these people, 'Now I've come to settle finally this question of the line.' Well, we thought he was going to say: 'You will *not* reenter it. It *is* national park. It *will be* forever. By government law.'

"Instead of that, he stood up and said, 'I've come to settle this question finally'—I'll never forget—he said, 'Where do you want the line?' And they pointed and said, 'Right in *there*, right in *there*.' And they pointed a line cutting across the present boundary taking almost half the Lamai. *Right across it!* The regional commissioner stood up and said, 'As from this moment, you can have it. Move back in there.' There was a great roaring cheer from the Wakuria.

"Naturally, Stephenson and me—we were sitting in a national parks car—*we were flabbergasted!* So we pushed off for Seronera. We wrote immediately to the trustees, to the director, and someone wrote to Grzimek explaining exactly what had happened. Grzimek got his underground working, letters out to everybody, and their letters suddenly began coming in. Then it got in the local press. You can look it up back in Nairobi. . . ."

I did:

March 7, 1972—A vital section of the Serengeti National Park has been taken over by the local population who are reported to be moving in and drawing land plots in the area. The area being taken over for settlement is west of the Mara River and is bordered in part by the Kenya/Tanzania International Boundary. It is the northwestern part of the Lamai Wedge. It comprises an area that was a late addition to the park. It was added by the Tanzania National Assembly after the government realized its important role in the annual wildebeest migration.

These animals end their migration in this area before dispersing, many of them across the border into the Masai Mara game reserve in Kenya. The decision to take over this section of the park, believed to be roughly 75 square miles in area, was taken at a meeting held in Northern Tanzania on February 28th.

It is understood that the local regional commissioner agreed to this meeting's demand that the area be taken over by the people. The request was given the approval of the local T.A.N.U. party. People started moving into the area immediately.

The influx has been reported at the Tanzanian National Parks headquarters in Arusha, and the trustees of the Park are said to be discussing the matter with government officials in Dar es Salaam. . . .

. . . According to one informed source, the new settlers—believed to be mainly of the Wakuria tribe—have been cutting down trees and marking plots in the area.

Rangers operating in the area have been instructed not to make any arrests for offenses against the National Park Act until the situation is clarified.

Tanzania is engaged in a program to give more power to the regional administration. Commissioners are taking more and more decisions formerly referred to the central government.

There is concern that if the decision to take part of the Serengeti is ratified it will lead to a similar action by other local commissioners.

The Serengeti has been described by international conservation bodies as the greatest national park in the world. It is one of the biggest tourist attractions in East Africa.

"You've no *idea* what it was like after that," Turner said. "In three weeks' time, they'd marked off their gardens right across the center of the park. They were cutting trees to build their houses, cattle were in, dogs chasing game! Everything! The whole area of Lamai is about two hundred and twenty square miles, and they'd taken almost *half* of it. Grzimek now was fighting desperately. It is such a serious thing, you see, if a piece of the park is cut off. Where does it ever stop? This is the beginning of the rot!

"Finally the whole thing was taken back to Parliament and we got the decision. There would be no agriculture and no housebuilding in the park, but people would be allowed to take their cattle in the park for grazing. So meetings were held in these areas, the houses were destroyed, and the building materials were taken out. But the people were allowed to go back in.

"To this day, I think, cattle are allowed to graze in there. They go in the morning and come out in the evening. Very difficult situation."

"Are they still there?" I asked.

"Well, when I left they were, but I haven't been over for six months. I don't know."

Turkoman rugs hang on the walls of the Turners' living room, and as he pauses now, sipping Kay's wine, the ambiguity of Vivaldi's "Concerto Grosso for Four Violins" is the only sound. Turner is not optimistic. Lamai is reflective of even larger problems. The same people hemmed in between the park and the lake are pushing downward toward the Grumeti, at the northern border of the western corridor. It is even worse in the Maswa reserve to the southwest. "When the Game Department made that big buffer zone down by the Maswa side of the park, I marked out the boundary. It was a magnificent buffer zone—exactly what we wanted to protect the migration. *But,* then it was up to the Game Department to keep the people out. It was not within the Parks Department's jurisdiction.

"I fly down there three months later, and there are twenty huts inside the boundary. I report this to the Game Department. They go down and the game scouts are beaten up by the people. I fly down a year later, and there are a hundred and fifty huts moving steadily toward the park boundary. Goodness knows how many there are now. In nineteen fifty-nine, when I put the western border in from Banagi to the Mara, the nearest settlement was eight miles away. It's *solid* human settlement now. They've plowed their last rows right up to the boundary—cotton, maize, millet, the rest of it.''

"But Serengeti is still some sort of tourist attraction, isn't it? Isn't this reason enough for the government to enforce the borders?''

"No, you see, it is complicated by the Customs Department's attitude toward tourists. They are *discouraging* tourists!'' Apparently there is rivalry between the Customs Department and the Tourism Department of Tanzania. Since tourists must enter the country through the Customs Department, which is unsympathetic to the interests of outsiders, there has been enough harassment to persuade some tour operators in Nairobi to bypass Tanzania altogether—despite the desire of their clients to see Serengeti and the much greater concentration of wild animals in Tanzania.

"As a tourist destination, this country could beat Kenya into the ground if it wanted,'' Turner said. "There is more game here by far. I've hunted all three countries, *I know!* But the feeling is, the Tanzanians just don't want to compete. In the last ten years under John Owen, they've built these magnificent parks and hotels—and *now* they aren't going to welcome tourists? Friends of ours—Americans—hired a truck, Land Rover and so on for a camping trip through our parks. They got to the border, where they had one permit missing—for the damn tentage! The customs seized their lorry and said, 'If this permit isn't here within two weeks, we are going to auction the lorry, everything, here in the middle of Arusha!' These people still had their Toyota, which luckily hadn't been seized. They motored back to Kenya and immediately booked passage home. They said, 'Never again!'

"The danger is obvious. The constituents of politicians in places like Lamai are going to see there are no tourists and say, 'Why *can't* we enter this area?' And the regional commissioner can't say, 'Because it's bringing us the necessary revenue.' Because it *isn't.* *There's no one there at all!* When that day comes, that literally is the end. Because if ever these parks are cut up, even in small pieces. . . . When *that* starts, with the land hunger here, you know—that's it.''

During my time with Myles and Kay Turner at Mount Meru, my

camp was situated in the woodlands of the park, a short drive along the mountain road to Arusha; and on the day between our evenings together, I had gone down the mountain to see Derek Bryceson at park headquarters, returning to attend a small cocktail party of expatriates at another tiny house within the mountain park shared by two aging botanists, Desmond Vesey-Fitzgerald and Mary Richards. Mrs. Richards was eighty-eight. She would be leaving Africa soon because she had cataracts and found it hard now to make her way about. In her tiny room, bare as a nun's cell, she slept with a Winnie the Pooh doll on her pillow. Also present, by remarkable circumstance, was an animal trapper and former warden named Max Morgan-Davies who had been on temporary duty in Ngorongoro fifteen years ago when Michael Grzimek's fatal accident occurred. Myles Turner and several of the expatriates joined us, and they talked about what had happened.

"It was early in the morning," Morgan-Davies said. "A warrant officer came up to the lodge and reported to the hotel manager that Michael had had an accident. We made arrangements for the body to be collected and a park lorry was sent down to Ildonyogol. Bernhard was down in the crater. . . ."

Someone recalled the message sent Grzimek by the game warden. It read, "I am sorry to tell you that Michael has crashed in the aeroplane and been killed. He is lying at my house."

"I followed on down to sort out the plane," Morgan-Davies said, "to get the plane ready for the aviation people to make their inspection of it. I spent the next three days down there."

Myles Turner said, "Keith Thomas, acting chief game warden of Tanganyika, hauled him out of the plane. He happened to be down in the crater at the time. Max was the next person to see the whole thing. But Keith took the body in a sack to the top of the crater. It was unrecognizable. He wouldn't exaggerate—he had been a paratrooper in the war. He said this was something—an instantaneous death."

"The first thing I noticed," Morgan-Davies said, "Keith had hacked the plane open, and you could sit inside where Michael was—and the first thing I noticed was that the throttle was wide open, which gave me the impression that he probably hit this bloody vulture—at not too high an altitude, from all accounts—and went into a dive. And to try to pull himself out, he put full throttle on and didn't make it. The bloody engine was right inside the seat. Must have gone down at a hell of a rate."

Someone else remarked that birds were a great hazard to light aircraft in East Africa. The Grzimeks had written of the problem in an article for a wildlife journal. John Owen had flown into a crane once, and Hugh Lamprey, the best pilot among them, had narrowly escaped disaster when he collided with vultures twice within two days flying over the Serengeti.

"Another thing about the Dornier," Myles Turner said, "the controls were all on the leading edge of the wing. The Cessna's, for example, are halfway back from the leading edge, you know. You can knock a hole in a Cessna before you hit any wires. That was the thing about the Dornier that was changed later." We were standing outside the house by a Land Rover. It was a strange conversation, rural, like farmers exchanging small details about an accident that happened yesterday. Someone else joined the group of us: "They say at the service next day the old man stood straight as a rod. Didn't shed a tear."

The mosaic grows, pieces appearing, like the unexpected account at Vesey-Fitzgerald's of Morgan-Davies, from witnesses of another dimension, from different places, different times. Much later, in a study of elephants by Iain and Oria Douglas-Hamilton, I would read in New York this strange account by Oria of a related event in the course of a Sunday afternoon's flight in their small Piper Pacer to an obscure corner of the plain not very far from the houses of Myles Turner and Vesey-Fitzgerald:

> Down we came to a few feet from the ground, racing along at high speed, ready to pull up at the slightest danger till Iain found a good place, went round to land, and we touched the rough, uneven ground, running alongside the road. The plane came to a standstill, the engine was switched off, and we remained seated in complete silence. All we heard was the sound of wind running along the surface of the earth. . . .
>
> I turned towards the straight track and saw a slim figure with a white cloth over his head, moving along fast, kicking up the dust. It is always strange to see a solitary man in a vast waste; one wonders where he comes from and where he is going. . . . The man came up and shook our hands, his face sweating, black and shiny. I could only understand a little of what he said and thought he was explaining that he had seen us suddenly drop down from the sky but he pointed to the hill, and said "long ago."

THE LAST PLACE ON EARTH

Then the others arrived. . . . The men kept on pointing to the hill and telling us about a plane that had come here a long time ago—though some said it was just the other day. It had fallen, killing all the people in it. The men told us they ran to the place but no one was alive, it had broken in many pieces. We explained that we had not crashed but only wanted to walk in the hills. Two men said they would accompany us and take us to the plane. I could not understand what they were talking about for there was no sign of a crashed plane. . . .

We followed a cattle trail, where the grass was coarse and long and scratched our legs. It was incredibly hot and I was feeling sick. About 30 yards from the road we came upon a piece of black and white striped tangled metal, still being pushed along by the wind. To my horror, I realized what it was, and could not believe my eyes that out of all those thousands of square miles we should have chosen this very place to land.

Iain and I stopped and looked. Above our heads we saw vultures twisting and turning in the currents, gliding along-side and over the cliffs. The few remains of the black and white plane were strewn all over the cliffs. Children had played with pieces. Animals, as they passed by month after month, must have sniffed them, kicked them and rubbed themselves against them. The frame of one of the seats still survived, as did a piece of the tail, and bits of the wings. . . . And that was all that remained of Michael Grzimek. . . .

There were no clouds, the plains were streaked with waves of heat, I saw things turning in the sun. Even the aeroplane seemed to have melted away and as I sat on that rock in the midst of nowhere, I felt that Michael and the people who lived here were lucky to begin life and sometimes end life in a reversal of time towards wilderness.

SIXTEEN

Even for an agrarian society like Tanzania, seeking self-sufficiency, oil can be as precious as food. "From 1960 to 1972," the ecologist Lester Brown has noted, "the world price of a bushel of wheat and that of a barrel of oil were nearly equal, ranging from $1.35 to slightly over $2.00. A bushel of wheat could be traded for a barrel of oil in the world market place. In late 1973 the price of wheat soared past $5.00. For a brief period a bushel of wheat could be exchanged for two barrels of oil. Then came the Christmas Eve, 1973, oil increase by the oil exporting countries—the second doubling in price within the year—and the price of oil soared above that of wheat, reaching $8.00 per barrel. . . . The poor countries importing both wheat and oil suffered the greatest damage. The many countries having no valuable raw materials of their own to export exhausted their limited foreign exchange reserves in a matter of months and several were on the verge of bankruptcy."

In 1974, Tanzania faced her greatest crisis in ten years as a new nation. Because of drought, in 1973 and 1974, there had been a severe food shortage. Tanzania held a deficit in balance of payments of a hundred million dollars. The largest donation of outside assistance for drought relief was thirty-eight million dollars from the United States. While her exports of coffee, hemp, sisal, and cotton had not risen in value, her oil bill had quintupled over the preceding two years, from twenty million to a hundred million dollars.

"Whatever reason you choose for keeping wild animals," I asked Derek Bryceson, "there isn't enough money to maintain your parks, is there?"

"What do you *mean*, there isn't enough money?" Bryceson answered sharply. "Of *course* there's enough money. It depends on your choice and how you're going to spend the money available. Of *course* there's enough."

"Do you have enough for park vehicles?"

"I don't have all I want but I have enough."

"For anti-poaching?"

"Yes, it's not just me doing the anti-poaching. I've got a special unit of the army set up for this purpose, and I've got a unit of the police set up for this purpose, so that, with ours, there will be the three departments coordinated by national parks." I wondered how long he would stay in the first-person singular.

"But the supplying of park equipment—the planes, the bulldozers, and so on—has to come from outside donations, doesn't it?"

"Fine. How many planes have we got? Four. Let's have a look at this in light of the facts. The Serengeti Research Center and the Gombe Research Center in southern Tanzania, where Jane Goodall works, are run mainly on overseas funds. Donations, if you want to call them that. As for the national parks system itself, of which the research centers are part, the amount of assistance we've received from the outside is not negligible, and it is very welcome. But my policy is the same as our national policy in all other fields. In other words, we run the parks system ourselves *for* ourselves. *If* we can get assistance from the outside, that's great. It means we can do a little bit more a lot better than we could have done without it. But without it, we will do it—one way or another—because it is our choice. It is our determination and decision that we will *do* it. Therefore *we will do it!*"

Like most of the others, Bryceson is soft-spoken, but there is an edge to his answers, as though he expects to be disputed. Perhaps it is only the manner of a professional politician speaking on the record. . . .

"Now people come in and they help, as old Grzimek has in replacing that aircraft we crashed the other day. He came by and I told him of the circumstances, and I said, 'Look, it makes it pretty awkward for me *not* to have an aircraft at my constant disposal. Can you help?' And he immediately said, 'Yes, I'll fix it.' There's an aircraft for sale, and he's fixing it.

"But this isn't to say national parks would collapse if I didn't have an aircraft. It wouldn't. I'd do what has to be done with the remaining aircraft."

"What about the income from tourism?"

"Okay. We've made a certain investment in tourism in the past. Right or wrong, the investment has been made. Now we want a certain return from that investment. *But*—we have been seeing things in Kenya: we have seen that alongside the development of tourism there comes a number of corruptive practices, and we don't like this. We do not *want* tourism to become a very important source of income to us. We don't think this is something we should allow for the good health of our country. We like it to assist our economy, but we don't want it to be essential to our economy."

"Where is tourism in Tanzania's economy?"

"One-fifth."

"That's rather a stiff decision in terms of the needs of the country, isn't it? If tourism delivers a fifth of the country's income, and the country is not solvent, then that, too, is a factor to the people, is it not? Isn't the welfare of the country deprived?"

"Yes, but the needs of the people are more important than the needs of the country's income. And the economy is part of the need but not the whole of it."

Tanzania is one of the twenty-five poorest countries on earth, with one of the highest birthrates; per capita income is about a hundred and twenty dollars. Yet, although the press is controlled and there are political prisoners, Nyerere's government is recognized widely as one of the most democratic in Africa and as one least beset by political corruption. Since independence, the salary differential in wage earnings has been reduced from a hundred to one to nine to one. In contrast to Amin (who has a private jet) and Kenyatta (whose personal holdings include thousands of acres of prime farmland and a gambling casino), Nyerere lives on a salary of six thousand dollars.

Julius Nyerere's hold over the imagination of Derek Bryceson is total. In the mid-fifties, as Nyerere began to emerge as leader of the independence movement in Tanganyika, Bryceson, then an expatriate farmer, wrote a letter to a local magazine denouncing Nyerere as a "racialist" prejudiced against all but black residents of the community. Shortly thereafter, the two men met, engaging in conversations lasting over three days and resulting in the total conversion of Bryceson to Nyerere's cause. Bryceson sold his farm to Dr. Michael Wood and entered T.A.N.U. After independence, he stood for Parliament in the capital district of Dar es Salaam and won his seat with one of the largest majorities in the election (as has been the case in other elections since). He became, successively, Minister of Mines and Commerce, Minister of Health and Labor, Minister of Agriculture, and now he was the director of the national parks. That he is a white man, and the last of importance in an East African government, is incidental—at least to Derek Bryceson.

They make unlikely allies, Bryceson and Grzimek: an ex-R.A.F. pilot and a former officer of the Third Reich; a farmer and a zookeeper; a Minister of Agriculture and a conservationist; a politician and an ecologist; an English expatriate and a German vying for the favor of an enigmatic and ascetic Tanzanian. But all the more unlikely even still for their bitter feuds over recent years. Bryceson is the man who tried to turn the better part of Ngorongoro over to Masai cattlemen, and the overflow of the Serengeti migration to the cropper Ian Parker's Wildlife Services Ltd. in the Loliondo reserve.

In the first instance, angrily, Grzimek had gone about as far as he would allow himself to in the African press. Commending the black Africans for their enlightened policies, he had focused his bitterness on Derek Bryceson: "It was Tanzania's last European governor, Sir Richard Turnbull, who started the rot by allowing his administration to cut Ngorongoro out of the Serengeti National Park. Now it was the only European minister, Mr. Derek Bryceson, who had finished the job."

"Absolute nonsense," Bryceson had responded.

But as Grzimek had mildly observed the other day in Molo, whereas Bryceson as Minister of Agriculture decided people should move into the parks, as director of the national parks he now helps to decide they should move out. In the first hour of our meeting, in fact, Bryceson seems almost as faithful now to Grzimek's philosophy as he is to Nyerere's. Bryceson says he believes in educating the people to their wildlife heritage at both ends of the age scale—the schoolchildren by cinemobiles, posters, classroom instruction, and free visits to the parks; and the politicians by persuasion. He cites as an example of his progress the most recent meeting of thirteen hundred T.A.N.U. representatives where specific proposals to end poaching were adopted, certain evidence of the nation's growing desire to conserve its wild animals. Bryceson believes now in the use of tented camps within the parks instead of permanent hotel lodges (like the one he approved in 1967 for the floor of Ngorongoro Crater). He doesn't sound like the old Bryceson so much as the same old Grzimek.

It is ten days since I left Grzimek at Molo in Kenya, and Bryceson has just now come back from the flight with him to Rubondo along the western border of Tanzania. Rubondo is the island in Lake Victoria which Grzimek has been stocking with miscellaneous animals since the sixties, when he first flew down eighteen chimpanzees collected from European zoos and set them loose. Since then, he has added rhino, elephant, various gazelle, and he plans soon to import gorilla. Having maintained Rubondo through his various funding sources over the years, Grzimek wants Tanzania now to take it over. Gazetting it as a national park is the best way, and Bryceson's concurrence as director of parks is essential.

Bryceson: "So before doing anything about it, I said to Grzimek, 'Let's go up and talk to the people up there and find out what their view of it is.'

"Rubondo is part of the Geita district. I had written the district commissioner, had told him we were coming and that I wanted to discuss the possibility with leaders of the districts concerned. The district commissioner collected the T.A.N.U. chairman, plus the area commissioner, plus about fifteen other various leaders and civil service representatives, and we all met on Rubondo Island. They came over by boat, and Grzimek and I flew in.

"Well, their reaction was interesting. The district chairman of T.A.N.U. said, 'Geita district is a very big district, with more than a million people. It is very good agriculturally. Our land is being taken up for civilization, almost totally now, and the district is completely covered. If we don't make Rubondo Island into a national park, we will wake up one morning and find that we have no national park anywhere near the Geita district. And this means our children in generations to come will have nowhere to go to see the animals as they were in this country long ago. And so that we in Geita district have wanted Rubondo Island to be a national park for some years.' "

Bryceson looked pleased. It was not difficult to imagine Grzimek's reaction.

"So I said, 'Fine.' And all they have to do is pass a resolution, which they have done; and the regional commissioner is in accord. And then it goes next to the provincial government, which will put the resolution to the Parliament, which will undoubtedly pass it because it comes from the people concerned. And then it will go to the President for his signature, and then it will be gazetted in the official gazette, and then it will become a national park.

"All our parks put together, including forest reserves and game reserves, make a land mass of approximately twenty-five per cent of this country." Bryceson smiled.

Things are running more smoothly now than in the old days under the expatriates, Bryceson says. "When I retired from government and was appointed to national parks, which was at my own request, I must say a lot of people wondered what the hell was going on. A lot of them said, 'Well, this is the end of national parks. He's an agriculturist, and his interests are agriculture.'

"When I entered national parks, we had seven parks. Now we have nine, and I expect to have eleven by the end of the year. This is apart from the fact that the whole atmosphere for national parks has swung totally by a hundred and eighty degrees. Parks is now *accepted* by the people as part of the country." Bryceson smiled.

"One of the first things I had to try to do was to nationalize the national parks. We have a number of first-class young men coming up now. We have managed to put them in charge of all the important parks to replace all the British expatriates but two, and they are finishing out this year. As of the end of the year, the parks will be totally Tanzanian. At the same time, we have been conducting a tremendous public-relations campaign based on the hunger of the people for a recognition of the cultural background of the country, to show how fortunate we are to have all this as part of our heritage. Other countries, such as the European countries, have not preserved this cultural heritage, and now they find themselves *without* wild animals. So we have to look around, take notes, and see that this doesn't happen with us." That Bryceson is a politician elected to office by the people of Tanzania is the reason he is sure he can be more effective than other expatriates. There appears to be no doubt in his own mind that he has already proved his effectiveness.

He has his own version of events surrounding the Lamai Wedge controversy. He had just been appointed director of parks when the issue erupted throughout East Africa. "Cattle were being allowed in on a daily basis," he says. "The herdsmen had started to move into some of the areas and build huts. So I got onto the local administrator in the district, and they sent the police in to burn the huts down and take the cattle out. It was important the police do it rather than the park officials. I was determined the action be taken by law-enforcing authorities from the district where the people came. And this they did without any problem at all."

"Is there now such cooperation between the Department of Parks and the local authorities?"

"*Now* there is. Previously the parks tended to be a foreign organization within Tanzania. The director was an Englishman. All the senior park wardens were British, and they ran parks rather as a little outside organization. Each man had a sort of personal kingdom in his park. . . ."

Bryceson is seated at the dining-room table of Parks House in Arusha, once occupied by John Owen. He is silver-haired and pale, with a V-shaped grin. He has a bad limp and walks with a cane—the result, I assume, of his wartime injury. Several Tanzanians about the house hover unobtrusively in attendance, like stewards in officer country.

His whiteness glistens.

"John Owen couldn't speak Swahili. To the Tanzanians, the very language he spoke symbolized the colonial culture they had sought to escape. It was impossible for him to establish any kind of relationship; the more so when there were other disputes with the parks, either on higher governmental *or* local levels. And the senior wardens, all British, were a new type of police force, roaming about, trying to catch the people hunting, collecting water, cutting firewood, or grazing their cattle. The parks were not popular with the people." Bryceson himself speaks Swahili fluently. Earlier in the morning, he had stopped in the street to pass the time with a toothless ancient before driving me to Parks House in his minibus. The old man had responded with great warmth.

"But what about expatriates who have demonstrated expertise in the formative stages of the parks?" I asked. "If there are individuals who have committed themselves to this country's interests, as you yourself have, and have helped build the parks system, isn't it shortsighted now to let them go?"

"It is only shortsighted if we can't replace them. But if we can replace them, why do we keep them?"

"Because of expertise."

"But we *have* the expertise. And no expatriate can deal with an African as effectively as another African."

"What about yourself?"

"Ah," he said, "but I am African."

By now I myself knew too much of the expatriates' role in Serengeti to let Bryceson's casual dismissal of the recent past go by so easily. And yet, if one could for the moment take him only on the face of what he said, if one could forget the resigned melancholy of Owen and Turner now as against their dedicated past efforts to save the Serengeti Plain, his position seemed sound—and, again, consonant with Grzimek's view: Africa's animals were for the Africans; they alone could save them. But Owen and Turner were still too fresh in my mind. Gingerly I pressed for a nerve.

"What do you think of Grzimek's effort out here?"

"He has drawn world attention to the problems of wildlife conservation. What he has done through his television show in making people aware of the situation has been fantastic."

"Has he been of assistance to you in rallying local support to the cause of wildlife?"

"He has been of assistance in some cases, and absolutely not in others. With respect to the Lamai Wedge, for example. Grzimek was amongst the people who shouted very loud in the world press, gave voice to forebodings and doom for the national parks, said this was the beginning of the end, and so on. He wrote some rather ill-considered letters—that cattlemen being let in marked the end of Serengeti. . . . Well, you see, he shouldn't have done that without coming and finding out from *us* exactly what the situation was. And if he had, I'm sure he would have seen that there was no cause for concern. There are tribes about the Serengeti who are pastoralists. Because the area is subject to the vagaries of rainfall, you get a year like this one when rain is insufficient for the cattle and they may not have enough water, or enough feed, and they will die.

"Normally, in these times, we just come to a friendly agreement, and they put their cattle in the park until such time as the rains come again and they can feed outside. It is not done except absolutely *in extremis,* because it is against the law. It is an unwritten understanding.

"Just the other day, in fact, I was on the radio to the park warden of the Serengeti and I told him he should allow Masai from the Loliondo area into the northeastern part so long as the situation demanded. They were in a very bad way and a lot of the cattle were dying. But in fact we had heavy rains over the whole of that area about that time, so it didn't prove necessary after all.

"But you see, we have to do this. In the first place, it doesn't do the parks any harm to do it, and in the second place, it would do the park a lot of harm not to do it. Not ecologically, but it would put us on very bad terms with our neighbors."

"If the law can be suspended at will, what good is it?"

"It depends, of course, on the strength of the parks as an organization, and we are certainly strong enough for that."

This part didn't sound like Grzimek.

As he said, Bryceson was a politician. In 1969, as Minister of Agriculture, he had taken precisely the same position as above when he sought to release three thousand and forty square miles of Ngorongoro to cattle grazers and farmers, and his justification had been the same: "It won't matter, it will do no harm to the wild animals."

In Nairobi, a man who has been a close observer of all the expatriate factions of the past decade heard out my report of the better part of Bryceson's remarks and said: "A poor show. Of the nine parks Bryceson cites, and two still to come, all were completed or in the planning stage at Parks before Bryceson came in. Bryceson just picked up a rolling ball. He makes no mention of the money John Owen raised, or the establishment of S.R.I. Let's not forget that in nineteen sixty-five there was no such thing as the Serengeti Research Institute. The important thing was to show to the world that research was worthwhile doing in the Serengeti. John Owen did that.

"But the main thing is, the significance of Lamai seems *lost* on him. It was the first attempt at regional decision making which affected the parks. In decentralizing, the national government had given power to the regions. The regional commissioner *on the ground* had declared that that part of the national park would no longer be a national park, that since it had originally been a game reserve, the people had the right to make that decision *on the ground*. The question of 'unofficial' grazing rights never came up at *all*. The point was, park borders, having been created by Parliament, could only be *changed* by Parliament. The only reason the Lamai Wedge is still in the Serengeti National Park is that Grzimek created so much fuss that nobody at the national level was willing to take it to the national assembly and undo formally the park boundary.

"In retrospect, however, and to Bryceson's credit, it was resolved very well. He worked out the compromise, and what he says now—coordinating local people with park policies—makes good sense. In the long historical perspective we may find in fact that Bryceson came in the nick of time on the political issue. If he does no more than that—tries to stabilize the situation in those regions—that is quite something. It is very important for parks to be on good terms with people living on the boundaries. So far as I know, this exists nowhere else in the world. What worries me about him is the fact that he is *no more* than a politician. The fact that he says he

THE LAST PLACE ON EARTH

has set down the proper course is not enough. The gap between promise and performance is too great, as he demonstrated as Minister of Agriculture. He suffers from the problem of all politicians. Too often it takes a crisis before any responsible action occurs."

But it was Bryceson, not I, who brought up the second great issue confronting the Serengeti Plain, that of cropping the game; and, curiously, he raised it in circumventing a question about population growth about the borders. Bryceson had spoken of the government's methods in moving people for better land utilization.

"Do you see these pressures about the borders of Serengeti diminishing because of the possibility of opening other areas for farming?"

Bryceson must have misunderstood me. He said, "I'm hoping that we are going to be able within our park system, as between the park on the one side and the other game reserves on the other, to come to a joint system whereby the park population is maintained. The overflow uses the game reserve from time to time, and there can be a cropping of animals as is possible from an ecological point of view and may even be necessary from an ecological point of view. The cropping can take place when the animals move *out* of the park in their normal perambulations."

"Through poaching?" I couldn't believe he was about to advocate cropping officially.

"No, scientifically based, organized cropping which will take place outside the park in the game reserve areas those times of the year when the animal populations move out of the park."

"Whose theories are being followed on this?"

"We are trying to learn more now about the possibility of animal populations to carry sustained-yield cropping, and various methods of cropping which may be used. There is very, very little known about this. There has been very little of it in this country. The Serengeti Research Institute now is leading this research. A man named John Bindernagel is in charge of it. He is a Canadian scientist who has worked on cropping in Uganda and studied it in Zambia. . . ."

This part didn't sound like Grzimek, either.

SEVENTEEN

Back in the West, Man's Way with the plants and animals that surround him is ingenious and yet so commonplace that one must make a special effort to register the fact. In upstate New York where I live, an apple grower tells of a new graft which will yield on the branches of a single tree seven varieties of apple simultaneously. A conservation teacher at our local high school remarks disinterestedly on the control of deer population, the community's most visible wildlife: it is held to the desired level by extending or reducing the hunting season. Birth regulation of domestic species is an even more exact science. To assure insemination of a valued cow by a prize bull, a farmer says, coition is mechanically assisted with such predictable commercial success that its unlikely failure may be insured for upwards of a million dollars. An item in a weekly news magazine: "One group of researchers showed it is possible to transplant the genetic material of one cell into cells of a wholly different species. Another group has managed for the first time to synthesize an animal gene. . . ." It is a measure of man's progress in manipulating natural processes that even the more remarkable of these developments arouse little wonder. In the West, Man's Way is entrenched and irreversible; too late in the day to question.

But not yet in East Africa. I mentioned the routine regulation of deer population in New York State to Richard Leakey and asked him if such techniques were not now internationally accepted.

"Yes, they are," he said. "It is simply that in East Africa the business of cropping is still seen as an open question. The position here is extreme, running from sentimentality to open greed. At the far end are the wildlife zealots who don't want to see anything killed, and at the other the meat producers who regard game as a source of profit. There is no aspect of the question here free of ambiguity."

In 1973, at the Serengeti Research Institute, in the first symposium of all the scientists in East Africa (there were then more than a hundred), research studies were presented on buffalo, fish eagle, dik-dik, free-tailed bat, talapia fish, elephant, ostrich, mar-

240

abou stork, impala, black rhino, lion, topi, wildebeest, zebra, and rodent pests. One of the few areas of agreement among the scientists was that the mechanisms which cause population regulation are different in different species and may even be different in different populations of the same species. It was agreed, in fact, that it was difficult to show that regulation was occurring at all—an essential factor in the process of cropping.

Ian Parker, the game cropper and leading exponent of Man's Way out here, is more certain about such matters, and he views as sentimentalists all those who want to preserve wild animals for any purpose other than as a commodity. "Damn it! All this bleating about the environment! Can't they see the whole of living is the ability to counteract the hostile elements in the environment? And that the hostile elements far outweigh all others?"

And:

"Conservation is a phenomenon on its own. The science of animal production, which is my interest, is a phenomenon on its own. That they overlap is untrue. Essentially what it boils down to is that conservation is the preservation of *all* life. Animal production, of which human survival happens to be a part, is the wresting as much as you can of the environment for the use of your chosen species. And the species which man can use are very few. As you sophisticate animal production, so you wrest more and more of the environment for that purpose, and you deny other animals access to it. It is a question of competition."

To the Nature's Way faction, some of whom are sentimentalists and some of whom, like Grzimek and Owen, decidedly are not, Ian Parker is a lively Serpent in the Garden. All the Nature's Way people fear most the adoption of Parker's "science of animal production" within the borders of the national parks. Since most of the animals left now reside in or around the national parks, and Parker's methods could conceivably yield more income to the East African nations than tourism, and since government officials like Derek Bryceson are speaking ever more favorably of such methods, these fears are not just the doomsday fantasies of zealots.

Always embattled, Parker seems to enjoy the role of antagonist. In a running dispute with Daphne Sheldrick, wife of the Tsavo warden and a leading exponent of Nature's Way, he wrote:

> ... the crux of the controversy is the dichotomy between emotional feeling and the process of reason. It is apparent in many human affairs; those whose position is based on one

usually deride those based on the other. Daphne Sheldrick reasons with the best, but ultimately takes her stand principally on feelings and intuition.

Others, of whom I try to be one, have strong feelings (very similar to the Sheldricks') but endeavor to subordinate these to the rather lifeless process of reason.

It is instructive to observe that our civilization places a premium on the latter and we are conditioned to pursue its course. Nevertheless our history is a succession of unreasoned acts initiated by our feelings. Therein, perhaps, lies the lesson.

One outraged Nature's Way writer, smarting from a Parker attack, characterized him as a male baboon and social dinosaur.

But the controversy over cropping in Nairobi, which has leaned heavily in past years to the side of the Nature's Way expatriates, is coming now to be seen as more complex than many among them would like to admit. It is, indeed, a testament to Ian Parker's fierce and effective advocacy of Man's Way, directly counter to any argument advanced by the Nature's Way adherents, that he is not instantly dismissed because of his vested interest. He is the chief executive of Wildlife Services Limited, a consulting organization in East Africa dealing in all those aspects of commercial exploitation of wildlife which conservationists most condemn: the sale of ivory (government-approved), skins, and hides, and the butchering of wild animals for the commercial meat markets. Parker has done business in all three East African nations; has acquired more expertise than others in the techniques of cropping because he has done more of it than others; and he has appeared before the British Ecological Society, among other scientific organizations, to explain his theories on the management of plants and animal life. A former game warden whose experience was gained in the field, he is considered to be among a handful of experts on the biology of elephants and of various other species he has cropped. He imposes rigorous field standards for his projects, and he claims to have rejected more cropping schemes than he has accepted.

Moreover, Parker and his theories more recently have come to gain the support of the growing body of international ecologists who simply see no way out for African man, beast, or environment other than through some systematic approach to the harvesting of wild animals. It is a consensus of benignity which is no less worrisome to the Nature's Way faction. "What is really needed," has said Dr. Leslie Brown, the former chief agriculturist of Kenya, "is careful management of the wild stock so it can produce the maximum yield to feed the African populace." Curry-Lindahl, the Swedish ecologist for the United Nations Environmental Protection Agency, goes further: "Buffalos, hippopotamuses, rhinoceroses, giraffes, elephants, zebras and large antelopes of many species [could] provide a rich source of food if utilized wisely. Normally they cause no damage to the vegetation and land in spite of the enormous quantities they eat. Many species increase in size more rapidly than cattle, are immune to sleeping sickness and have none of the other ailments that often affect cattle. They also have a much bigger rate of survival, owing to thousands of years of adaptation to their environment. As producers of meat these wild animals could easily surpass the cattle, qualitatively as well as quantitatively. . . ."

And Norman Myers is even more specific: "The Serengeti migration could produce perhaps 40 million tins of canned meat each year without any decline in the total wildebeest, zebra, and gazelle numbers below the present two million."

On a personal level, Ian Parker has said he enjoys wild animals and for his own pleasure does not want to see them disappear, but he thinks this may be a selfish attitude. If material justification cannot be found for them, they will have to go. We are seated in the terrace lounge of the New Stanley Hotel, which is packed with holidaying tourists, mostly Americans, drinking and chattering all about, trying to look casual in their new, crinkled khakis. It is our second session together, coming after my swing through Uganda and down to Mount Meru. Parker is an intense man. He shows little interest in either the beer or the food set before him and is wholly oblivious of the cacophony that surrounds us. He could as easily be speaking at a wildlife meeting in Hertfordshire. In shorts and sandals, with briefcase documentation at hand for his impatient correctives, frowning past the table and measuring his words, he seems a curious figure: East Africa's inverted ascetic, a Saint Francis of the abattoir.

Parker has known Grzimek since 1961 when Grzimek and Alan Root visited him at his thatch-roofed cottage on the bank of the Galana River in eastern Kenya, at the edge of Tsavo Park. Over a cement floor, the walls of Parker's house have been built waist-high and then left open to the roof so that the swollen river in the long rains can pass through, leaving the basic structure intact: on one such occasion, a hundred yards of the bank had been torn away in fifteen minutes. What is left of the bank now is a promontory, upon which the cottage is perched, reaching into the water like an elbow of grass so that you can sit out in the soft air at once protected and yet part of the soft Tsavo night. Ian Parker built the cottage himself. It is the house of a man who has romantic notions of what life in Africa should be like but is unwilling to leave it at that.

After dinner that evening in 1961, Parker offered to demonstrate to Root how he could catch a crocodile by hand. "You dazzle it with the beam of a flashlight," Parker says, "and grab it by the head. We found one three or four feet long, but it was all underwater. Like a bloody fool, I grabbed it by the tail. In a flash, it had me by the hand. I let out a yell and threw it against Root's chest. Old Grzimek heard this terrible bellowing and came down to see what was going on. I had a lacerated hand. We had no anesthetic, and he reckoned he hadn't sewn anything up since schooldays. After he had taken five or six stitches, I reckoned he hadn't, too."

Parker's theories spring out of a source different from Grzimek's. "One of my greatest interests is the process of logic. I'm always bugged by things which are illogical, and I gain security out of a logical argument. When I first joined the Game Department, I was aware that a lot that was said about conservation was difficult to justify in logic. You had to make acts of faith, accept blind certain dogma. This worried me more and more because I had become involved in the new ideas of animal production, making animals pay. Which pulls for *logic*. My first concern was: Can these matters be handled technically? There were tremendous battles to get the opportunity to try one's ideas. Similar projects were going on with a couple of Americans in Rhodesia, but their research wasn't applicable here. Just moral support. But it was something new—a lot of people were talking about these questions, and I went into business to develop my ideas.

"Many people come to me now and say, 'Are you for or against cropping?' As far as I'm concerned, that's as sensible a question as saying, 'Do you prefer screwdrivers to wrenches?' Cropping is only a technique of management. All animals respond to artificial reduction by overcompensating their birthrate. It depends on *how* you modify the population structure as to what results you get. You modify cattle population to get maximum reproduction. It's the

244   THE LAST PLACE ON EARTH

same with many game populations. But it is equally possible to modify production so as to get *minimum* population. These are all technicalities. The major argument shouldn't be on this level at all. Conservationists reveal the weakness of their faith when they couch the question in these terms."

He seemed very sure of himself about such matters. An elephant can live as long a life as a man, and its regulatory mechanisms, as the Serengeti symposium indicated, are subject to wide variances according to an indeterminable number of influences. "How do you know the degree of cropping of elephant that can be maintained over a long period of time?" I asked.

"This can only be demonstrated by practice, and no one has as yet practiced it." Parker and his associates have acquired their own data to support their theories on given species: herding characteristics, age and sex distributions, grazing habits, social structures, and so on. "Conservationists are stonewalling when they say there is insufficient data," Parker said. "If you are worried about the animals in the parks, the real question to ask is: What are the *objectives* of the park? That has been the problem at Tsavo, as it has been everywhere else cropping has caused controversy. The trouble comes from the tendency of the park administrators to ignore the conflicting tendencies of various species within the park.

"Nature is a process of continued change," he said. "There is no set rate to it. It starts, it stops. It is irregular, but it continues to change nevertheless. You find that one of the possible objectives of a park is that it be maintained as it was at a given point in time. Fair enough. However, your management of the park will then be geared to *oppose* whatever trends there might be in that system, and that entails *techniques* of management. By man.

"In Tsavo, as an example, it had been put out and accepted by many that what they were trying to do was to keep a replica of the Nyika bush in climax—a general term for the ecosystem there.

"All I said in respect of this was if you want this Nyika system to exist as it was when you established that park, then you have no choice but to oppose the major trend of what the elephants are doing. They are removing the trees because the elephant's density is too high to maintain that system. Therefore, you must reduce the elephants to a level at which this doesn't happen. However, there is another way.

"It is quite as logical, quite as valid a goal, just to let things go, leave the elephants alone and see what happens. But *then* you must put in the rider—which the conservationists never do—that if you allow the park to freewheel, you are willing to run the risk of losing other species whose existence is very much part of the Nyika ecosystem. In Tsavo, one species of plant, the *Euphorbia roebecchii*, is virtually eliminated, the baobab tree is disappearing, the *Sansevieria* is gone. Then, of course, you are rather stuck with the concept of preservation, aren't you?"

Some hunters believe there to be a mysterious form of communication between the shooter and his prey; aim the gun, and the quarry bolts. Scientists also suspect this strange intercourse—the quickening of adrenaline in the predator is sensed in some unknown way by the prey. The story is told out here of a hunter tracking an elephant which, with certain knowledge of what it was doing, headed in a straight-line path over a hundred miles to the border safety of a national park. Underlying these strange phenomena are the persisting questions raised by the Serengeti Research Institute: Would a herd of wild animals oblige the cropper by mechanically replacing its number with the amount artificially removed, replenishing itself from some inexhaustible source of response to man's order? Were such replenishable reductions measurable, as Ian Parker believed? Would Man's Way work in East Africa?

"Cropping is NOT the answer," Grzimek had stated conclusively to Omar, the director of Uganda's national parks, at Kabalega. "The Tsavo experiment, for example, was a failure."

"The Tsavo experiment" is the pulsing center of the cropping controversy—the beginning point of the Nature's Way argument— and has continued to be so since it first arose almost a dozen years ago. Before leaving for Uganda with Grzimek, I had heard it cited by others in almost the same cryptic way, conclusive to one side or the other, but most often the other, for the Serengeti expatriates tended to lean as far away from the Tsavo experiment as from Man's Way in the West, which it reflected. Its history is worth noting here.

In the same drought of 1961 that had aroused John Owen's concern for the wildebeest in Serengeti, a similar concern had grown among the park authorities at Tsavo National Park in Kenya, an extremely arid region that hovers perilously close to being dry-bush wasteland. There were thirty thousand elephants at Tsavo, one of the largest elephant reserves in East Africa but, under the circumstances, too large for the vegetation available there. (Tsavo also has the largest stock of black rhino.) An adult elephant may consume as much as seven hundred pounds of forage a day. They knock down the trees and strip the bark from those left standing. Because of the fragility of the African savanna, destroyed woodland turns quickly into plain, and while this is favorable to some species—the ungulates, for example—it is deleterious to others. If the cycle is allowed to continue, plain may turn into bush desert. Thus, the elephants' population problems, unmanaged by other means, could cause them to destroy their own habitat and that of other species, like the rhino, as well. In the extreme, there would be no animals left to see, no tourist income, and no financial support for the parks.

Working in Uganda at the time was the British zoologist Richard M. Laws, who was having some success in the long-term reduction of elephant and hippo populations. Earlier, he had gained recognition in the commercial cropping of seals and whales in the Antarctic. Kenya invited Laws to Tsavo to advise the park. In consultation with Laws, park officials authorized a sample cropping of three hundred elephants, to provide data for the study of population structures and breeding patterns of the herds. The animals were slaughtered and processed with great efficiency, and the meat was sold off for human consumption. Subsequently, Laws determined that there were ten separate population groups of Tsavo elephants, and he felt that to prepare a comprehensive survey it might be advisable to take off as many as three hundred animals from each population group—a maximum of three thousand elephants to be destroyed. At this point, the Tsavo experiment turned into a scandal. The shooting of three hundred elephants was bad enough, but the prospect of killing as many as three thousand within a national park was intolerable to conservationists, and not for sentimental reasons alone.

In the course of slaughtering the initial three hundred, to keep panic from spreading throughout the entire elephant population, the croppers had removed whole families of the animal, forcing a new consideration: in order to compensate for their diminution, would those families remaining begin now to overbreed at some unknown (perhaps unknowable) rate? If so, one expatriate warned, the park would then be faced with the necessity to crop even more, and the ramifications of that decision in a complex ecosystem, where so many different species had roles to fill, could not possibly be assessed. Even the removal of the elephants physically from the park, for example, might further disrupt the balance of the ecosystem by depriving the earth of their decomposing minerals. On the other hand, the elephant population, if left alone, conceivably would reduce its own excesses in adjusting to the park's carrying capacity—Nature's Way. At the height of the controversy, Richard Laws resigned from the study and left Kenya.

Whatever natural regulatory mechanisms were, or were not, at work among the elephants, however, a massive drought in 1971 went far beyond Laws's cropping proposals, destroying between seven and ten thousand of Tsavo's elephants, reducing the total herds by as much as a third. The Nature's Way faction immediately claimed vindication of its views. Most of the casualties were calves and mature females, reducing the population not only immediately but for an indeterminable time to come. The woodlands had survived, and the species, in collaboration with the unpredictable forces of nature, had indeed corrected its own imbalance.

But Parker and the Man's Way faction would not so quickly yield. By allowing the animals to starve, instead of managing their reduction through controlled cropping, they argued, the parks had wasted almost three million dollars of resources in meat, leather, and ivory. Furthermore, there was insufficient evidence to prove the elephant had achieved a balance within its environment (which, because of the elephant's migratory instincts, was artificial in any case). Acrimony followed.

"They accused Laws of being a crook," Parker says. "They said he only wanted to kill elephants. The sort of thing they *still* say today is that he had always been involved in the spilling of blood, and that's *all* he was after. Actually, Laws was a proponent of cropping and manipulating of the population for predetermined goals. He is able to demonstrate that when his recommendations were followed on harvesting seals, the seal crop *and* the seal population went up. But they ignore his successes."

In departing, Laws left behind a statement which hangs over the East African community today like a frozen shadow:

Personally, although I genuinely wish there were no necessity for killing these magnificent beings, I believe that humane and efficient reduction towards the possible solution of the problem is preferable to the uncertainty of decades of slow death of elephants through malnutrition, disease, and stress caused by drought, starvation, and overcrowding.

Laws went on to become director of the British Antarctic Survey, but his close associate and stoutest defender in Nairobi, Ian Parker, has carried forward his theories and still draws the fire. Among the Nature's Way faction, Parker is known as the man who did the shooting of the first three hundred elephants from the herds of Tsavo National Park (with automatic weapons, in a very few minutes); two thousand elephants and three thousand hippo in Uganda's national parks; and who, in 1968, at the height of the Tsavo experiment, signed a contract with Derek Bryceson to crop wildebeest and other species in Loliondo, on the outskirts of Serengeti National Park.

What could he tell me about that cropping project in 1968 in Loliondo, at the edge of Serengeti?

"We were to set up sustained-yield cropping of plains game and elephant—a whole spectrum of animals," Parker says. "John Owen was radically opposed because we would be working next to the Serengeti Park. Then the government wouldn't stand by its contract, and so we pulled out. Bryceson represented the government. He favors these possibilities. There's a man at S.R.I. now, conducting a feasibility study of wildebeest cropping."

Parker's company would have paid the Tanzanian government for rights to crop the Loliondo district, but when the government equivocated, Parker withdrew. He does not conceal his exasperation. "What is so obvious about all this is that food is the greatest use of wildlife on this continent. And it is by orders of magnitude that run to hundreds. If we make one unit of cash out of wildlife, then the use that could be made of ten thousand units by peasant people is enormous ... and this is consistently and absolutely ignored by conservationists."

"But certainly you would draw the line when it comes to the production of leopard-skin coats?"

"You mean because they are luxuries, like diamonds and gold?"

"Yes."

"If business is based upon leopard skins, it is sustaining human life. The use of East African animals is strictly up to the East Africans. To this continent, ivory is worth between seventy-two million and a hundred and forty-four million dollars annually. People say you are exploiting your resources. *No!* You are *using* your resources, and by systematic harvesting you could be even more successful. These are all currencies within man's social structure. You can't argue it on that level. Anyway, you will find people here who want to kill crocodile irrespective of market considerations because they are predators and capable of taking human life."

"But as population increases, the threat of predation decreases."

"No. The threat of predation *increases*. You are hemming the predators in. From a world view, sure—as the population increases, the predators must decline. But the process of decline takes place where the predators are, and it is inflicted by the humans in this area who must deal with this local, very steep increase in contact. *That's why they get rid of them!* What it boils down to is, if you wish to avoid their interaction with human density—and this is the prime component of our interaction with all other life, human density—what you have to do is make sure animals cannot interact with humans. There's no use in people coming here talking about the value you're getting from tourism with all this game when you've just lost a child the night before to hyena. I reckon there is a death a week that way—out in the sticks where you never hear such reports. You must realize that the people who want to preserve the game for idealistic purposes are directly opposed by the people who *live* with the game."

"Grzimek argues that if there is a constriction of Pleistocene mammals to this one area, then what's left becomes a world reserve, a treasure of human culture. He cites the example of the Acropolis in Athens, where a hundred years ago farmers would use its stones to build their houses, and where agriculture was as important to the people as it is here today. But when the community eventually realized the value of its possession, they preserved it, and today no one would touch it."

"A biased argument."

"Why?"

"For a start, the area of land occupied by the Acropolis is minuscule. Secondly, Greece is making a very substantial profit from it, and this cannot be said for the game."

"What? Tourism is Kenya's largest source of income!"

"The loss to local agriculture from wildlife is twice the income from tourism. I challenge you to go around East Africa and see. You've done it now. How many times have you heard how much damage the game does?"

"I haven't heard of any."

"No, and you will not, because no one has ever quantified it,"

Parker said. "However, take just one species—the elephant. The game departments of East Africa kill over six thousand elephant a year in protection of human life and property. *Why* do they do this? All you need to do is get a few facts on elephant biology. Elephants are gregarious. The game department doesn't take action until the elephant does something first—as few as possible are shot. Each elephant is a member of a herd of, say, six to twelve. For each elephant shot, there is from six to twelve times the damage being done. A peasant crop may be only an acre or so. How much damage of this sort can be sustained? And that's just the *elephant*, the most spectacularly visible of the game. However, they actually cause less damage than others—baboon, bush pig, bushbuck, buffalo, waterbuck, duiker, lion. . . ."

"Is all this not a very real political problem?"

"Yes, of course. That's why you get politicians from the game area who vote against the game and against the parks. It is in *their* districts that poachers get the lightest sentences."

(In the distance, a poignant echo: *"But elephants can't vote, and lions can't vote. . . ."*)

"It is my contention, and I can demonstrate it, that the material loss from wildlife in energy, food, and crops, as well as in cash, is much greater than the revenue from tourism. This loss is sustained by subsistence-level people who tend to be just outside the monetary economy."

"Is it your belief that the elimination of wildlife would cause the country to thrive?" I asked.

"I'll answer that question with a question," Parker said. "How do you think Britain would do today if its pristine wildlife were restored?"

Parker surprised. His strongest arguments were in the people's interest. Killing for food, he said at one point, was the most efficient use of wildlife by the peasant—he even objected to the term *poaching* when the game was used for such a purpose. How could he escape the conclusion he was arguing out of vested interest? "I get my business from the parks and the conservation policies I attack. Why should I do that?" There seemed little of Grzimek's program Parker could agree with, even that which has been demonstrably effective. I mentioned both Bryceson's and Grzimek's reference to instances where Tanzanians had requested their land be made into national parks.

"Absolutely! Have you *seen* the publicity that's gone into selling parks to these people? Do you know the worst thing you can say to one of these chaps? That is, if he's not civilized? *'If you don't accept this, you aren't civilized, because that is what civilized people do!'* "

But if Parker considered himself a pragmatist, and if he did not want to see the game go, and if he believed the problem for the parks to be the proper setting of objectives, what would he do to preserve Serengeti?

"First of all, the Serengeti belonged to people—to the Masai—and by a paleface act they were kicked out of it. The Masai have a growth rate of just beyond two per cent, slightly lower than the national average, but all those people in the south and the west—the Waikoma, Wasukuma, the Wakuria—they have the *highest* growth rate in Tanzania. They are breeding at the rate of three to four per cent per annum. The greater the population, the less of a drought it will take to produce extreme drought effects. This intrusion at the Lamai Wedge, for example. The need to use the Wedge *must* rise. All those people are confined to Lake Victoria and have no room to expand. The western boundary is now defined by huts and fields. You can tell where it is, because cultivation comes right up to it. There are between one and four million people down there. Can you tell me what is going to happen to those people?"

"John Owen says the park grasslands are too fragile to sustain cattle and wildlife simultaneously, that there is too little water."

"Bullshit! The Masai did it and have done it—not for a hundred years, but for *thousands* of years. There is little water, so they moved in and out seasonally. But now they're *shut* out. The only thing is to fix the humans, stop them from increasing."

"What about moving them out?"

"There *is* no other place to go. Comparatively speaking, these people are on desirable land. We are heading into an extended dry period. Assume the human population doubles and triples there and the people somehow manage to eke out survival until a really classic drought comes, the sort to which East Africa is given. Their only hope will be to graze the Serengeti. When that point comes, *no* government elected by the people is going to deny those people access. The conservationists would ask them to draw the line between human life and animal life, and that is impossible. As the population goes up, less of a drought will be needed to reach this point. Population will bring these droughts to a point closer together. The Serengeti will be eroded. The whole phenomenon has nothing to *do* with wildlife. It has to do with *human density.* Period."

Human density is the essential component of Parker's analysis, and he angrily denounces the conservationists for evading the issue: "The Duke of Edinburgh, when he was interviewed on Australian television, let it be known beforehand he would not countenance any discussion of human population control. The Stockholm Environment Conference decided it would not consider such things. At a recent conservation meeting here, some of the members said population growth is 'not our brief.' They chose to ignore it. Leslie Brown challenged me to take an intrauterine device and fit it to a Masai woman. Very funny. A very erudite man, the former director of the Serengeti Research Institute, Hugh Lamprey, said, 'Well, we must conserve something while we still have something to conserve.' *That's* the way *he* faced what I'm saying.

"And that sets conservation for what it is—a waste of time. The Grzimeks of this world make it all too simple a question. Conservationists ignore human destiny, and they ignore hostile elements within the African environment. By doing so, they sow the seeds of their own destruction. To ask the Africans to try to keep Africa open is to try to cure cancer with aspirin."

"Does Derek Bryceson share your views?"

Silence.

"Derek Bryceson," I said, not sure he had heard me, "does he share your views?"

Parker remained silent.

"Julius Nyerere?"

"Nyerere's concerns are overwhelmingly with the welfare of humans. Of all the philosophers on this continent, he is the most clear-cut and honest. He says wildlife is a resource for the people and how the people make use of it is *their* show. And currently the best use of it is food.

"In Tanzania, the hierarchy look on wildlife as a source of damage. They say, 'You are trying to make us accept something which causes us grief. From many points of view, in many areas, it is bad. You say we must preserve it because it is a source of revenue. But surely, doing something for money which is bad is no less than prostitution.' And it *is.* Conservationists like Grzimek have to review their whole argument. The case they are selling today is not one whit different from the glass beads traders sell to Africans."

While Grzimek had stated his opposition to interference of any sort within the national parks, it occurred to me somewhat belatedly, as Parker was growing ever more indignant over such deceits, that Grzimek must have seen value in cropping techniques in certain cases. I recalled now what he had said about his own methods of assuring the survival of Canadian seals and Nile crocodile. He had forced both industries to hire scientists to oversee the harvesting of both species. I mentioned this to Parker. Would these instances be compatible with Parker's views? "Sure," he said. "*Absolutely!* This reveals a glimpse of Grzimek that delights me. He's a pragmatist, all right. You see, Grzimek underneath is an extremely cold, practical person. He has chosen his political weapons with tremendous thought, while realizing at the same time that he has to take several faces. I think he also realizes ultimately this may be his personal downfall, not that he gives a damn. Because there is going to come a point where the overstatement of conservationists, of which he is one, will turn full circle to ridicule them. What it all boils down to is, there are *two* sides of the question. What one seeks to do is to put conservation in a balanced context of human life, the wresting of existence from a hostile environment. But it has been sold by others in an unbalanced fashion—as all pros and no cons. And there are many cons."

Parker fancies himself a philosopher, and at this point he left the ground of Serengeti and East Africa altogether:

"Every established civilization has practiced conservation. The Egyptians went so far as virtually having parks and park wardens. The Assyrians, Babylonians, Persians, Romans, and many European peoples have all had conservation laws. It is not generally known that William the Conqueror's oppressive game laws were a prominent factor in the background to events that led to King John signing the Magna Carta. Conservatism is a recurrent phenomenon which comes about at a certain stage in the growth of the civilization. It is always when civilization heads toward its apogee that conservation comes in, and conservatism is always expressed by the same social strata. It is invariably the higher strata that are pro-conservationists and come up with the idea; it is always the lower strata that are basically opposed to it. Because it can only be practiced at *their* expense. So when people say now, 'We mustn't make the same mistakes that our forefathers made in eliminating the game'—*all* this just goes by as hogwash.

254   THE LAST PLACE ON EARTH

"What is more interesting is to get down to these foundation drives. Why do people do this? This, in turn, leads you into a perspective on politics and human relations which is as fascinating to some people as it is horrifying to others. You can see very concise and clear-cut compartments. It is not very difficult to demonstrate the aggression behind conservation. Very simple indeed."

"Do you honestly think wildlife in this stage of our civilization represents a hostile threat to man?"

"Definitely. By the question you ask, you haven't defined *wildlife* to yourself. It is all life that is not tamed—microbes, diseases . . ."

"Let's just deal, then, with the remaining African animals. Elephant, rhino, wildebeest . . ."

"You are trying to steer me onto mammals, the so-called higher form of life. People do this because they are nearest to man, the easiest to anthropomorphize. You see yourself in them. You're using animals to view yourself. You attribute to them all manner of human concepts."

"Some see value in that alone."

"Why didn't we preserve them, then, in Europe and America? It was because we couldn't afford them. So why should you have them here, when they pose exactly the same threat? For some, they are hostile; for some, they are not. It depends upon your circumstances as to whether they are hostile. I may aesthetically like viewing animals, but why should I impose my aesthetic desires on others? The guy who lives in the field sets about doing exactly what my forefathers did—to get them the hell off his land, where they're a nuisance."

"Where do you share Grzimek's views and where do you depart from them?"

"We probably share the same views on the fundamental level but depart on ways to manipulate the public."

"Surely he will not agree with you about any of this?"

"No. Grzimek would go along with the logic, except that he has made a decision to stop. He has said, 'I like it. I want it. I consider it a value to *me* and to mine, and I'm going to persuade those guys over there that it is a value to *thine* that I might enjoy it.' And that's where he brings the argument to a halt. He doesn't want to go on with it. Or if he did, he would resort to metaphysics, the world beyond. . . ."

Once more I tried with the Serengeti. "Say the objective of the park was just to preserve the ecosystem as it is there now. How could you see practical management achieving that goal?"

"Well, this is where we enter into the horrendous aspects of what conservation really reveals of man's condition. Because what it all boils down to is, if *that* was my objective, there would be no recourse other than saying to the humans, 'Tough on you, you're finished. This is an objective I want, and it means you're going to die because you have become too many. It's *you* who became too many, not me or the animals.'

"I delight in this because it forces the issue, brings us to what it's all about in conservation. Brings us to the nitty-gritty of the human condition. It has nothing to do with conservation, but conservation gives you this skylight into the problem.

"I had a session with the Audubon Society once, the little old ladies in tennis shoes. I told them about the elephant problem, and I told them it was man-made. I pointed out that it wasn't an elephant problem, it was a human problem. So let's forget elephants, I said, and get down to the human problem.

"I told them that within a decade biologists would justify what Hitler did, and there was a great shout immediately: 'Ah, *push* off. Don't be *crazy!*' So, I said, I would come back to this.

"And I got onto population growth and the difficulties involved in controlling it—how you can control it at the top end of society but not at the bottom end, because it is the lower strata's biological safety valve. They're right up against the bread line. Biologically, the only way out is to reproduce as many as possible. It's very difficult to educate a person against his inherent drives. The dialogue went on. Finally they agreed that you *couldn't* educate them to control their numbers. So I said, 'Now the ball is in your court. What are you going to do?'

"So they said, 'Well, we'll just have to *force* them to do it.' I said, 'How are you going to do that?' So they said, 'We're not sure.' And it went a bit further, and then they said, 'We'll just cut off aid.'

"I said, 'Yeah, that's *exactly* what you'll do. One way or another, you'll run out of the ability to *give* aid or you'll make the decision to cut it off. And if you do, it is automatically the death warrant for millions of people. Now the going term for this is *genocide*. And that is what Hitler did. And I haven't had to wait to hear scientists support it. You people yourselves have come up off the floor and said that if the people are not sensible, we will ultimately have to

THE LAST PLACE ON EARTH

resort to it. You are countenancing it yourself. Go on, be horrified!'
They said, 'We didn't mean it like that.'

"I said, 'From the point of view of the guy who gets the death
warrant, it doesn't matter whether it is the gestapo shooting him or
you starving him. What does he think is the difference between you
and Hitler, when you've cut off his aid? He'll think of you in exactly
the same way.

" 'Only, from your point of view, if you once thought Hitler was
bad and you thought you were good, and you'd never equate
yourself between the two, you have to understand that to a third
party there is literally no difference at all. And that's where we're
at, folks.' "

EIGHTEEN

I had allowed myself a last few days in Nairobi, but it was troublesome time. I had learned more than I could quite manage, but not yet enough to discern a possible reprieve for Serengeti, even within the immediate months ahead. I was glutted with contradictions, quite lost within the expatriates' own confusions. This morning had been given over to Ian Parker's angry excoriations which, coming now after Turner's pessimism and Bryceson's too-facile reassurances, were impossible to dismiss. Parker's analysis had been *political:* he had simply refused to acknowledge any scientific controversy over the question of cropping. Nothing inconsistent about this, I had thought afterward. At one point, he had dismissed the Serengeti Research Institute in a sentence: "After fifteen years of scientific research out here, costing millions and millions of pounds, *nothing* has been achieved in the application of research to the management of wildlife." As for the passion of Bernhard Grzimek, what was left after Parker, mainly, was its extravagance.

I hadn't been able to locate Hugh Lamprey, the scientist; in truth, I had given him up. No one knew where he was, or what he was doing, or when next he might be in Nairobi. It hadn't seemed now to matter quite so much—Parker's harsh predictions had served to foreclose the pathetic efforts of the rest of them. I could not suppress a feeling of my own abandonment of this mythical place, but reality is a relentless enemy of passion; I was myself at too low a point to resist the outcome at hand, whatever its character, and I was ready now to return home.

Yet, in keeping with so many of the surprising turns to this journey—almost as though the ordeal of Serengeti now was pursuing me—as I tried to sleep through the hot afternoon to dampen Parker's perverse "logic," someone knocked on the door of my room, and: "I am Hugh Lamprey," my visitor said. "I received word that you were trying to reach me. . . ."

We walked down to the terrace of the Norfolk and I ordered Dr. Lamprey a beer. He is a tall, sturdy man with an impassive face but eager eyes. One senses an immediate empathy, as though it will not be impossible to find some common ground. I decided quickly I must lean hard on that assumption, and I was not to be disappointed. He proves open to my questions and meticulous with his answers, his manner that of a patient teacher whose occasional frustrations arise only from his obligations to the accuracies of discipline.

On Grzimek, for example (it is the most convenient and obvious starting point):

"Grzimek is a splendid man. Quite incomparable for his growth. Among many other things, he changed from a conservationist into an ecologist. But you must remember where he began—as a veterinarian, which is a comparatively narrow scope, and he grew from there to an ecologist. There are no people like him."

Still ensnarled by the definitions of others, I stopped him here. Derek Bryceson had said the only difference he saw between a conservationist and an ecologist was that the latter was now a more fashionable word than the former. How did the distinction apply to Grzimek?

"It is an important distinction. The conservationist in an earlier stage might have been called a preservationist. But now he recognizes you may have to manipulate wild animals and their habitats to preserve them. The idea of preserving had been to leave them alone completely. Conservation today is preservation with management. . . ." (*Management.* Even the conservationist believed now in manipulations by man! . . .) "The *ecologist* is a scientist who studies the interactions of different components of nature. He studies structures and functions of nature seen as a whole. Nature is organized on different levels—on the molecular level, on the cellular level, on the tissue level; on the whole animal and plant level; on the population level; on the biotic-community level; on the ecosystem level; and, finally, on the biosphere level. At each stage there is organization; otherwise the system could not work. As you look at successively larger and more complicated aggregations of animals and plants, the organization becomes more difficult to characterize. But it is there nevertheless. This is the organization which ecologists attempt to study. And these are Grzimek's concern today, although I doubt he would describe it in those words." (But, in fact, he had come close: "... *The animals belong to our planet, and the planet belongs to the animals, too. They are part of nature, and we are part of nature. We must realize we are animals, too....*")

Could Lamprey somehow bring it all together? I catalogued my perplexities. Against his own definition of ecology, if man should interfere in a climax region like Serengeti, the whole system could collapse—this was said to be the basis for Nature's Way. But the wardens of Serengeti had shot elephants within the park to save trees; and George Dove had treated Serengeti lions with antibiotics to preserve them. When was man's interference—his management— "improper"? Who were the antagonists out here, and who the protagonists? Against Parker's human-density component, what possible justification could there be for saving the animals other than as a source of food or as a commodity? And beyond the impoverished government of Tanzania, whose responsibility, finally, *was* Serengeti?

Where Lamprey stands on these vexing questions is in the existential land of direct contradiction, persistence beyond reason. He is tolerant of the extremists on either side of the cropping issue; of the people's need for the Lamai Wedge and the animals'; of the government's priorities and the scientists' concerns. Of the scientists who have come and gone over the past two decades, Hugh Lamprey is considered the most knowledgeable of the many aspects of Serengeti biology. Thus, of all the expatriates, because of this knowledge, he is the least expendable. Yet he is without rancor over his own exclusion through Africanization and does not speak of it (nor of Derek Bryceson who, within the past month, has maneuvered him out of attending an important scientific council meeting of the Serengeti Research Institute). Perhaps it is because he knows so much about the Serengeti Plain that Lamprey, the biologist who came down from Oxford in 1953 to advise on pest control in East Africa, is now one of the most temperate and cautious of all its well-wishers. And perhaps it is especially because he knows so much about the Serengeti Plain that his most urgent concern that it be preserved is for the reason, finally, that we know so little.

A good thing for me that he is at this moment in Nairobi. Sipping his single beer to extend his reflections—it will last him through the afternoon—Lamprey begins now to deal with my confusions.

"This is the awful part of it," he says. "Wildlife in East Africa is the interest of a large number of people, scientific and nonscientific, commercial and noncommercial. It is very difficult indeed to thread your way through the many conflicting opinions. You should recognize when you are dealing with extremes on either side—at one end, total sentiment, and at the other, hardheadedness and almost total skepticism. Unfortunately, the issues have become polarized. . . ."

"Parker says Grzimek is at one end and he is at the other."

"No," Lamprey said. "Grzimek is not at the far end. He has a lot more common sense than others would credit him for. He is very much more balanced about it all. Grzimek tends to be *seen* in the preservation camp. But Parker and his supporters *are* at the opposite extreme. They see themselves as the common sense, modernist approach to conservation. They think they see a long-term uselessness in the current conservation activities of others. My own opinion is that they go too far.

"What you'll hear from Parker is that we should have left the problem of wildlife conservation quite a long way behind us while we look at something far more important. Wildlife conservation is only one side of the real problem, which is correct, rational land use, human density, and how to come to some form of reconciliation of these incredible problems. Wildlife occupying areas of land is just one side of it.

"Whereas people like Parker will have looked at this problem in a very wide context, Grzimek is far more single-minded about it. His role in life is wildlife conservation. But he certainly isn't blind to the fact that it goes a good bit further than wildlife conservation, to the conservation of man."

Lamprey sipped at his beer and reflected.

"The distinction is this: whereas Grzimek is ready to try to tackle the more immediate problems, the ones he sees, the ones he understands, Parker sees the more immediate ones as being rather irrelevant—he wants to tackle things on a very much wider basis. And he rather decries the efforts of people who are trying to get at the immediate problems."

Another long pause and a sigh.

"I haven't got this very well—my sympathies lie with both of them, and you can't say either one is wrong. I think each of them should acknowledge that the other is doing a necessary job. The only thing I can't say that I agree with Parker about is the hopelessness of the general situation. Because if we start to acknowledge at this point that any trend is too difficult or intractable or, you might say—in the end—useless . . ."

"Futile?"

"*Futile*, and then don't do anything about it . . . I *can't* agree with that because from the past record a *tremendous* amount is to be gained at this stage by fighting a rearguard action. And this is why I believe Grzimek is right."

"Is it an oversimplification to say it all comes down to the choice of Man's Way versus Nature's Way?"

"No, it is not." Lamprey paused again, searching, apparently, for our common ground.

"Could you deal with their differences with respect to the Serengeti?"

"Yes, all right. The Serengeti. Let's go back to the first days at the Institute." And, interestingly, Hugh Lamprey chose the same central reference point as had Ian Parker.

"People began to ask," said Lamprey, " 'What are the *objectives* of a national park?' A most interesting stalemate was reached. The scientists were being asked how to manage the park, and the scientists said to the parks' administrators, 'Right, we may be able to advise you on management, but first tell us, what are your *objectives?*'

"For the first time almost ever, the administrators were faced with the question: What do you manage a park *for?* What do you want to achieve? Then questions came up one by one after that: Where is the park going? Is it changing from one direction to another? If so, is that desirable? The answer was, no one knew. So they looked at other national parks systems and tried to find one where the question had been asked before. And they found it in the United States, not posed very well and not for twenty-five years. But at least there was an answer, and the answer was: 'We want to maintain the U.S. parks in the condition they were in before the white man arrived.' Well, we went over this endlessly."

Presumably, the objective was to maintain the park in a natural state. But there finally can be no definitive answer to the question of what is "a natural state," Lamprey says, mainly because it is impossible to determine a time at which human activities and their influence can be judged to have become artificial. In 1972, at the Second World Conference on National Parks, in Wyoming, Lamprey himself had tried to deal with the thorny question of

262   THE LAST PLACE ON EARTH

objectives. In a paper he delivered before the conference, he reasoned that sustained biological activity, which is measured by ecologists as the flow of energy through a system, tends to peak where there is a great diversity of species. Thus, biological productivity and species diversity, he said, seem interdependent. The preservation of these elements is a worthy objective for a national park.

But, as Parker had pointed out, there are great changes always going on in a biotic community, some of which may work directly against productivity and species diversity. "If there is doubt about the course to follow and if there are apparently no management problems," Lamprey had warily observed then, "it seems better to do nothing, trusting in the self-regulatory properties of nature to maintain the status quo."

"The world's national parks *should* aim to conserve natural ecosystems," Lamprey was saying now. "I stated in my paper that the main objective is to conserve natural ecosystems insofar as this is possible, recognizing (a) that there are practically no natural ecosystems left, and (b) that it is practically an impossible task, but that we should *start* by trying to identify the criteria for naturalness and aim for them, knowing full well we can only achieve a compromise. "And this is where people like Ian Parker say, '*Why try?*'

"I would contest this, because certain areas of the world still maintain these natural ecosystems. The climax rain forest, for example. Then you have places like the Serengeti. It is remarkable because one element of it—the grasslands ecosystem—is still operating as a self-perpetuating system, and we can see the mechanisms operating there today. In this extraordinary African situation, which is unique, with richness unparalleled anywhere else, with a large mammal community which has arisen in the course of evolution due to a unique background where the situation of repeated changes in climate, repeated changes in vegetation, have produced successive opportunities for speciation—all of it has led to this tremendous adaptive radiation of large mammals, and birds as well. . . ."

Lamprey toyed with his beer and hesitated, almost visibly forcing his own perception.

"What one must keep in mind is that the world's plants and animals—and not as taken singly in species but in self-regulating communities—are gradually losing their identity and their capacity for self-regulation," he said. "Their capacity for self-*perpetuation!* At the same time, *species* are being lost. But it is not as simple as that. A species is genetically variable across the whole of its range, and it's *not* just a matter of losing a species which is so bad, it's losing even a *part* of a species. An important concept that has arisen over the last few years that Parker may not have understood is that it is *criminal negligence* to allow a population, a community, an ecosystem, or a species to become extinct. The world is going to be short of usable genetic material in the future. Any plant or animal—either the species itself, or a genetic variety of it, or a subspecies of it—which is lost, is lost forever."

The sun-bright terrace of the Norfolk seemed as distant now from the Serengeti as a beach house in the Hamptons. What was moving about Lamprey beyond his words was his desperate effort to harness his own passion, correcting himself, qualifying, paren-thesizing, all out of the constraints of discipline, but at the same time frustrating his momentum: the antithesis of Grzimek in manner—the connectives counted for too much—but ally to his conclusions, and he, too, was without a moment to lose.

"The view *must* be taken by conservationists—and I'm being dogmatic, I *really* shouldn't—that where it is possible, through taking a little trouble, to remind people to prevent the extinction of any element of nature—this *must* be done. Now when I say *any,* one may find reasons for exceptions, such as the smallpox virus, for instance—some disease organisms one would say perhaps we have to do without if we possibly can. But there aren't many such cases. These are in the minority. But at the other end of the scale, plants and animals and their ecosystems are gradually being eroded away. Some of them are on the point of extinction. Not only do you need to take that view," he said, "but you can extend it. Where you have something as remarkable and, for want of a better word, as *precious* as a self-regulating ecosystem, and which *need* not be removed, for *God's* sake, *let it go on!* The world is becoming increasingly man-regulated, increasingly more *difficult* to regulate, and I should say that every time you become committed to the management of artificial ecosystems, you introduce bigger and bigger problems. If it is possible to leave ecosystems to manage themselves, insofar as they can—since there are very few which are totally capable of doing so, due to human interference—then let us do so. For a *whole lot* of different reasons.

"The most cogent reason, I think, must be that one is trying

264   THE LAST PLACE ON EARTH

desperately to preserve for posterity—and I know I am arguing with myself here, but I'm trying to get at something—something that is *a record of nature as it has been!* Nature in its self-regulatory state. This is part of what nature conservation is seen to be. It is very hard to get it over as an objective in itself."

"No seeming practical application?"

"Exactly. But the practical application, as we see it, is probably there very far ahead for our descendants to make use of these ecosystems or their components. And it is a *social crime* to eliminate them, or even to damage them if we needn't do so.

"Now on the other side of all this is this extraordinary argument of Parker's that you *must* manage everything, you *must* make everything economically productive. Otherwise it won't survive, otherwise it has no relevance to human needs. I profoundly disagree with this. . . ."

Elsewhere in the world, others were similarly concerned for—in Lamprey's phrase—"a whole lot of different reasons." In 1975, Dr. Ian McTaggart Cowan warned the Pacific Science Congress to expect unknown troubles in unpredictable places from the persistent obtrusion of Man's Way into natural processes. "The loss of diversity is not merely a matter for sentimental regret, it is a direct reduction in the number of opportunities open to future generations." Wild lands "produce food, cover for other creatures, breeding sites for insects that may be essential for pollinating crops, and others that keep plant pests under control. . . . The spread over the world of the industrial objectives of Northern peoples can be seen as a most destructive event. Almost inevitably diversity is sacrificed to a spurious efficiency. . . ."

In the northeastern sections of Brazil, rain is sparse. The clearing of the eight-thousand-mile highway through the rain forests of the Amazon is to open new farmlands to refugees from the northeast. But now it is coming to be seen that once the forest is cleared from this seemingly fertile setting, thick with silt and humus, the soil loses its fertility. "When the forest canopy is rent by clearing the decline in soil fertility begins," reports Dr. Robert Goodland of the New York Botanical Garden, "and it is accelerated at a rate commensurate with the decrease in the overall amount of transpiration. Sunlight piercing the hitherto protected forest floor rapidly dries and oxidizes the litter and humus. Eventually this stops the normal decay, which reduces the return of nutrients to the soil. Then rain leaches some nutrients from the soil and burning vaporizes others." And yet, throughout the world today, tropical rain forests, which apart from their scientific interest as climax ecosystems, serve the world as significant sources of oxygen, are being destroyed at the rate of fourteen acres a minute.

In Kenya the government has encouraged soil erosion by permitting the sale of charcoal to the Middle East, where the trees are gone and wood fuel has become as precious as oil and food. In Nairobi, a sack of charcoal is worth sixty cents; in the Middle East, fifty dollars. An acre of scrub bush will produce a ton of charcoal, but after the wood is taken, the land is spoiled for good. The one-time profit from this resource is about four pounds, or thirteen dollars, an acre. In 1967, Kenya exported twenty-five hundred tons of charcoal; in 1970, thirty-two thousand tons; by 1975, eighty thousand tons—exponential destruction of its own environment.

But the principal constraint Lamprey was moving toward was man's ignorance of natural systems and the certain damage that follows his assumption of ecological omniscience or infallibility (Parker's insistence on the "logical" way). This, too, has raised concern elsewhere and, in two remarkable and otherwise unrelated inquiries, the expression as well of a new hope. One is to be found in the observations of Dr. Eric Kraus of the School of Marine and Atmospheric Science of the University of Miami, the other within *The Parable of the Beast,* a little-known book by John Bleibtreu. Both share Lamprey's concern over the illusion of assumed knowledge with respect to the environment.

"The management of the man-made environment always required a measure of anticipation," Kraus writes, "furs and firewood had to be collected before the advent of cold weather." Cultural evolution and reliance on scientific predictions have therefore strengthened our tendency to believe we can anticipate what is to happen. But now we exist in a technology which can produce global changes within a short time, and now "we have no long-term guarantee that a turn of the tap will yield fresh water without fail, or that the supermarket around the corner will always supply us with frozen vegetables regardless of environmental vicissitudes. Things can go wrong. In the long run, they almost certainly will go wrong, and will probably do so in rather unexpected ways." The "scientific" analytical method for predicting the distant future

266

doesn't work for three reasons: we can never know the present completely; we are unable to make accurate deductions from what we know; we are unable to know even how to ask the right questions.

A hurricane, Kraus suggests (he is a meteorologist), may commence from the wingbeat of a solitary sea gull. "All the water in the clouds now overhead will inevitably come to rest in the sea; but who is to say when it will do so after it has been incorporated in soils and rivers and living creatures and other as yet unborn clouds?" The trouble begins, Kraus says, because we have no actual experience with any completely isolated system—nor can we, for there is nothing we know that can remain physically in isolation, within our world or outside it. "Stars are born; clouds build up and grow; creatures keep on living and develop—all because they are not isolated and self-contained. This may apply even to the cosmos as a whole. Whether or not there is a spirit which interferes with it, the thing is so vast that any phenomenon that we can observe is always affected by influences outside itself." Scientists can agree on deductions drawn from a limited set of facts, but environmental phenomena proceed from a *limitless* set of facts. Yet science so pervades all our lives that it is almost unthinkable to approach any unknown phenomenon without an analytical, scientific attitude. It is our limitation with probability information on ecological or behavioral processes that concerns Kraus. It is important to our survival that we come to know of this limitation: "On the spiritual level it may provide a matrix of common deeper understanding and of a shared aesthetic feeling for the design of an evolving universe."

Within such an understanding does John Bleibtreu see the beginning of myth. Western man began to restrict his inquiries out of the Judeo-Christian belief in the duality of mind and body: intellect reposed within the mind; the body was separate, a vehicle for the mind. Thus did we come to lose our sense of shared identity with all other forms of biological life—until most recently, through a series of critical experiments and investigations into the world of nature. Among the sciences, it is the emergence of biology over physics and mathematics that poses now the greater challenge for man's understanding of self.

"We know that flowers bloom in the spring," Bleibtreu writes, "and that the swallows *return* to Capistrano, but as regards the conduct and apprehension of ourselves inside the phenomenon of time we are still entranced by the fallacy of western causal logic.

The fallacy involves the idea of closed systems. There are no closed systems in nature; everything involves everything else.

"The great reward of western causal logic has been technology and the manipulation of our environment. The loss has come about because we consider every act a closed system with short range predictable consequences. The result is therefore a loss of the meaning to act."

But now, Bleibtreu suggests, "We are in the process of creating a mythology out of the same raw materials of science in much the same way that the Greeks and Jews created their mythologies out of the raw materials of history. We have lately discovered there are forces abroad in the world to which animals respond. At one time or another in our evolutionary history, we, too, responded to these forces. They now remain mostly vestigial like the 28-day lunar cycle of human female menstruation. This new mythology which is being derived from the most painstaking research into other animals, their sensations and behavior, is an attempt to re-establish our losses—to place ourselves anew within an order of things because faith in an order is a requirement of life."

Bleibtreu then traces his "parables"—through studies in the perceptions of time of the cattle tick, which may wait in suspension up to eighteen years before its instant of biological fulfillment; through Lamarck's theories of volitional control by animals over the direction of their evolution; through von Uexküll's studies in anxiety and flight behavior (with implications leading to man's own self-punishing gastrointestinal disorders); through von Frisch's thirty-year observations of the honeybee's dance to discover the relationship of time and light to its directional codes—circadian rhythms (which man himself still dances to); through the experiments of various scientists with various animals resulting in theories of molecular memory; and many other concepts emerging now, all leading Bleibtreu to conclude:

> Love and hate, aggression and submission, need and satiety; one may see all these forces working themselves out quite simply and mechanically in the behavior of fish, reptiles and birds.
>
> Ethological systems apply there; it is as one ascends the ladder of psychological complexity, as one observes animals up through the class of mammals, up through the order of

268   THE LAST PLACE ON EARTH

primates, finally reaching man, that one finds what seems to be a progressive blurring of that which is innate, or given by the genetic heritage, and what is the individual experience.

But "blurring" is a poor metaphor; it seems more like an alienation or oscillation—an oscillation between the historical past embedded within the very flesh and bone, and the perceived existential present. At each moment of our becoming (becoming older, wiser, other than what we were in the previous moment) we are being acted upon alternately by a pulse of autochthonous existence and a pulse of consciously perceived and intellectually evaluated experience; each alternating pulse modifying the next, so that, as with the sound of a flute, we are conscious, finally, only of the continuum, the thin, beautiful and resonant sound of the self—the self, alive. . . .

We no longer see ourselves as belonging to one order of living being as separate from any other order of living being. We are all interconnected by the fact of existence, the fact of life. And this fact of life ties us irrevocably into the past as determining great parts of the present.

It is to the sound of this continuum, as well, that we must attend (so the new myths of biology advise us), for this is also the sound of the self, and we must listen in awe and humility, ever more aware of all that is contained within this sound, which we do not begin to understand. The new biology tells us to listen to all the sounds of the self, attend it in all its movement, internal and external, and also attend those reflections of the self that surround us and enclose us within the web of life. There is nothing new in this advice; every great myth of mankind has advised us to do precisely the same. But somehow the metaphors of this new myth can make a claim of credibility on the contemporary imagination. . . .

One listens to Hugh Lamprey and is reminded of isolated images occurring across East Africa—of a photograph, taken by her husband, of Oria Douglas-Hamilton holding their baby son out to be inspected by a wild elephant of Lake Manyara; of Alan Root nuzzling his spotted hyena; of Dian Fossey lying in the thick forest grass beside a gorilla, imitating its feeding habit and making its sounds until gently, inquiringly, the gorilla reaches to touch her; of Grzimek, the biophylactist, the showman of pity, patrolling the savanna in his minibus.

Hugh Lamprey was in basic agreement with Myles Turner and Ian Parker that the political problem of Serengeti's borders had become acute. "This is terribly serious," he said. "There are very strong pressures along the Lamai Wedge area to the northwest because the population is increasing at a fast rate. It is not just Tanzanians but a lot of Kenyans, too. An embarrassing situation. This has only recently become recognized as a place where people *can* settle. Growth is exponential, increasing rapidly because there is now land hunger everywhere. As the people come in so suddenly, the countryside ceases to be wild bush where the less adventurous don't want to go. The first pioneers have moved in now—those who are taking the risks—and once there, others will follow. The people in the southwest, in the Maswa area, are the second problem. They are illegally in the area. They light fires, which make the park's policies of fire control practically useless. But that's another story. . . ."

"Is it true that the wildebeest migration is central to the biology of the plain?" I asked.

"Yes, precisely. The wildebeest is half of the total animal biomass in the area."

"How will all this affect the migration?"

"The wildebeest population, I think, will go on adjusting itself as the total area available to it is reduced. It is simply that if this does happen, the park will become less of a viable ecosystem than it is now and there will be more strain on the center."

"What do you see as the possible future of Serengeti?"

"Given the pressure of the people, eventually it may come to this," Lamprey said, turning to the map (shown on the facing page).

"This part, the shaded area, is cultivatable. The people nearby farm and raise cattle. They impose pressure. So do the Masai in the eastern section about Loliondo, and the people to the south and west. What is left is not suitable for human use, and that part of it may be saved. Supposing in the more distant future attempts were made at sophisticated agriculture, the use of methods adapted to cultivating poor soil—irrigation, for example—and supposing people were starving in large numbers and it became imperative to find

THE LAST PLACE ON EARTH

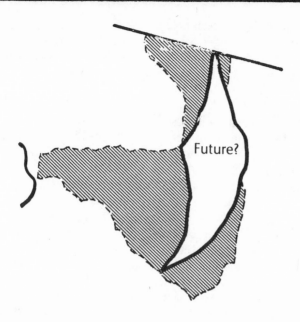

land. One can imagine, in the *far* distant future, nuclear power being used to pump water from Lake Tanganyika or Victoria and to spread it over large tracts of the land. But as far as I can remember, even then the greater part of the Serengeti is unfit for cultivation. [Myles Turner and Ian Parker believed otherwise.] So there is a strong possibility for its survival, even with the political developments that will occur.

"But the possibility of its survival as a *natural ecosystem*—I think that's fading out. Serengeti has this extraordinary capacity for self-regulation even when it goes on being reduced, but what it *can't* do is accommodate both wild animals and domestic animals at the same time. Because as soon as that happens, you get serious degradation setting in."

More bluntly to the point than the cautious Lamprey was Ian Parker: "When the severity of drought intersects with an intolerable pressure on the land, what government would say to its people, 'Fellows, I'm afraid you'll have to get your coffins ready because you can't go into that park'?" According to Derek Bryceson, border crossings were already happening and would continue to as unofficial policy; the strength of the Parks Department under his administration would keep them from getting out of hand. But how long could Derek Bryceson hold off the swell of human density, and when he could no longer, what then would be lost?

The scientists of Serengeti and elsewhere in East Africa are seeking to understand processes which are unknown within units of time still immeasurable. To alter these processes for whatever purpose short of Parker's charge of genocide is to arrest their natural development and erase that fraction of the biological past, ending forever the remnants of recognition by man of his own natural history. A social crime, Lamprey said. (Surely the end, hardly begun, of Bleibtreu's "new myth.") As he talked on of such problems, with airline pilots and stewardesses checking in and out of the hotel, the terrace packed with festive, excited all-white foreigners, it seemed almost inconceivable in this time of the mid-seventies, as the fashions of science had shifted from outer space to terrestrial biology, and with the funding reserves of powerful and wealthy institutions available throughout the West, that such a possibility seemed now inevitable; and not within the decade but perhaps upon the occasion of the next severe drought.

Grzimek perceived (and Niko Tinbergen demonstrated) that the study of wildlife is reliable only when conducted within its natural setting. The natural environment for the widest variety of visible mammalian species exists in the Serengeti Plain. That this is a world resource rather than just a local one remains the specialized knowledge of too few among the very many who might help. In money and time, the processes of investigation are expensive. From the Grzimeks' first eye counts of the migration only a few years ago, Lamprey said, the techniques today have progressed to the use of computerized aerial photographic surveys designed to accumulate population counts over generations of herd game. Conversely, the behavior of a single species may yield data only through years of patient, firsthand, visual observation: George Schaller spent three years studying Serengeti's lions, to be succeeded by Brian Bertram, who studied them for four years, and who has most recently been followed by David Bygott, who will, as have the others, drive out through the cool Serengeti mornings to the pride he seeks, kill his motor, sit and watch. Still in a relatively benign setting, the Serengeti lion population, meanwhile, continues to decline. And meanwhile, as elsewhere in the fragile East African savanna, the environment asserts its own pressures, changing swiftly and without warning. At Tsavo to the northeast, Norman Myers warns, the "ecosystem is swinging up and down in a manner scarcely ever

THE LAST PLACE ON EARTH

witnessed by scientists and on a scale that can hardly be imagined. It is a pity there are not more scientists to witness it; at present there are only three to keep an eye on . . . an area the size of New Hampshire, while the scientific community busies itself elsewhere with the thousandth piece of research on the white-tailed deer, disregarding an episode that must rank as a major phenomenon in the whole history of large animal biology."

At the Serengeti Research Institute, the financial crisis is constant and unrelenting. So far as he knew, Lamprey said, this would be the last year of major foundation funding. Quite literally, Tanzania cannot afford the Serengeti Research Institute, nor should she, with her crushing social needs, be obliged to support it. John Owen attracted seed money from various foundations with the assurance that tourist income would eventually increase to the point that the cost of operation (approximately a hundred thousand dollars a year) could be offset against it. But now the money had run out, and tourism, which was in decline internationally, was even the more weakened in Tanzania because of the costly intransigence of national policy.

"The Ford Foundation won't come back," says Lamprey, "because this is outside their scope. They are normally more interested in financing projects which have a more direct impact on human welfare." Throughout the world, as Grzimek angrily charged, the cause of wildlife is regarded as an object of charity.

"Is it finally the old clash between agriculture and wildlife carrying over to the foundations?" I asked.

"Yes," Lamprey said, "nearly every foundation wants to see its money used on the fairly immediate problems of agriculture or social welfare of people—anything that directly benefits the human population. It is a very large step to take for a foundation to investigate natural ecosystems, because the large proportion of the governing bodies of such foundations are totally inexperienced in this field. To most of them, it is unrelated to human problems. It is only in the last two or three years literally that the *real* need of studying the environment in toto, and how it functions, is coming clear. There is a great misunderstanding of the nature of ecology, of what is the true nature of the relationship between man and his environment. It is now necessary to re-educate agriculturists, sociologists, and ordinary people to the idea that one should be looking at the environment as a whole—and not just the environment of the human being and that part that he has an impact on."

John Owen was ingenious at scraping up the money to keep S.R.I. and the parks of Tanzania going. Derek Bryceson, who is a successful politician but a poor public-relations man, has that job now.

With varying degrees of urgency, adding one problem to the next, the expatriates closest to the concerns of Bernhard Grzimek had led me through the "morass of opinion" to an inescapable conclusion: the dual questions of animal rights and nature's way did not really, after all, pose a choice. All of it now was man's property, man's need, man's way—no choice. The park borders of Serengeti were established by man, invaded or protected by man, and the herds ran their migration through his sufferance. Man, his own ark. What use he would make of such possessions, what sacrifice to keep them, was the last question, as it had been for me the first, posed by Conway back in New York: "Will man save for tomorrow what he can use today?" Except that now, as I sat facing the worried frown of this wandering ecologist, it had come down from the abstract to a discrete time and place: save Serengeti for its values to the future, still locked tenuously within its borders, or utilize it by whatever means for the growing needs of hungry people just outside it? What had also become clear by now, more than ever, was this: whether through universal indifference, ignorance or gross neglect, Serengeti was no longer a matter of mankind's decision but Tanzanian man's decision.

But that, of course, was precisely where I had begun in Nairobi. The expatriates had been of value only as guides. The politicians in Dar es Salaam were said to be unwilling now to discuss such matters. Grzimek had traveled on, no longer available for the more complex conditions I might now pose, but that didn't matter so much either, for whatever questions I might have asked, he would undoubtedly have answered as he had all my others, several times over, and always the same way: it was finally the pride of the people that would prevail, and that was growing now all over Tanzania. No matter the degree of her poverty nor of her resentments over tourism inequities nor even of her need for more arable land, Tanzania could be depended upon to save for the world that which the world had squandered elsewhere. As to the problem of people multiplying about the borders, "It had never happened this way before—Julius Nyerere would *move* the people!" No matter that none of the expatriates shared his optimism on this last, crushing reality; Grzimek would be sure Nyerere could find a way.

Now that the money was running out and land hunger growing, the last reed all of them clung to was the empathy of Julius Nyerere—despite the sometimes conflicting evidence of the past to the contrary (when Bryceson as Minister of Agriculture had moved against the parks, it was presumably with Nyerere's foreknowledge), despite Ian Parker's version of Nyerere's position, and despite the devolution of government through Nyerere's *ujamaa* philosophy. But George Dove, Myles Turner, Derek Bryceson and John Owen, with remarkable consistency, had told the same story Grzimek had recited endlessly to anyone within earshot throughout the Uganda trip, and Hugh Lamprey repeated it now:

"An interesting change has occurred in Nyerere," he said. "He discovered that one of the things he can do to rest when he has a holiday is to become a botanist. He is interested in trees. Every time he goes to Serengeti, the Serengeti botanist comes out and goes around with him, and they have an afternoon or maybe only an hour or two of tree-spotting. He obviously enjoys it. He likes the peaceful side of nature."

As it had been true in the past, so it might continue into the future: only Nyerere could keep safe the Serengeti. But a most slender reed indeed against Parker's crushing prognosis and Nyerere's own desperations for his people. Against the cold facts of human density crowding Serengeti's borders, I thought, the expatriates' dependence on Nyerere's vacation hours at S.R.I. as palliative had about the same promise for the long-term future as Owen's bicycles and Grzimek's animal-art contest.

I told Lamprey I hoped to see Dr. Nyerere before I left, and if I did, how should I best ask him about his intentions regarding the future of Serengeti? He said: "I would try to put it this way: 'It's well known that Tanzania has created the greatest national park in the world. The Serengeti is absolutely unique. It is enormously appreciated outside that Tanzania values it so highly. Not only Serengeti but the other parks as well. I realize that it is not a simple problem in laying aside large areas of land, some of which might be used otherwise, but the world as a whole would say this is worthwhile. How do you view it?' "

Nyerere could not see me in East Africa, and when I wrote him the question some months later, he did not respond.

NINETEEN

But time has been friendly to Serengeti, after all. Many months after I left Africa, seeking through whatever means at hand to understand what I had seen and heard, I was to discover that the people of Tanzania have decided to preserve Serengeti, regardless of what the cost might prove to be. And at the Serengeti Research Institute, the Canadian John Bindernagel has concluded that the cropping of wildebeest is not economically feasible at the present time, and he has returned home.

But this is to get ahead of my account, for the reasons underlying these developments began more than fifteen years ago—before independence, and roughly during the years when the Grzimeks flew down to survey the Serengeti. They are primarily political. Because they proceed from the perceptions of Julius Nyerere, however, they may be regarded as philosophical as well. They have to do with Nyerere's present policies as President of Tanzania, a partial explanation of which had come to me from the expatriates. But Nyerere's aspirations were more ambitious than they had indicated. Through the fifties, the British had sought to prepare the new independent governments for self-rule by indoctrinating them into the colonial master plan for economic self-sufficiency: They should borrow money abroad to expand the production of local products (coffee, tea, sisal, and the like) for the world market. Such monies would be made available through foreign aid or multinational investment, perhaps both. The objective for each new nation was to achieve economic self-sufficiency as quickly as possible. Because it would take some time for a black ownership class to be developed, however, expatriates would be kept on hand to run things. Social services would be tended to when the system was working. True independence on the down-payment plan.

Tanzania moved away from this plan more rapidly than other African countries (many of which still follow it today), for several reasons: there were too few resources for the world market; outside financing created a business elite, widening the disparity between the quality of life in the city and that in the country; and outside assistance, whether through foreign aid or multinational investment, demanded fealty to outside interests. Instead, Nyerere turned Tanzania back to her own historic traditions of rural communalism—a modern version of the same village life Grzimek described our first night in Uganda. Urban growth would be discouraged, and whatever domestic savings became available would be invested in developing the land. Nyerere prepared a series of position papers. Beginning in 1962, the people would be moved about the countryside to develop his *ujamaa* villages. Cooperation, self-sufficiency, and mutual support would be stressed over individualism, competition, and profit. The educational system would prepare the people for better management of their land: the modern movement to the cities that was taking place elsewhere would here be reversed. Within their own communities, the people would control their community affairs; through T.A.N.U. they would make known their wishes for the national community. The preservation of Serengeti and other parklands was only a small part of the plan for land utilization throughout the country. *Ujamaa* was an idealization of the African way over the colonial way. More, it was the bold, considered rejection of political, economic, and social systems that guided the technological society throughout the Northern Hemisphere, the consequences of which were by now becoming all too clear: arms races with nuclear weapons; pollution and ecological imbalances; fuel shortages; the failure of political institutions; alienation; mindless consumerism. More was worse. Tanzania would head back the other way.

From wildly differing points of origin, Tanzania's discontents with "modern" ways had come to match those of many young people throughout the Northern Hemisphere. Nyerere's Tanzania was an African counterculture, the acknowledgment of limited resources; a reaction against the closed-circuit systems described by Bleibtreu and Kraus; a heroic effort to avoid reliance on material commodities whose consumers had been lured into believing the supply of essential resources was endless. By the early seventies, there was great interest across the continent in such notions. In Zaire, Mobutu would declare:

> Industrialized countries put the blame on those who have not
> yet reached that stage for not controlling the growth of their

populations, and emphasize the dangers of this especially in terms of shortage of food.

At the same time, however, they forget that their populations, although representing one third of mankind, consume ninety percent of the planet's resources. Their planes and their cars use up twice as much oxygen as does the entire population of the world. And it is because of them that the seas today are polluted.

. . . undoubtedly, an industrial society leads to material profits, but it also leads to the failure of mankind. For it impoverishes an irreplaceable asset: Nature.

. . . Every citizen in the world must defend his heritage, the area in which he lives, against those modern savages, the killers of Nature who do not hesitate to slaughter her to swell their own wallets. . . .

Among the few democratic countries left on the continent (not including Mobutu's Zaire), Tanzania would be seen by many as the only society systematically organizing itself against a time when the closed-circuit, technological society would have destroyed itself—in most extravagant terms, I was to find, Tanzania was regarded by some as a step toward post-industrial civilization.

While I had traveled through Tanzania several times in the past, I had known or cared little about her other than for my interest in the natural settings I had seen; but now, back home and realizing that the fate of Serengeti was inextricably tied to her political survival, I followed her fortunes through whatever fragments I could find. Although often helpless without foreign aid, Tanzania had systematically qualified the terms of accepting assistance to avoid domination by the donor power, refusing British aid on one occasion over principle, and ending aid from the Chinese after completion of the Tanzam railway, which the Chinese had largely funded. A gnat nipping away at the great elephant's ear to the north.

From my vantage in the other part of the world, I awaited the next development. When finally it came—a routine roundup in *The New York Times* in late 1975—it seemed to confirm Ian Parker's bleak predictions in every respect. Because of drought, the high cost of fuel, and the drop in the value of her own exports, Tanzania now hovered on the edge of insolvency and massive starvation. The United States had been expected to provide relief, but because

Tanzania had aroused the ire of the White House by voting against
U.S. interests in the U.N., the money—some twenty-eight million
dollars—would be withheld.

The end of Serengeti.

And yet something toward the close of the account leaped from
the page. According to the *Times* correspondent, Tanzania in the
fifteen years since independence had moved *nine million* people in
order to establish *ujamaa* villages. The italics might well have been
Bernhard Grzimek's. *Nine million!* Three-fifths of the nation.
Within this increasingly grandiose context, one began to wonder
seriously for the first time if it was possible that Tanzanian man's
way could after all prove to be—Nature's Way.

A wildlife administrator, Robinson McIlvaine of the African Wildlife Leadership Foundation, just back from Kenya, brought more
news:

"I don't know what they are doing for money at S.R.I. now. But
it's still going. The universities who send people out pay their way.
We are supporting the computer-monitoring service there. Tanzania
pays about thirty to forty per cent of the total operating costs. I
know of no foundation actively supporting it on the level of Ford or
Rockefeller. I don't know what's happened with the population
pressures about the borders, but there is a young Asian there now
making a study of them."

McIlvaine gave me his name—Feroz Kurji—and I immediately
wrote him asking how bad the pressure had become and what
would happen next. I received in reply a lengthy handwritten
document filled with abstruse terminology, complex references to
density levels and spatial structures, but also with news of an
extraordinary development:

Resulting from my demographic and land use analysis [of
Serengeti] was one central theme: since mobility was a major
feature of population dynamics and the prospects of numeri-
cal control were nil the major aspect in ecosystem planning
would in the near future be the "spatial" one, i.e., the
relative locations of the human/wildlife populations was
very important. To stop the rapid settlement diffusions and
encroachments into vital wildlife areas I envisaged that some
form of "spatial semistabilization" of settlement was probably the best. This would a) consolidate settlement into tighter
settlement nuclei, b) consolidation be aimed to remove

settlement in key wildlife areas, c) future growth and expansions would be around these nuclei and hence put restraints on the unplanned diffusion. The "semistabilization" would be due to the fact that under populations growth some spatial expansions would be necessary but not be the major mechanism for relieving increasing densities in an area. But such a recourse involving 2 million people as of 1967 suggested to me that it was impractical and I should "shelve" the idea. Well, I was wrong!

In 1974–75 the Ujamaa Program bought the Serengeti (and other Tanzanian conservation areas) a major reprieve for the immediate future. Settlement consolidation was carried out into "development villages" and in some areas, e.g., south of Ruana river all settlement was moved to give a 8–14 km. cleared zone (mid-dry season wildebeest & topi area). In the Maswa consolidation is taking place into three major villages; on the whole some forms of spatial controls have been initiated. There occurred within the context of the rural development strategy for the whole country to facilitate the provision of basic social infrastructure. *On the local level the choice of village relocation areas often resulted in the considerations of wildlife requirements and hence settlement was moved, where possible and necessary, away from essential wildlife habitats.* [Italics mine.] I think that the move into development villages has been a great benefit to the interests of wildlife conservation from the "spatial" point of view and thus has considerably eased human pressures on many wildlife areas. I am in the process of trying to assess the "spatial trade-offs" that have resulted from these developments and my initial impression is that it has provided a turning point in conservation history in the country in that an opportunity has been created within which conservation as a form of realistic long-term land use can be assimilated into overall land uses into a compatible framework and it is now up to conservationists/development planners to further solidify these links on a realistic basis. The latter can only presuppose the existence and availability of adequate information from research involving long term monitoring of human as well as wildlife activities. The "villagisation" policy seems to me a strategy where the interests of wildlife

THE LAST PLACE ON EARTH

and the national development objectives are *not* at cross purposes but complement each other to create conditions for the long term viability of wildlife conservation. . . .

Grzimek was right.

When I first arrived in Nairobi, the expatriates had been astir with talk of Alan Root's new film on the wildebeest migration, most of them agreeing it was the finest documentary ever made on African wildlife; but it wasn't shown in the United States until well over a year after my return. As I watched it now on my television set, returned to the routine of my own affairs, I fretted throughout— the imperfect colors of the set, the miniaturization of the great herd, the absence of the Roots' presence except through their camera as they hovered in their silent balloon over the animals below, the periodic commercials reducing the phenomenon to yet another night's television fare—all of it somehow trivializing the unlikely circumstances I had witnessed there through the terminal phase of the expatriates from 1969 through 1974, the encounter with the improbable Grzimek, ending with Kurji's account of Tanzania's massive relocation plan. Who could imagine the circumstances attending the migration I now watched on the screen? All of it had become rather hopelessly cinematic in my own mind anyway: an unlikely fiction for my fellow-viewers, I thought. Only partly because Root's camera could move through but two dimensions, as I watched now in the last minutes the infinite animals in refraction, stretching to the horizon of the plain yet all pressed within the nineteen-inch screen, I found my own conclusion taking over with its own dissolves and montages, with closing sounds and images and list of names pieced from the fragments of gossip borne back across continents and from the random scenes of my own memory of the East African past:

JOHN OWEN: retired, living now in Tunbridge Wells, England . . .

HUGH LAMPREY: working for the U.N. Environmental Protection Agency to arrest the spread of the Sahara desert . . .

MYLES TURNER: moved to Malawi . . .

THE LEAKEYS: Mary Leakey discovering in Serengeti yet another "true-man" fossil, this predating the most recent discovery of her son, Richard, by one and a quarter million years, moving back the possible time of man's origin to three and three-quarter million years . . .

GEORGE DOVE: moved to Australia . . .

MICHAEL WOOD: moved to Nairobi . . .

DEREK BRYCESON: continuing as. Director of Tanzania National Parks, recently married to Jane Goodall . . .

IAN PARKER: trading no longer in ivory or skins; still available for proper cropping schemes . . .

ALAN ROOT: recuperating in a Nairobi hospital from a goring by a hippopotamus . . .

GENERAL IDI AMIN DADA: self-appointed Field Marshal, President of Uganda for life . . .

JULIUS NYERERE: principal in negotiations to liberate Rhodesia . . .

BERNHARD GRZIMEK: engaged now in a public-opinion campaign against the manufacturers of turtle soup . . .

Then, to a movement through time beyond the confinements of the imagined screen, to the persistence of Serengeti, its devious elusive collaborations to sustain all life within it, and now seeking to draw even the human community of modern Tanzania inside its plan, the shared complementary existence of plant, animal, climate and soil: a retrograde movement reaching back across the aged rocks and lava-bed grasses, past the crocodile sentries to the Mesozoic Age, pressing toward the lost moment before tools and the trouble began, past the wildebeest migration of two million years ago along the route traced downward through sediments by the Leakey mother and son to the times before man arrived—two million years? four million?—and then beckoning to Julius Nyerere's Wakuria and Wasukuma and Masai to erase the mistakes by turning again through natural ancestry to the constant lands before—within the closing distance of the Northern Hemisphere—the electricity shuts down. Tanzania trying now against the force of motors in the West to pry open the door leading back to the affirmative past. Serengeti, the last place.

But time is invisible, and so I began again.

In my last week, heading south from Nairobi, I had driven the macadam road to Arusha passing hundreds of bloated cattle carcasses destroyed by drought, too many for the vultures to tend.

THE LAST PLACE ON EARTH

The day before there had been flash floods and many had drowned. Boris had said that when the cattle have learned to subsist on tough dry grass, when the rain finally comes, the new grass springing to life is so rich it can kill them. At the border town of Namanga, a Kenyan guard said he would keep the door open so that when we were turned back we would not be delayed. Sure enough, Tanzanian customs seized our rented vehicle for insufficient clearance papers. We were obliged to spend the next day in Arusha and stand trial; were fined and permitted to enter the country the day after, arriving at the foot of Ngorongoro near noon. The drive up the eastern side of the caldera is sharply vertical, rising higher swiftly, so that at the hairpin bends of the dirt track it is possible to see out over the Great Rift Valley at intervals, each time the horizon widening until one is certain he can see the earth's curve. Upward through rain forests and then onto the edge of the crater, a distance of about a hundred and ten miles from Arusha, perhaps three miles away from the crater lodge, where for the first time in my several trips along this way I noticed the monument to Michael Grzimek erected fifteen years ago. It is a simple stone obelisk about eight feet high. A bronze plaque at the center reads:

MICHAEL GRZIMEK

12.4.1934   to   10.1.1959

He gave all he possessed for the wild
animals of Africa, including his life.

Bougainvillea bloom about its base, but there were as well a wreath of dried flowers set beside the live plant and a plastic sprig of pine cones at the top. A sash of white silk was draped over the apex of the obelisk. In gold letters, it read: DEM HELDEN DER SERENGETI DEUTSCH TIER FREUND. The plastic sprig was fixed to the edge of it. At the lodge, I asked the captain in the restaurant who had put the banner there. He said Grzimek had passed through last week, and he had put it there. Still, with Serengeti, it is the sense of place which persists with the greatest visual clarity. But there are many dimensions to memory, and it remains difficult for me to order the sequence of real time from the file of views I carry of other times there. Was it after seeing Michael's memorial, or the time before, that we saw from our tent the pride of lions filing obliquely through the grass of Seronera? Was it the first time there that we stood on the hood of the Land Rover surrounded by the migration, watching the animals bowed to graze, filling the horizon in every direction?

Of small consequence to this arrangement. Whenever it may have happened, my last memory scene is the last now in sequence. I had met a young forester named Denis Herlocker from the University of Washington who was working on the study of soil composition in his office laboratory at the Serengeti Research Institute; he was going over aerial maps with his young and eager Tanzanian assistant. He suggested that on my way out of the park I visit the test soil pit he had established at Olemangi, some forty-five miles north, to the west of Klein's Camp just short of the Kenya border. He had to leave immediately but his assistant would go along and guide me from the main road to his station next day. It turned out to be a four-hour drive and the countryside was familiar to me—through the northern extension added to the park in the late fifties, the dry grazing grounds of the wildebeest—so long as we held to the main road. When we turned off on a tiny dirt track to the left, although I hadn't known it at the time, we were heading toward the Lamai Wedge. For a time the countryside was harsh scrub brush, like the soil of Arizona, although more rolling, a series of small hills. We passed a bush fire spreading at a slow leisurely pace over these hills, some gazelle and a few zebra grazing the charred stalks in its wake. Then quite suddenly the far side of the next hill was covered with white grass reaching in height to the window level of the car and extending beyond the crest of the next hill. There must have been a light breeze moving across it for in my memory the grass drifts and ebbs. Over the next hill it was the same, and the same over the hill after that, and more until we came suddenly upon enormous eland, shoulder-high in the field, four of them. Larger than cattle they turned their heads only slightly toward us and then sprang away in giant leaps, all four feet off the ground; graceful and twitching, nimble as tiny Tommies. On we went over more hills of grass, and beyond the next in the same fields there were seven giraffe, staring at the intrusion, and then they walked together, long necks pumping, away from our track. Denis Herlocker was waiting for us, standing on his Land Rover to see over the tall grass. He led us to his soil pit at the top of one of these hills and went to work with his assistant measuring out samples and sifting them into cellophane bags. A creek branch lined with trees wound to the rear across the hilltop, and between Herlocker's soil pit and the stream there was a family of baboon undisturbed by our presence. We had brought box lunches from the lodge at Lobo, and we ate from them quietly, sitting on the fenders of the Land Rover in the high, dry heat, watching the baboons. Now, about fifty yards behind us, at the edge of the track we had followed and over which we would return, two rhinoceros emerged, nose first, grazing slowly out of the high grass into full view. We finished; Herlocker and his assistant would move deeper into the woodland to tend another soil pit, and we turned around to start back. There was no way to go cross-country because of the uncertain terrain beneath the grass, and so I drove slowly toward the rhino hoping we might get past without rousing them. But they are mean-tempered animals, irritable and inexorable; they tend to charge a threat rather than flee it. They were some thirty feet in now and as we passed alongside they broke into a trot parallel to our course over the potholed track. There was no way to go faster, and for them no need; at any point, turning left, they could charge the side of the vehicle. They seemed extraordinarily graceful. We moved along together in this fashion no more than a hundred yards but for what seemed a very long time, down the grass hills and up again, sharply upward and with gears grinding, down again, our prehistoric escorts galloping through the grasslands of Olemangi, weighing the whim of their own course until they began to veer off to the right, still pounding along at our speed, and then they had become partly obscured, and then finally lost to the deep grass.

AUTHOR'S NOTE

Pete Turner first invited me to Africa. For the purposes of this book, William Conway suggested some of the people I should see there, and he recommended David Ehrenfeld's *Biological Conservation* (Holt, Rinehart and Winston, Inc.) as a helpful book to read before going. The principals of this account, as should be evident, made much time available to me. So did Philip Thresher and Kai Curry-Lindahl of the United Nations; Andrew Jaffe of *Newsweek;* Boyce Rensberger, now of *The New York Times;* John McDougall, of the Nairobi *Daily Nation;* James Willson, a Kenya hunter; and George Adamson, the conservationist.

There are many books that relate to the concerns of this one. Some that were extremely helpful to me were: *Ngorongoro—The Eighth Wonder,* by Henry Fosbrooke (André Deutsch Ltd.); *The Long African Day,* by Norman Myers (Macmillan Co.); *Africa, A Natural History,* by Leslie Brown (Random House); *Among the Elephants,* by Iain and Oria Douglas-Hamilton (Viking Press); *Portraits in the Wild,* by Cynthia Moss (Houghton Mifflin Co.); *The Tree Where Man Was Born,* by Peter Matthiessen (E. P. Dutton & Co.); *Africa Emergent,* by John Hatch (Henry Regnery Co.); *We Must Run While They Walk,* by William Smith (Random House); *The Serengeti Lion,* by George Schaller (University of Chicago Press); *The Parable of the Beast,* by John Bleibtreu (Macmillan Co.); *The White Nile* and *No Room in the Ark,* by Alan Moorehead (Harper & Row); and of course all the books by Bernhard Grzimek, cited earlier, most especially *Serengeti Shall Not Die* (E. P. Dutton & Co.).

Nearly every back issue of the excellent local magazine, *Africana* (published by the East African Wild Life Society), contained some reference to the troublesome controversies over East Africa's animals. The African Wildlife Leadership Foundation's *News,* a quarterly periodical, was similarly helpful.

I am grateful, too, to those who, by reading and responding to my manuscript, took so seriously my effort to tell the story of Serengeti. These were: Dr. Bernhard Grzimek, Boris Tismimiezky, Myles and Kay Turner, Andrew Jaffe, Roxanna Sayre, Tom and Sarah Ferrell, Gail Godwin, William Conway, Gay Talese, and Tom Wolfe. At expense to their own projects, Dr. David Ehrenfeld and Dr. Hugh Lamprey went even further by supervising my revisions until I could understand—and thereby hope to make comprehensible to others—some of the biology of the Serengeti Plain.